I0651449

Thomas James Mathias

A Translation of the Passages from Greek, Latin, Italian, and French

Writers

Quoted in the Prefaces and Notes to the Pursuits of literature...

Thomas James Mathias

A Translation of the Passages from Greek, Latin, Italian, and French Writers
Quoted in the Prefaces and Notes to the Pursuits of literature...

ISBN/EAN: 9783744763530

Printed in Europe, USA, Canada, Australia, Japan

Cover: Foto ©Thomas Meinert / pixelio.de

More available books at **www.hansebooks.com**

A

TRANSLATION

OF THE PASSAGES FROM

GREEK, LATIN, ITALIAN,

AND

FRENCH WRITERS,

QUOTED IN THE

PREFACES AND NOTES

TO THE

PURSUITS OF LITERATURE;

A POEM,

IN FOUR DIALOGUES.

———————

[*Price Three Shillings and Sixpence in Boards.*]

A

TRANSLATION

OF THE PASSAGES FROM

GREEK, LATIN, ITALIAN,

AND

FRENCH WRITERS,

QUOTED IN THE

PREFACES AND NOTES

TO THE

PURSUITS OF LITERATURE;

A POEM,

IN FOUR DIALOGUES.

TO WHICH IS PREFIXED,

A PREFATORY EPISTLE,

INTENDED AS A

General Vindication of the PURSUITS of LITERATURE, from various Remarks which have been made upon that Work.

BY THE TRANSLATOR.

Νοῆ—

—σαι καιρος αριστος.

Εγω ΙΔΙΟΣ ΕΝ ΚΟΙΝΩ σταλεις,

Μητιντε γαρυων παλαιγενων,

Πολεμον τ᾽ εν ἡρωϊαις αρετᾶισιν,

Ου ψευσομαι.   *Pind. Olymp. O.* 13.

THE SECOND EDITION.

LONDON:

PRINTED FOR T. BECKET, PALL-MALL.

1798.

PRINTED FOR T. BECKET, PALL-MALL,

In One Volume Octavo, price 8s. 6d. in Boards,

A NEW EDITION,

Being the EIGHTH, *Revised, of*

I. THE PURSUITS OF LITERATURE,

A SATIRICAL POEM,

IN FOUR DIALOGUES,

WITH NOTES.

II. A NEW EDITION, BEING THE FOURTH,

Price One Shilling and Six-pence,

OF

The IMPERIAL EPISTLE from KIEN LONG,

EMPEROR OF CHINA,

To GEORGE THE THIRD,

KING OF GREAT BRITAIN, &c. &c.

IN THE YEAR 1794.

Transmitted from the Emperor, and presented to his Britannick Majesty by His Excellency the Right Hon. George Earl Macartney, of the Kingdom of Ireland, K. B. Ambassador Extraordinary and Plenipotentiary to the Emperor of China, in the Years 1792, 1793, and 1794.

Translated into English Verse from the original Chinese Poetry. By the AUTHOR of the PURSUITS of LITERATURE.

With Notes by various Persons of Eminence and Distinction, and by the Translator.

~~~~~~~~~~~~~~

A

PREFATORY EPISTLE

ON THE

PURSUITS OF LITERATURE,

&c. &c. &c.

ADDRESSED

To L. B——, Esq.

~~~~~~

Post resides annos, longo velut excita somno,
  Romanis fruitur Musa (*Britanna*) choris:
Sed magis intento studium censore laborat,
  Quòd legitur medio conspiciturque foro.
Illi conciliat gratas impensius aures,
  Vel meritum belli, vel *Stilichonis* amor.

~~~~~~~~~~~~~

A
PREFATORY EPISTLE,

ADDRESSED

To L. B——, Esq.

Τῷ πανυ.

Intended as a General Vindication of "The PURSUITS OF LITERATURE, a Poem in Four DIALOGUES, with Notes;" from various Remarks which have been made upon it.

Δει μεν, μη τας πολλας των εξηγητων μιμαμενας, ξηρον και ελλιπη τον τοπον διαλειπειν· μηδε ωσπερ ετερας, αμηχανον ὁσην απεραντολογιαν επεισαγειν. Αλλα δει αυτο μονον το προκειμενον Συγγραμμα προστησαμενας, ὑπ' οψιν αγειν τοις σχολαζασι την Προθεσιν, διερευνομενας το ειδος, την ὑλην, τα δογματα συνηρημενως, την δι' ὁλα τα Συγγραμματος διηκασαν των λογων ὑποθεσιν. Ὁυτω γαρ αν τοις ακασσι γενοιτο καταφανες το παν βουλημα ΤΩΝ ΔΙΑΛΟΓΩΝ.
Ex PROCLI *Commentariis in* PLATONIS Πολιτειαν. Edit.
Gr. *Basil.* 1534. pag. 349.

DEAR SIR,

I HAVE been informed that repeated requests have been made to the publisher of "THE PURSUITS OF LITERATURE," for a Translation of the passages from various languages quoted in the Notes to that Poem. I wish the Author had translated them himself; but as that cannot be the case, I have, at your immediate desire, endeavoured to give you some idea of their force and full meaning. As you are of opinion, that my attempt will not be disagreeable or unsatisfactory to many persons, who are

a 2

not

not peculiarly conversant in Greek and Latin, I have consented to print and publish them.

The Author of the work had perhaps too much respect for his readers to obtrude a translation upon them. But that circumstance is no reason why *a friend* to the Author, and to the general diffusion of the learning, principles, and illustration of the work, should decline it. They who are best acquainted with the difficulty, will most readily excuse the errors and mistakes. I have not thought it expedient to present you with a poetical version of the passages from the Greek and Roman bards, for various reasons. But independantly of every other consideration, I conceive, that a translation in prose always gives a more adequate and precise idea of their strength and meaning, than the most finished attempt in verse, to those who are not acquainted with the original language.

The Author of the Pursuits of Literature seems to have produced them to enliven, to illustrate, and to enforce his doctrines and opinions. I think also, it was his purpose to recall and fix the attention of the publick on those finished models of ancient learning, the great directors of taste and judgment, and to their best disciples and imitators in the modern ages. I wish so useful an intention may have its effect.

As to the various languages employed in the work, it may be observed,that a noble peer of this realm has lately followed his example. I know not with what propriety. The Earl of Abingdon has regaled an illustrious *Lady* of the house of Courtney, not only with his own English, and that of the Orator of the University of Oxford, the Reverend William Crowe, but with Greek, Latin, Italian, and French in the original languages, from Aristotle to Citizen Gourville. And he has actually performed all this in one short

4   philosophical

philosophical Letter to Lady Loughborough.(a) Who shall
hereafter blame the Author of the P. of L. or my zeal to
explain his quotations ?

Since the publication of those ingenious and witty compositions by Tickell and Sheridan, " Anticipation, and
The Critick;" there seems to be a species of pleasant
ridicule on most translations of *detached* passages. I expect
to be told by some persons that, like Colonel Barré,
" I am translating for the Country Gentlemen." By
others it may be insinuated, that " Egad they think the
interpreter is the hardest to be understood of the two." (b)
Especially as the Author of the Critick *now* deserves himself the same compliment with his own Mr. Dangle, upon
his talents for criticism, and *his interest with* THE DIREC-
TORS *of the present* FRENCH THEATRE.

But if I have only to encounter the objections of real
criticks, like yourself, in the ancient languages, my sufferings, I think, will be light. I only hope you will receive
it kindly, and still continue to think me, " a very civil
gentleman-interpreter, trying to make myself understood:" (b)

I have as much curiosity as ever I had to discover the
Author of the P. of L. and I have read most of the pamphlets
and criticisms on the subject. Whoever he may be, he has

a 3   at

(a) A letter to Lady Loughborough from the Earl of Abingdon, in consequence of her presentation of the colours to
the Bloomsbury and Inns of Court Association, 1798.
(b) Sheridan's Critick, act 1. sc. 2.

at least been honoured with great attention by the publick. As no man has ever yet owned the composition, and the author is declared to be still U N K N O W N, every supposition and conjecture has been examined with a minute diligence, and every mode of *proof* has been tried ; but in vain.

It is the advice of Cicero, in his first book on the Duties of Life, " Ne incognita pro cognitis habeamus." It is also generally allowed, that conjectures are at best too light a pretence to allow a man to assign a name in publick. But notwithstanding so obvious a truth, some pronounce with a random boldness, others give signs instead of names, and then plume themselves on their discoveries.

"In so many words, in so many syllables, or in so many letters," is the old and approved argument of the SHOULDER KNOT, and has admirable use in the present case. The actual concealment however remains the same. In point of proof, and rational, well-supported conjecture, it is agreed by most persons of sagacity, and fairness of character and understanding,

" That putting all their *proofs* together,
'Tis three blue beans in one blue bladder."

Various have been the attempts to discredit the work. Criticism, in the true sense, has never yet been exerted ; *(c)*

but

(c) I am rather inclined to except " The Remarks on the P. of Literature, in a Letter to the Author. Printed at Cambridge." It is the production of a polite and accomplished

but intemperate, angry, and smarting scribblers, in prose and verse, have issued forth in little swarms. But it has been well observed, that exceeding fierceness with perfect inability and impotence, makes the highest ridicule.

From among these angry and smarting scribblers, I shall select the Author of " The Progress of Satire, an Essay in verse, &c. the second edition ;" not for any merit whatsoever in his composition (for it is remarkably dull) but merely for the singularly petulant malignancy, and imposing air which pervade the whole. The infamy of such misrepresentation is in it's own nature perishable, and the folly transitory; but, for the sake of the *example*, if I have the ability, I will make them immortal. This Author I shall hereafter call for shortness, or for want of a better name, THE PROGRESSIONIST. Whether he and his co-adjutors scribble in verse or prose, they prove themselves to be either of that fabulous race of " men, whose heads do grow beneath their shoulders," or of the number of those unfortunate persons, " whose brain is shaken out of it's natural position."

They are perpetually mistaking one thing for another. With the nature and signification of words they are wholly unacquainted. It would be a process in infinitum to define the words which they use, as Mr. Locke has well observed en the names of *simple* ideas. In their vocabulary, satire means encomium, and severity, good-nature. They might as well stile the law of a country ill-natured, because offenders are punished by it. With regard to anonymous

                   a 4   writing,

plished scholar, written with urbanity, but not with any great force of argument. I have just seen a full answer to it, and therefore I have nothing to observe. The Answer is stiled, " A Letter to the Author of that Pamphlet, by a Country Gentleman, formerly of the University of Cambridge."

writing, satirical or political, opinions are various. But I think it was said wisely and justly by Junius * to Sir William Draper; " After voluntarily attacking me under the name of Junius, what possible right have you to know me under any other?" The Author of the P. of L. has not indeed given even the shadow of a name to himself; but as THE PROGRESSIONIST has been contented also to attack him under the title of the Author of the P. of L: it may be as fairly and as justly demanded, " what possible right can The Progressionist have to know him under any other?" But for one anonymous writer to call so vehemently upon another to give his name to the world, must be added to that number of absurdities which he has bound in sheaves, and stacked so plenteously in Mr. Bell's shop.

The Progressionist seems to be in one continued raving dream upon a bed of torture, under the influence of irritation and malevolence. I believe he sees double suns, and double booksellers shops. He is something between Pentheus and Orestes, yet perfectly harmless. What his literary sins are, I know not; but at least he seems to suffer for other people's transgressions. He rants and foams, that other folks follow his own example, and still keep their names to themselves. He has not even the sense of Mr. Dabble, the Dentist, in the exquisite farce of the Humourist, and never puts a plain question to himself, " What have I to do with the violence of *Sir Antony*'s temper?" He has indeed a strong passion for the *grinders* ; yet like Mrs. Matador, in the same farce, (as will be seen hereafter) one would think, " he *glories* in having *his teeth drawn*." But he has a higher original.

Like the great Knight of La Mancha, he comes forth as Redresser General of literary wrongs, and has an unlimited

Commission

Commission to act in the same manner, and nearly to the same effect. He is said to have received the Order of his calling in a regular manner. He passed through every ceremony of literary knighthood, having kept watch in compleat armour from head to foot, according to the rites of chivalry, during one whole night over a pile of books, ranged in order on the counter in Mr. Bell's shop, in Oxford street. For at present booksellers have no chapels in their castles for the purpose. But it was observed, that no person attempted to meddle with the books, which might easily be accounted for, if I were to mention their names. The age of *literary* chivalry is not yet gone.

The Progressionist was then let loose upon the world, and sallied forth mounted on a *Provisional* charger, though a Knight without a name. Yet he threatened much; and in his first *Essay* had nearly the same success with his great original. You remember the adventure of the countryman and his poor boy Andrew, who suffered more severely from the interference of the Knight in his behalf. " The boy departed weeping, and the master remained behind laughing. And *in this manner*, says Cervantes, the valorous Don Quixote redressed that wrong." I refer you to the volume itself, in which is recounted the pleasant manner observed in the knighting Don Quixote. The speech of self-congratulation on that occasion, the Progressionist is said to have spoken, and applied to himself with a *very few alterations;* after he had first recommended himself to his patroness, or literary Dulcinea; and then published to the world his " Progress of Satire," and completed the destruction of the Author of the Pursuits of Literature. The passage is this: " Glad above " measure for his success, *accounting himself to have given* " *a most noble beginning to his feats of arms*, Don Quixote " did travel towards his village *with very great satisfaction*

" *of*

" *of himself*, and said in a low tone of voice; " Well may'st
" thou call thyself happy above all other women of the
" earth; O! above all beauties, beautiful Dulcinea of
" Toboso, since thy good, fortune was such, to hold subject
" and prostrate to thy will and desire so valiant and *renowned*
" a Knight as is, and *ever shall be*, Don Quixote of the
" Mancha; who, as all the world knows, received the order
" of knighthood *but yesterday*, and has destroyed *to day*
" *the greatest outrage and wrong, which want of reason*
" *could form, or cruelty commit.* To day *did he take away*
" *the whip out of the hand of* THAT PITILESS ENEMY,
" who did *so cruelly scourge*, without occasion, THOSE
" DELICATE INFANTS." (*a*) I am told The Progressionist
wished to have the Reverend DR. PARR behind him as his
Squire, and offered to find the Doctor *a very good Ass* for the
purpose; but *that delicate infant* resisted all the proposed
honours of Barataria, and would not quit his village.

On Dr. Parr's refusal to act the part of Sancho, and the
impossibility of procuring a proper Squire, The Progressionist
quitted the plains of *La Mancha*, and appeared as, the
successor and rival of *other* Knights Errant in fields *nearer
home*.

It is curious to observe, how THE PROGRESSIONIST
strives not only to imitate, but to prove himself the legitimate
descendant, of various heroes of the Dunciad. He has
revived all the trash which was vented against Mr. Pope, as
will appear by a short comparison. The prophecy of the
bard of Twitnam has been verified:

" See the dull stars roll round, and *re-appear!*"

The leaden power of Saturn has prevailed over Mars and
Jove,

(*a*) *Shelton's* translation of Don Quixote, b. 1. ch. 4.

Jove. Jerningham and the Progressionist have risen in the opposite quarter of the heaven, and Gifford and the Author of the P. of L. have looked up, and read their lot *united* in those cœlestial signs.

Perhaps it is but doing justice to their Authors, if I mention a nameless pamphlet or two, which probably might never have escaped from the lumber-room, or shop of the Bookseller, if my obscure diligence had not extracted and preserved them. The Authors think themselves very laudable in their intentions. All of them, and the Progressionist in particular, have verified the Arabian observation, that whenever learning is introduced into a brain, whose texture is not adapted to receive it, a fermentation ensues, till the whole is exhausted. Though perhaps the writer of the P. of L. never read them himself, I could have assured him, that they are but a second edition of Mr. John Dennis, Mr. Oldmixon, and the soft-flowing Welsted! If you turn to the Prolegomena of the Dunciad, the testimonies *in favour* of Mr. Pope, are nearly the same as the more modern compliments of these poetaster-cricks.

> All black, *Tartareous*, cold, infernal *dregs*,
> Adverse to life!

Mr. John Dennis thus begins of Mr. Alexander Pope. "His precepts are false and trivial, or both; his thoughts are crude and abortive; his expressions absurd; *his numbers harsh and unmusical*; his rhymes trivial and common; instead of majesty, something that is very boyish; and instead of perspicuity and lucid order, we have too often obscurity and confusion." Hear another description of him by this most ancient of Criticks. " He (Mr. Alexander Pope) is a little affected hypocrite, who has nothing in his mouth but candour, truth, friendship, good-nature, humanity and magnanimity. He is a great lover of falsehood, &c." Once more attend to the

furious

furious Dennis. " He (Mr. Pope) is a creature that reconciles all contradictions; *he is a beast and a man*; a Whig and a Tory; an assertor of liberty, and the dispensing power of Kings; a *Jesuitical* professor of truth, a base and foul pretender to candour." As I intend only to give you a specimen, I shall not proceed.

How beautifully has THE PROGRESSIONIST,* dilated and expanded his predecessor's ideas! With what reverence, I will not say servility, but homage, does he tread in his very footsteps! It is the love of Lucretius for Epicurus! Not the desire of contention, but of honest affectionate imitation. Scarce one idea of his own if you change the names of the works.

It is the very spirit and essence of Mr. John Dennis, and the soft-flowing Welsted, with now and then some of Curl's *better* part, and a palpable *imitation* of some of the most finished strokes in a late modest and simple-minded Translator of Horace. But now attend to *The Progressionist.* •

" It (i. e. the Poem on the P. of L.) is scarcely ever elegant,
" but sometimes it has a degree of poetical spirit; at other times
" it is not only prosaic, but vulgar. Sometimes his declamations
" in the notes *appear* eloquent, at others frothy and
" puerile; on some occasions his sarcasms are pointed and
" just; on others wretchedly trifling, or deliberately ill-
    " natured.

* See " The Progress of Satire, an Essay in *Verse*; with notes, containing remarks on " The Pursuits of Literature;" *second* edition; with this modest and *complimentary* motto to the English Nation:

   " What if *an addle-headed Public* praise
   The proud conceited Pedant's rumbling lays,
 · Shall *we* not weigh his insolent pretence
   In *juster* scales—the scales of *Truth and Sense?*

" natured. In his most laboured effort at sublimity he is
" *in part* successful, but in *some parts* inflated and obscure.
" To cite the feeble and prosaic passages in the Pursuits of
" Literature, would be *to repeat* almost half the book.—
" The purity and propriety of the English language are often
" grossly violated.—Some of these improprieties he has lately
" corrected.—I call his Muse shapeless, because nec pes nec
" caput uni reddatur formæ. Indeed the whole passage in
" Horace describes a work similar to the P. of L.—Many of
" his vulgarities are noticed in *a very sensible Essay** called,
" Impartial Strictures on the P. of L. He has been well
" denominated a Jesuit," &c. &c.—This is but a specimen.

Considering that the Progressionist is so strong an advocate
for decorum, *(and that he has not given his own name to the
publick)* the terms of reproach are scattered with a very liberal
hand, or rather heaped up, on a person whom he is pleased to
call " *his adversary*." Now here I would observe; that it
does not appear that the author of " The Progress of Satire"
ever published any other work whatsoever but that *celebrated*
Essay ; and I do not find the remotest allusion to the " Progress
of Satire," in any part of the P. of L. It must therefore of
necessity require much ingenuity, or perversion of mind, to
prove that one man can be an adversary to another, who is
equally ignorant of his person and his pamphlet. I am
confident that the Author of the P. of L. never knew him, or
thought of him. If that Author had ever condescended to
stile any man *his adversary*, he would have looked in
another quarter.

A writer, like the Progressionist, has all the follies of poetical
childhood

---

* Great writers always quote one another ; and in return,
his *impartial* Brother sends us back again to that *very sensible
Essay*, the Progress of Satire. See Impartial Strictures, p.
25. Par nobile!

childhood with the vices of satirical puberty. I have already honoured him too much by extracting some prose parts of his pamphlet; but I absolutely refuse to paralyse my page with a line of his versification. The touch of the Torpedo could not be so fatal to it. I subject myself indeed to ridicule, when I think for a moment of such men as Warburton and Lowth, when I am toiling over " The Progress of Satire." Yet the Babylonish, or rather French, captivity into which true learning and good poetry are fallen, suggest the words of Lowth. " I do call, (says that illustrious scholar) the age " itself semi-barbarous, if you please; but I do not call " Ezra *a semi-barbarous Poet*, for I maintain that *Ezra is* " *no Poet at all**." When we turn from Warburton, Lowth and Pope, to the Progressionist, I feel we reverse the journeying of the Hebrews. From the Land of Promise, we are passing to the desert.

Surely the Author of the P. of L. acted wisely in declining the puny contest. Had he ever begged an interview, or made overtures for a timid negociation, I hope even the Progressionist would have had the spirit to have treated him with contempt. But that Author knew too well the ground on which he stood. He felt, that the arms, as well as the supplies, were in his own hand and disposal. I know not whether he would have adopted the expressions of Warburton; but I am sure some of his friends would be ready to do so for him. Warburton said; " Of all the Bœotian phalanx who have " written scurrilously against me, there is not one, whom a " writer of reputation would not wish to have his enemy. To " my Authorship they are heartily welcome. Rome permitted " *her slaves* to calumniate HER BEST CITIZENS *in the day of* " *triumph*."†

The

---

* Lowth's Letter to Warburton, p. 77.

† Preface to Pope's Works.

The Progressionist in the very out-set of his march halts a little. He pants even in the Preface, and lashes himself (by no means like the British lion) with his own *tail*; for the Preface and the Postcript are both equally candidates for this appellation. The middle or body of his *work* (I mean *his whole Essay* in verse, with all it's appendages) is quite innoxious. He has indeed a great mind to hurt and bite, and annoy; but having more mind than ability, the effort dies, where it might be expected, in the very beginning.

It would have been happy for himself, had he rested in his prime question. He would have saved his friends and himself from much additional contempt. He says, with some *Christian* self-complacency to the Author of the P. of L. " Have you, (*I will stake* THE WHOLE CAUSE upon *this* " issue) invariably done unto others, as you would wish that " others should do unto you?" Whoever feels the nature of human infirmity, has already answered the question, and borne testimony to the folly of the man who could be weak enough to propose it. But the *intention* of the question, and the region to which he would fain consign the Author of the Pursuits, are easy to conjecture. He reminds me of " The Night-walker, or Little Thief" in the Comedy of Beaumont and Fletcher ; and has his nurse, servants, bell-ringers, and sexton all ready for his interment. Nay he seems willing to follow him to the world unknown, and even to anticipate his sentence.

Still there is always something unfortunate in the imitations of inferior writers. Indeed they seldom discover the proper object of imitation. Sir William Draper was an ingenious man, and a good scholar, but imprudent in his conduct. He had zeal without knowledge, and boldness without discretion. He voluntarily attacked *Junius*, '' whose shoes' latchet, the

" Progressionist

" Progressionist declares, the Author of the P. of L. is not
" worthy to unloose." The wanton and impious levity of
the allusion I leave him to reconcile with decorum. The
Progressionist is here an unhappy rival to Sir William, in
putting questions from the Scriptures. If I had been the
Author of the Pursuits, I would have said with Junius,
" Such a question, Sir, may perhaps discompose the gravity
" of my muscles; but I believe it will little affect the
" tranquillity of my conscience."

The only question is this; whether an Author, of whatsoever
description he may be, deserves satirical censure. If he does
deserve it, the point is settled; if that is denied, the parties
are at issue. The Satirist writes for the publick; and the
precepts of Christianity can never be violated, when strict
publick justice is inflicted in any manner. I should feel
myself clear on this charge, if I had been the Author, without
the assistance of a Casuistical Professor of Divinity. I should
pass over this, and most other of his objections, from the
debility of the argument; but a respect for the English Nation,
which has honoured the work on the P. of L., inclines me to
repel the malignity of the accuser, and the irrelevancy of the
charge.

I know what every Author must expect, who submits his
labours to the publick. If he will write, criticism and her
sister, Satire will seldom be far off. He knows the conditions;
nor can I see how *Christian* precepts are violated by their
application. No man ever seriously objected to the monthly
severity, or lunar caustick, of our Reviews. If the
character of any Author is implicated with his book or his
conduct; his character, book, and conduct must often be
examined and fall together.

The

The pleasantry of Dr. Johnson, (than whom no Author was ever attacked in his character. and writings with more spleen and injustice) may be certainly heard in this respect. He tells us, that "the diversion of baiting an *author* has the sanction of all ages and nations, and is more lawful than the sport of teazing other animals, because for the most part he comes *voluntary* to the stake."* But *now*, if a ci-devant Lawyer translates Horace; or a Dilettante writes heavy verses on *the Progress* of Society (the very name of *Progress* we see is infectious); or a Doctor in divinity republishes obscene poems; or commentators make indecent notes on Shakespeare; or men in their old age turn schoolboys, and publish their Greek exercises; and they happen to be censured; what are we to hear? An appeal to the Decalogue, and the Sermon on the mount.

I allow much for the impotence of irritation, when a patient, like the Progressionist, becomes feverous and shakes. I expect not to find legitimate argument; nor am I surprised when I look in vain for truth and logick. If I have carefully perused the Pursuits of Literature, I perceive much playfulness and humour, which can hardly be resolved into ill-nature or insolence. I do not wonder that the Progressionist has confounded them. It is perfectly consistent with the nature of his understanding, and perhaps of his education. Dr. Cornelius seems to have been concerned for his second son. " When ideas (of the same species) copulate, they engender *conclusions*, said philosopher Crambe; but when those of different species copulate, they bring forth *absurdities*." But the Progressionist seems to have forgotten, throughout his whole pamphlet, the ninth proposition of that celebrated philosopher on syllogisms, namely, that " an hypothetical

b   proposition

* Rambler, No. 170.

proposition is only a contract or promise of marriage, and that from such THEREFORE there can spring *no real issue.* *

It appears that the instances of *playfulness* and humour in the P. of L. are *exactly eight* †, in the estimation of the Progressionist. He seems at least to remember his Accidence, and *can* tell how many parts of speech there are. He says with great selfcomplacency, " Is this *playfulness* &c.?—Is this, &c.?—Is this, &c.? It might be replied, Certainly not. So curiously happy is he in these selections, that scarce one of *the eight* appear to have been intended as playful or humorous. All of them seem to me severe, serious, or monitory. But the Author has himself given so full and compleat an answer to this part, in his " Introductory Letter," that more is unnecessary.

It is rather surprising, that so much should be required of the Author of the P. of L. It appears, as if a kind of perfection had been expected in his work. Are there no *blemishes* in Horace and Juvenal ? no personal reflections, which were well understood in their time ? Was there ever any Satire, addressed to a Nation at large, which was not in some measure *personal*, at the time in which it was written ? Are there no observations rather flippant, and sometimes imprudent, in the finished satires of Boileau and Pope ? I believe no satirical Poet was ever wholly exempt from such *blemishes*. I would not defend the faults or defects of one writer, by those of another. But I would ask with great temper, whether in any Satirical Poem of the same extent, and variety of subjects, *so few* instances of imprudence, or impropriety, or inattention can be produced, as in the Pursuits of Literature. I very candidly declare, I think it impossible. If it were of sufficient importance, I am of opinion,

that

* Memoirs of Scriblerus, chap. 7.
† Progress of Satire, 2d edit. Preface.

that each instance might admit of a vindication, if it were adviseable to produce the ground, the authority, and the reasons for which, as I conceive, they were introduced. In a revolutionary age, a Satirist has to contend with dangerous tenets publickly professed, or privately favoured; with novelty, prejudice, folly, impudence personified, false learning, insolence, the rage of system, erudition misapplied, frivolous conduct, unthinking levity, open wickedness, and secret designs. Men, therefore, as well as their measures, and their doctrines, must be marked, and held forth to the publick observation. They who have made such objections, are wholly ignorant of the nature of the time. But if such objections are indeed just, " Down, down, proud Satire! though a realm be spoiled."

I always thought that some little reprehension was due to the Author of the P. of L. in a few instances. I will meet The Progressionist, but not half-way. I cannot encounter such a Major Sturgeon in poetry, in all his marchings and counter-marchings, and particularly in this last expedition.

I think it was improper in the Author of the Pursuits to speak slightingly of Mr. Abbot, a member of parliament, a gentleman of learning and great respectability of character, for his intended Digest of the Laws. But the Author of the P. of L. seems to have withdrawn his censure very readily, and upon an early conviction of it's impropriety. It appeared but in *one* edition of the Fourth Dialogue, published *separately.* Yet I still maintain, that a publick caution to the ablest man in the kingdom, is not unuseful at such a time as this; nor can the Progressionist be acquainted with the motive, which might have given rise to it. But with such a writer repentance and amendment are but evidences of increased guilt. *Gaudet monstris, mentisque tumultu.*

As

As to the subject of the Roman Catholick religion, and the various discussions on the French emigrants, and particularly the priests, the Author of the Pursuits stands in need of no additional vindication. In all his notes, and in his introductory letter, he has given a full, perfect, and compleat explanation of his publick sentiments. I think it satisfactory. In my solemn opinion, his motives were honest; his caution justifiable; his reasons forcible and convincing; and the measures he recommended, appear to have been dictated by sound policy and charity, and the true humanity of a Protestant statesman. The late proceedings in Ireland are the best (and as I am persuaded, an *unanswerable*) commentary on his text. I refer you to his own words, and arguments; for I will not discuss the matter again needlessly. The moral babble of the Progressionist on this occasion might be natural enough in the mouth of Mr. Jerningham.

In my full and most unequivocal belief, the Author of the P. of L. never intended any ridicule whatsoever on " *The Literary Fund.*" Nothing but malice or stupidity could misrepresent him in this instance, and the *playful* allusion to the *Sportula*. He was speaking of Mr. Boscawen's Horace, which he did not admire; and that gentleman being a Commissioner in the *Victualling* Office, appears to have suggested the allusion, which gave offence, when tortured into a hidden meaning. And very probably when the Author found it so unaccountably misunderstood, he omitted it. I am convinced that a man of his disposition never could have cast a reflection either on that, or on any other useful institution whatsoever. If Mr. Boscawen published his translation of Horace, I suppose there is no statute of pains and penalties for those who are so unhappy as to disapprove of it. I join with the Author of the P. of L. in his opinion of the translation.

translation. I speak impartially; for I have not the slightest acquaintance with Mr. Boscawen: I know not even his person.

If *such* is the scheme of interpretation and allegory, which is to be introduced into this country by the Progressionist, I shall soon expect to see him *prove*, that the *Art of Cookery*, by that excellent and useful citizen Mr. John Farley, is one concealed *Satire*, from beginning to end upon the *literature*, and government of this country, under the form of *receipts* and made dishes. There is one of them which, I am sure, the Progressionist will assert and *prove* to be directed against him and his *pamphlet*. The reader of taste will perhaps be of the same opinion. It is called, " THE CALF's HEAD *Surprized*." The metaphorical culinary citizen informs us, in page 116 of his * valuable work, that " THE CALF's HEAD *Surprized*." is an elegant *top*-dish, not very expensive †. He recommends us to *prepare* it, by raising off the skin with a *sharp-pointed* knife, and as much meat from the bone *as you can possibly get*; so that it may appear like a a *whole* head when *stuffed*; but be careful not to cut holes *in the skin*." He then recommends a mixture of pepper, the best *(Attick)* salt, and other *pungent* ingredients; and he says, " pour a little of it into the ears, and the rest *into the head*." This severe style, and the clear allusion to the Progress of Satire, is too evident to admit of a doubt. Hercules is not better known by his foot, than the Progressionist's pamphlet from Mr. Farley's receipt. If such is the

tendency

---

† Art of Cookery made plain and easy to *every* understanding in the kingdom, by John Farley, Cook to the London Tavern, 8th Edit.—N. B. It is said to be among the tracts recommended by the Hon. the Commissioners of H. M. *Victualling* Office, for promoting good living, &c. &c.

* Progress of Satire, *price* 2s.

tendency of the book, Mr. Pitt and Mr. Dundas will do well to look with caution, in their visits to the London Tavern, on the designs of *Citizen* John Farley and his dangerous compositions. From *these* interpretations I shrewdly suspect that the State apprehends as much danger from Mr. Farley, as the Literary Fund does from the Author of the P. of Literature.

As to the charge against the Author of the P. of L. of having admitted any expressions of an *indecent* nature, I think it perfectly ridiculous. The passages which are brought to support the opinion, may be again submitted to the reader. The following is termed by the Progressionist " grossly indecent." It should be first recollected, that the passage itself is declared by it's Author, " to record the political conversion of Lord Loughborough to Mr. Pitt's party." This is done under the imagery taken from the serenata of Acis and Galatea. The lines are these :

" Nay Thurlow once, 'tis said, could sing or swear,
Like Polypheme, I cannot, cannot bear ;
For, ah ! presumptuous Acis wrests the prize,
And ravishes the nymph before his eyes ;
Such feats his honour little Pepper saw,
In all the pride of musick and of law. †

When the meaning of the passage is declared, and the allusion to a well-known story so fully understood, it exceeds all power of face to be grave at such a charge.

Dr. Johnson, in his Dictionary says, to *ravish* is to *take away by violence*, and he quotes Shakespeare for the illustration :

" Their

† P. of L. Dial. 2. v. 35. read also the note.

" Their vow is made
To ransack Troy, within whose strong immures
The *ravish'd* Helen sleeps."

I make no doubt, that THE OPPOSITION, and that good man,
Mr. Fox, thought this *ravishing* of so able an assistant, or rather
leader of the party, a direct and most *indecent* felony on the
part of the minister. In my opinion, the Poet supposes a
little more than the truth, and succeeds in fiction. I
conceive *the Nymph* was willing to be won, yet not wholly
unsought. I know nothing of that reluctant amorous delay,
with which Lord Loughborough resigned his *legal* charms
to Mr. Pitt. The minister well knew by whom the armour
of that political virgin had been often tried. Blood and
war were to be her dowry. Her bridal gown was soon
changed into the sagum of a siege-directing Chancellor.
If this be *indecent*, I shall leave it to the cabinet at St.
James's to justify the assault. If I had been the Author of
the P. of L. I should be in no pain for the Panel.

The Progessionist affirms, that " Sir James Bland
Burgess, Baronet, is ridiculed for not having made his
Poem lascivious and indecent." The passage itself is
the best answer. The Poet speaking in the Second Dialogue,
that he *could* do, such and such things ; among them he says,

" Or to Cythæron from the Treasury, move,
And like Sir James Bland Burgess, murmur love."*

I refer you to the whole of the note upon these lines, of which
the following is a part. " Sir James says of Cupid, " That
boy and that boy's deeds shall not pollute my measure." The
Author of the P. of L. says; " Now when I consider what
Virgil and Tasso have said and sung of " that boy and that
boy's deeds," it is a *little prudish* in Sir James Bland Burgess,

Baronet,

* P. of L. Dial. 2. v. 63. and the notes.

Baronet and Poet, on such a subject to have such fears. A poet may be a little playful." I believe there is not a Court in the whole world, not even a Jury of the Muses and Graces in the island of Love, who would not acquit the Author of any charge, but that of pleasantry. I think the Progressionist has not quite forgot his *former* character in La Mancha, and has yet some secret Dulcinea of Toboso, whose charms he has sworn to defend and maintain againſt the whole universe. I shall not be surprised to hear of some new freaks in the Brown Mountains.

. The Progressionist next informs us of some " infamous allusions respecting Mr. GEORGE STEEVENS." For my own part, I am totally ignorant of any " infamous allusions," whatsoever to that most accomplished Editor of Shakspeare. I have examined the P. of L. again and again, and can only find, that Mr. Steevens is called the Whipper-In of the Shakspeare Pack of Commentators. He is complimented for his learning and abilities; and reprehended for the indecency of some of his illustrations of Shakspeare. His very early visits to London from Hampstead, to correct his edition of the poet in 1793, gave the Author of the Pursuits some sportive apprehensions for his classick purity. And why? Because Aurora might have mistaken *Mr. Steevens* at so an early an hour for her own *Cephalus*. Risum teneatis ?

The Author of the P. of L. has not attempted to penetrate Mr. Steevens's retirement on the Heath of Hampstead, or to pry into the mysteries of his closet. The retreats of virtue and erudition were ever sacred. The consolations of solitary reflection are reserved for men of uncorrupted integrity: they need not to fly from their enemies, or from themselves.

They

They have a claim to private affection, seconded and confirmed by the publick esteem. In all the busy agitations of literature and philosophy, they remember those honourable principles which have uniformly directed their conduct; they remember them, and are at peace. As I cannot discover what *allusions* the Progressionist insinuates, I am under the necessity of dismissing the charge. If he should think proper to specify them, time might be found for the discussion. Till then, I am silent through ignorance. The Editor of Shakspeare has no need of such a pen as the Progressionist's in his defence. If Mr. Steevens himself should be inclined to present the world with *a History of his own life and writings*, he could not leave a more instructive lesson to posterity.

The indignation of the Progressionist next rises to a more than ordinary height, when he thinks of that ornament of the Court of King's Bench, Mr. *Barrister* Erskine. For my own part, I think no one appears to have wished health and spirits to Mr. Erskine more than the Author of the P. of L.

> " And while the busy *Hall*
> Attracts him still to toil for power or gold,
> Sweetly may He his vacant hours possess
> *In Hampstead*, courted by the western wind."*

But it seems the Progressionist is very angry at the mention of Mr. Erskine's Materia Medica. If indeed the poppy were described on the brow of a *poet*, he would understand the propriety of it: but if the opium is said to sink into the skull of a *Lawyer*, we are told, that all shame is lost.

The

* Armstrong's Art of Health, B. 1.

The Progressionist, in the fury of his zeal to prove that he himself is sleepless, appears in an attitude copied from Bedlam, or Parnassus:

> Fire in his eye, and papers in his hand,
> He raves, *recites*, and maddens round the land.

If Mr. Erskine has read his defence by this real enemy to his reputation, I well know what he would think and say, when such stupidity is offered for wit, and any narcoticks (but his own) for restoratives.

> What drop or nostrum can this plague remove?
> Or which must end me, a fool's wrath or love?

But, after all, what are these sarcastick and contemptuous terms on Mr. Erskine? What is this note so "unworthy of a gentleman or a scholar?" If I had been the author, I should not offer any other apology, than *the words upon the record*, produced and read in court. The Clerk may now read them, if he pleases.

> "In state affairs all Barristers are dull;
> And Erskine nods, the opium in his skull."*

If I had written them, I should be most in pain for the first line. Consider, how discouraging, how unkind to the Professional Gentlemen in the House of Commons. It is delivered as a self-evident proposition. There are indeed many exceptions to it; and the question is *now* rather nice, and perhaps dangerous. Erect your ears! From Lincolns Inn to Bloomsbury, "The hum of *either army* stilly sounds!" The Author of the P. of L. must surely have forgotten himself.

We all remember, when THURLOW and WEDDERBURNE were called into Parliament, how soon they proved
what

---

* P. of L. Dial. 4. p. 360, 7th edit.

what manner of men they were. They separated the lawyer from the statesman. It was a proud day for the Bar at that period. Never before were such irresistible, overbearing powers and talents displayed by the official defenders of a Minister.

Hos mirabantur Athenæ
Torrentes, pleni et moderantes fræna theatri.

Lord North indeed, when he appointed Thurlow and Wedderburne his Attorney and Solicitor General, meant no more than to give spirit, eloquence, and argument to his measures; but in effect he hung a millstone on the necks of all their successors. This by the way.

I proceed to the second verse and the comment upon it.

" And Erskine nods, the opium in his skull."

The note begins thus. " MR. BARRISTER ERSKINE is " *famous* for taking opium in great quantities; (I have " often heard him speak in praise of it) and if he proceeds " in this manner, it is apprehended that his *political* facul- " ties will die of too large a dose, of which there are some " symptoms already." Here is the assertion. A plain matter of fact, acknowledged and approved by Mr. Erskine himself, and the Author of the Pursuits only expresses a kind apprehension, and solicitude for the consequences. The words " Mr. Barrister Erskine" seem to be repeated, merely that Mr. Erskine might always remember the publick opinion, and never consider himself as a statesman, but by way of eminence, *The Barrister.*

I can see neither contempt nor sarcasm in the observation. I think it indeed rather adulatory at the expence of his brethren: They are all declared to be dull in state affairs; but some powerful cause seems necessary to produce dulness in Mr. Erskine. There may be also a gentle admo-

admonition or some allusion, more than meets the ear. We
are told, that the highest Rulers in that Nation, which is
most celebrated for an attachment to Opium, are seldom
inclined to bear any brothers near the throne. And this is
an allegory.

But the Progressionist, who generally draws his
logick from Dr. Cornelius, seems strangely to have
forgotten a grand rule of Philosopher Crambe, "That
there can be no more in the conclusion than there was in
the premises." But in argument he redoubles his veneration for him, by strictly adhering to another dictum of
his great Instructor, namely " that the conclusion always
follows the *weaker* part."‡ The understanding of the Progressionist seems indeed to be in such a state, that I do not
think it expedient to awaken or even to disturb it. Sleep
is the beſt restorative; but there is a sleep, which is unto
death.

It is allowed that Mr. Erskine is a man of talents and
great eloquence; and has made more extensive conqueſts
in his profession than any of his predecessors. Be it so.
Expende Annibalem! Every honour is paid to his genius,
and professional rank and distinction; but his *political*
eminence and ability are absolutely denied. In the hall
of Æolus he is declared supreme; but the command of the
trident, which he had vainly and so unaccountably
assumed, is wrested from him.

When THE STORMS are once set at liberty, Mr.
Erskine knows, that wisdom and power are often inefficient
for their control. They are represented, by the Poet, as
in one perpetual struggle against *authority*, reluctant and
terrible. It is a cavern vast and spacious, a prison houfe,
where they are chained down in confinement. But when
⸺ the

‡ Memoirs of Martinus Scriblerus, chap. 7.

the spear is thrust into the side of the mountain to unloose them, and they are unloosed ; the day and the sky disappear ; darkness is interrupted by the lightning alone, and general destruction and desolation seem to be inevitable. In France, and in every country which France has invaded, deceived, revolutionized, and plundered, this picture of political storms has been realized.

But Mr. Erskine, *though he knew all this*, did not feel his heart humbled. His voice, his talents, and his doctrines have been all exerted in strange union against the best political interests of Great Britain. I agree with the Author of the P. of L. that his pamphlet on the French war is flimsy and puerile. I am still more inclined to think it reprehensible and dangerous ; it is full of misrepresentations. There is not one mark of a Statesman's mind impressed on any page. Mr. Burke first read the writing on the great wall of France, and made known to Europe the interpretation thereof.

Mr. Erskine forgets, that the French themselves require something more than the talents of a *Barrister*, however brilliant, to *direct* their councils. An honourable and useful profession in a free country, is Mr. Erskine's undoubted right. Let him remain there with credit to himself, and advantage to others. I hope never again to hear that eloquence, so successful in defending the religion of his country in her courts of law, employed against her safety and her government. His vanity may deceive him ; and it is indeed deceived, if he thinks that Barras or Talleyrand, by any future order of a Directory, would " clothe him *in scarlet*, and put a chain of gold about his neck, and make a proclamation concerning *him*, that he should be the third ruler in" the new Republick. No. They would soon forget the tinsel of his eloquence in

the

the sterling weight of his property. There is no security against the Goth or the Gaul. The mystery of their morality and of their politicks is penetrated, and revealed in open day to every inhabitant of the civilized world.

Periere làtebræ
Tot scelerum; POPULO VENIA EST EREPTA NOCENTI;'
AGNOVERE SUOS!*

There is a fatality which attends the Progressionist whether he marches through Weſtminſter Hall, or loiters in the Treasury Chambers; whether he appears as a Nuncio from the ancient Vatican, or in the weeds of Dominick from the Castle at Winchester. His judgment and understanding keep pace with his natural politeness. He provokes a discussion, which might have ceased; and revives a controversy which, but for his imprudence, might have rested. Yet as he says, that he intends "to ſhew the *artifice and malignity* of the Author of the Pursuits of Literature in their *true* light ;" the friends of that work will be pleased when the charge is repelled. The respect due to the English Nation who have honoured it, and whom the Progressionist, with his usual courteousness, styles " *the addle-headed publick*,"† may require some justification. The hand of friendship and affection for the truth and importance of the work will, I trust, be able to effect it.

The conduct of the Progressionist frequently resembles that of Sir William Draper, though without one trait of the learning and ability of that undaunted Knight. The defence of Lord Granby by Sir William, and the zeal of Major Scott for Mr. Hastings are almost proverbial for their consequences. I am also of opinion, that if the Reverend Dr. Warton had been abandoned by the Progressionist,

* Lucan. lib. 4. v. 192.
† *Motto* to the Title Page of the Progress of Satire.

gressionist, it would have been esteemed as no breach of friendship by the learned Editor of Pope's works.

I have just re-perused the whole of the objections made by the Author of the P. of L. to Dr. Warton's edition of Pope, and the comments on those objections by the Progressionist, and his *Impartial* Brother. Sancho and Quixote were not more faithful to each other. The Castilian gravity is happily tempered with a sententious proverbial buffoonery. They seem equally zealous for the helmet of Mambrino, and the doctorial robe of Joseph Warton. They find a few spots upon the divine ermine and academical scarlet, and by an aukward attempt to remove them, the marks become indelible, and sink into the very grain. They exert all the sinews of the body, but fury and violence, as usual, relax those of the mind. The terms, " insolence, brutality, cowardice" and some others, are so familiar in their mouths, that the colour of their forehead is not more conspicuous than the ground of their hearts.

Let me ask them: have they ever weighed seriously the period in which we live? Have they felt the *necessity* of guarding with greater and still increasing vigilance, every *avenue* to moral corruption? We are reminded now more than ever of the *conceit* of the fabulist, not inelegantly applied by the orator of Byzantium.† " Sorrow is made more permanent. The clay, of which man was formed, was not tempered with water, but with tears." The miseries of all civilized states are multiplying in every form, and springing up from sources never yet conceived. New fountains are opening under our feet, and they cast forth waters of bitterness. Channels must be prepared to carry them off the land in every

† —Λυπην εμμονωτεραν. Τυτο ὁ Αισωπος λεγει· των γαρ πηλον, αυτω ὁ Προμηθευς, αφ' ὁ τον Ανθρωπον διεπλασατο, υκ εφυρασεν ὑδατι, αλλα δακρυοις.

Themistii. Orat. 32. p. 359. Ed. Harduini, 1684.

every direction. Time and the hour have not yet run through the roughest day, which Great Britain and Ireland ever experienced. Among the causes of many present calamities, I fear we must number the intemperance of Literature in one kingdom, and the neglect of culture in the other. I think it was very wisely observed by Mr. Pitt, in the House of Commons, that ignorance and want of instruction dispose the mind to revolution and rebellion. It is equally true, that the dreams of a heated brain, the meteors of modern philosophy, and the beatifick visions of experimental statesmen and *accredited* scholars, have produced the same fatal tendency. We have lived to see no mimick desolation. Palaces have been unpeopled, battlements have been shaken, fortresses laid prostrate, and every polished edifice defaced and mutilated.

The mine was laid and sprung originally by *Literature*, falsely so called. And when the strict and unbending principles of morality are relaxed or discountenanced, and the passions let loose and inflamed by licentious language and luscious imagery, the ruin is soon compleated. The horrors are realized, and fiction is no more. At such a period as this, are we to rise and watch, or to be for ever fallen?

If I had not a greater regard for Dr. Warton than the Progressionist has, I should copy the whole note on his edition of Pope's works, from the Pursuits of Literature. I think *every* charge in that note may be substantiated. In particular, the charge of having published the scandalous Imitation of the *Second Satire** of Horace, against the last injunctions and directions of Mr. Pope himself, admits of no defence whatsoever. There is a shamelessness, as well as folly, in some parts of the Progressionist's defence, which I could not have expected.   The

* The *Impartial* Brother of The Progressionist says, that " Dr. Warton is reprehended for publishing the *Satires* of Pope." Strictures, page 27.—I only notice it for the wilful misrepresentation of the *plural* for the *singular*.

The Author of the P. of L. well knew the humanity and characteristick of an Englishman; and the respect due to age and learned repose. I am convinced, he felt a veneration for the hoary head, and the laurels of a veteran. He seemed to regret, that all scholars have not preserved the same consistency and propriety with Mr. Bryant and Mr. Melmoth; but he most certainly expressed himself with that warmth, severity, and earnestness, which the interest of his country seemed to demand. De Republicâ graviter querens, de *Homine* nihil dixit.

The Author of the P. of L. put this plain question: " Am I to spare publick criticism (of an *edition* of Pope's works) because of Dr. Warton's age ?" And he asks, Is it in the title page of the edition ?" or he might have added, " Is there any allusion to it in any part of the work ?" If the edition is not designed to supersede, by it's excellence, the use of Dr. Warburton's, or any other, the argument might be changed in some measure. But there is no compromise, no qualifying circumstance whatsoever.

The Author of the Pursuits expostulated with Dr. Warton on the impropriety of seeming to laugh at, or to decry, the use of moral satire, and the endeavours after a reformation of manners. He also strongly condemned the Doctor for the *tendency* of many of his notes, to favour those fatal opinions, by which Europe has been overthrown. The Missionaries of the French Propaganda are in every country. Troy was not in greater danger from the arts of Sinon, than Prussia at this moment from the Abbé Sièyes.

The Author of the P. of L. said also, that Dr. Warton praised VOLTAIRE too much. Surely whoever is fully acquainted with the desolation and misery which Voltaire's

c   writings

writings and princ;ples have effected, will be surprized at the
mildness of the term, by which they are characterized. " I
have always been as ready (says Dr. Warton) to censure his
inconsistencies, as to praise his talents." * Any person who
has read Baruel's Memoirs of Jacobinism, will be astonished
to hear of the *inconsistency* of a man, whose actions,
writings, and principles formed one regular, *consistent*, and
undeviating plan for the destruction of all religion and
established government. I should have expected another tone
and other language from a Doctor in Divinity.

I remember that Doctor Moore, in his View of the French
Revolution,† tells us, it was Voltaire's misfortune not to
be a believer in Christianity. He told us well. He says also,
that his attempts to overturn the established religion of his
country, cannot be excused. Why, well too. But he and
Dr. Warton both concur in a strange observation, on the
respect with which Voltaire treats Christianity in all his
Dramas. ‡ Dr. Moore calls it a *peculiarity.* But what does
that prove ? Dramatick characters surely must be drawn con-
sistently. A writer of plays must not openly outrage the
government or religion of his country ; more especially in a
Roman Catholick kingdom. Neither the police, nor the
audience, would suffer such characters and such representa-
tions on a publick theatre. Besides, an open, apparent
respect and recommendation of Christianity was an essential
part of Voltaire's plan to overthrow it. He was an actor

himself

---

* Warton's Pope, vol. 1. Life of the Author, p. xxxviii.
note.

† Vol. 1. p. 24.

‡ Dr. Warton's Edition of Pope, vol. 1. Life of Pope,
page 38. " Voltaire was an *Unbeliever ;* which however
never appears in his tragedies."

himself in every thing. *Cujuslibet rei simulator et dissimulator.* The people knew nothing of the amulet, or horrid formulary, which he wore under his cap, and signed in every letter to his private friends. The " *Ecrasez l' Infame,*" had not then been made publick. What could they know of his interior? On his knees before the Romish mass in a publick church; with a Confessor openly maintained in his house; with a chapel in that house, and regular daily service in that chapel; with every exterior reverence and obedience to the national religion and catholick superstition; the kiss of Judas was fidelity, when compared with the calm, deliberate, secret, exterminating hypocrisy of this arch Theomachist.

The first Traitor lived to repent, that he had " betrayed the innocent blood." The Sanhedrim of the day told him, " What is that to us, see *thou* to that." He cast down the money before the priests, and elders in the temple, departed, and perished by his own hand. The Sanhedrim of France, when they met, had indeed nothing left but the ashes of *their* Founder to canonize. What they could do, they did. They acknowledged *his* work, and *his* services, being so done and so allowed. If they had been inclined to take *his* pieces of silver and gold, it would have been very *lawful* for them to have put them into the national treasury, for it was THE PRICE OF BLOOD. They might have been still more consistent. They might at least have taken Ferney from his heirs for the use of the martyrs of the Revolution, and called it " The field of blood," unto this day. Upon my word, Sir, we are insulted with mere words on these subjects; when one Doctor calls them *peculiarities;* and a Divine of the Church of England terms them *inconsistencies.* I understand not these prudent submissions, these polite fears of giving offence to any literary cabals in this, or any other kingdom. I would court no favour, no patronage, no applause from those persons, whom upon what Dr. Moore terms the

" *Elite*

" *Elite des Philosophes,*" * the chosen elect of the modern philosophy.

If the name of Dr. Warton, and his age, and his merits are registered in every ountry, and in every climate, where the voice of English poetry is heard, and the name of Pope and his works venerated, the Progressionist might indulge his vein for panegyrick. He comes forth with such determined fierceness and prowess; he claims for Dr. Warton, whatever does or does not belong to him in all the territories of literature, with so sturdy an earnestness, that you would think neither a field, nor a blade of grass, nor an ear of corn belonged to any other person. He has all the boldness of a celebrated *advocate,* whose speech is recorded by *a female historian* : " Good people, if you do not declare and confess, " that ALL these lands and fields of corn belong to *my Lord* " *Marquis of Carrabas,* you shall all be cut as small as " minced meat." † I imagine we are all as terrified, as the peasants were, with the threats of *this Cat in Boots.*

Yet perhaps in this little island there *may* be found readers of Pope, who, in the fine language of The Progressionist, are ignorant, that " Dr. Warton has been for nearly half a " century one of the brightest ornaments to the classical "' literature of his country." I am persuaded that many men, many women, and many children, are certainly ignorant of this truth (which the Author of the P. of I. never denied to a certain point), and yet they read Pope. If The Progressonist had plain sense, he would have changed his interrogatories, which admit of so easy an answer. He

would

* Dr. Moore's View of the French Revolution, vol. 1. p. 23.
　　† Mother Goose's Tales of the Master Cat, or Puss in Boots.

would have found that the praise of classical erudition was granted liberally to Dr. Warton; and the defects of the critick rarely attracted any censure. If the Progressionist had thought, as well as written, he must have seen, that it was not the age of *Pope's Editor*, but the *Divine* who forgot his age, and the obligation of his profession, that was the object of his censure. In a vigorous, chearful, and respected old age, like Dr. Warton's, I discover no excuse for his conduct; and he who had so usefully and so honourably presided over the morals and learning of youth, could not have been ignorant of the tendency of so inflammatory and shameless a composition, as the Imitation of the Second Satire of Horace.

The question indeed is not, whether Dr. Warton is a man of learning and ability (which the Author of the P. of L. has not denied); but whether by unpardonable inattention, or by carelessness, or by design, he has not forfeited the publick esteem as *Editor of Pope's works*. He has suffered them to be degraded and contaminated by the insertion of some writings, which no readers called for, many had forgotten, and the greater part never knew. Some abler defence, than the Progressionist can make, is required. The evidence of the book is before us; the Doctor is taken *in flagrante delicto;* the protest of Mr. Pope is upon record; the decency and dignity of an Editor demanded a compliance with that protest; the character of the English Nation was violated, when the licentious were gratified, the virtuous disgusted, and the unsuspecting perhaps corrupted. Upon every principle the action was wrong; and it constituted a criminal offence in a moral and literary court. The Author of the P. of L. addressed himself not so much to Dr. Warton, as to the publick. I think he was, and is, right. The offence, (if I may use, by analogy, the terms of law,) was not bailable; no defence was

set

set up by the person accused, or by any man acting by his directions; and I maintain, that the Author of the Pursuits acted wisely and justifiably in following it up, and prosecuting the Doctor to conviction. The Reverend Doctor's office was to support morality, and to discountenance whatever *tended* to destroy, weaken, or discredit it. The maxim of the law is wise, true, and solid: *Quando aliquid prohibetur, prohibetur et omne, per quod devenitur ad illud.*" The Doctor and The Progressionist may answer this at their leisure.

The Author of the Pursuits is speaking of all the readers of Pope in every part of the world, where the English language is either spoken or understood. Whatever poet may be neglected, *his* works are studied. On the banks of the Ohio and the Ganges, his numbers are heard with delight; and to the inhabitants of those distant shores that author would vindicate the fame and consistency of the poet. In my opinion, The Progressionist has hazarded something more than the character of his understanding. I would also suggest to him, that " in justice to his friends, " his future labours should be confined to the care of *his* " *own* reputation." *

When Virgil had consigned his immortal work to destruction by his last injunction, Augustus interposed in behalf of the poet, and of all posterity. The gratitude of Italy has been, and will be, re-ecchoed by every civilized nation, till time shall be no more. But the request of dying men, and in particular of the virtuous and the eminent, should meet with sacred attention. By that declaration, Mr.

Pope

* Junius, letter 5.

Pope left his works to the world (I use his own words) " *as*
" *Mr. Warburton* * *shall publish them,* WITHOUT FUTURE
" ALTERATIONS." He certainly provided for his own
reputation, and the consistency of it, by this direction ; and
he departed in tranquillity. I think Mr. Pope has found an
avenger of the wrongs his memory has suffered ; and it
remains for The Progressionist and Dr. Warton to
reply :

" Id cinerem, aut manes credis curare sepultos ?"

For my own part, I am not so schooled in ancient or in
modern classicks. In the very winding sheet of the poet
there is verge enough to trace the characters of his virtue,
and of repentance for his errors.

Lighter charges require fewer words. The Author of the
Pursuits reprobated Dr. Warton, and in my opinion justly,
for having exhibited a contemptible, smuggled likeness of
Mr. Pope. As to the propriety and kindness of this conduct,
I refer to Dr. Warton's own words. " The portrait was
" drawn *without his knowledge,* when he was deeply engaged
" in conversation with Mr. Allen in the gallery at Prior
" Park, by Mr. Hoare, who sat at the other end of the
" gallery. *Pope would never have forgiven the painter had*
" *he known it.* He was *too sensible of the deformity* of his
" person, *to allow the whole of it* to be represented. This
" drawing is THEREFORE *exceedingly valuable.* †" And
THEREFORE the kindness and moral delicacy of Dr.
Warton are exceedingly remarkable and conspicuous.
In kindness to Dr. Warton, I sincerely hope that no
critick

* Mr. Pope's last Will and Testament.
† Warton's Pope, vol. 1. p. ix.

critick will hereafter give the Progressionist fresh materials for writing in his *defence*.

The Progressionist is unwilling that any figures on the literary canvass of "*his adversary*" should be unnoticed or untouched. He wishes to re-animate them all. He has a dexterity bordering on the *Andröides*, and Automata of the day, and pretty much after the same manner. He pulls the strings, and the puppets dance, and sometimes continue longer on the scene than could be wished. The Author of the P. of L. contented himself with drawing a picture of life, as it is. The Progressionist would fain exhibit the figures distorted; and as he has often obtained for himself " the Praise of Folly;" has no objection to the caricatures of Holbein *.

He appears to great advantage in the character of A CONJUROR, *or* RAREE-SHOW MAN. His glass magnifies or diminishes at pleasure, but the objects are very clear. When he has prepared his little machinery, the company are admitted, and he begins.

First, he presents to your view at full length, the figure of *a Bishop*, drawn from the plains of Salisbury, with the happy genius of Stukely himself. He puts a wine-glass in his hand; by magick turns his port into *circulating* claret; next gives him a twist round before the spectators, writes his name on his back, and dismisses him.

Then, *presto*, A BARRISTER, from the fatigues of a long state-trial, and " incessant exertions" for Horne Tooke, Citizen Hardy, Thomas Holcroft, John Thelwall, and the whole crew. A bell rings, and up comes an apothecary with *opium* for Mr. Erskine, and the dregs for his clerk. A

chariot

* See " Erasmi Moriæ Encomium figuris Holbenii."

chariot next appears ; the door opens, and Mr. Erskine, in a kind of convulsive lassitude, falls back into his seat. A little mob of figures rises, takes off the horses, and drags *the Barrister* fast asleep into Serjeant's Inn, where he wakes just time enough to make the citizens and citi*zettes* a speech; he gives a yawn, and reposes again. He then wakes, and chants first a kind of *Graduale*, composed for the chapel of an intended republican *Conservatorio*, but without much *counterpoint*. Last, with a *voce di petto*, accompanied by one of his *virtuosi da camera*, the Barrister sings out various *stanzas* from his pamphlet on the French War, selected for the purpose; but perceiving how little effect they have, and finding his *portamento* drowned by an increasing chorus of " God save the King," louder and louder throughout *all the Inns of Court*; he drops his voice and his pamphlet together, and is carried off fast asleep, as before.

The scene shifts ; and lo! an Under-Secretary of State, with a *Microcosm* before him. A distant view of *Eton* college, a transparency in the manner of Loutherbourgh. He tells the audience, that the Under-Secretary wrote and thought when he was a boy, and spoke when he became a man ; and makes the spectators observe how very trifling the difference is between the little, and the great world, and the moral of the piece,

The Progressionist, or Raree-show man, next presents us with an auction room, with booksellers and their shop-men, and various other scholars round the table, who generally plead ignorance as to the value of the books, till a Doctor in divinity explains and nods ; and he particularly takes care that the spectators shall know who the Doctor is. It was observable, that in the title page of one of the *old* black letter books,

books, there was a figure of Prodigality, contented at last to feed *on husks* in a foreign country; but the company in general were so struck, or offended at the print, that *only one gentleman* would bid for the book.

The next change of scene is to a hall, or committee-room. A phantom rises with *seales* in his hand, inscribed " *Truth and Sense.*"* He puts into one the Baviad and Mæviad, the Pursuits of Literature, and some of the Anti-Jacobin newspapers; in the other the second edition of the Progress of Satire, the Impartial Strictures, some leaves from the Reviews and the True Briton, and Jerningham's poems for a make-weight, but all in vain; the art of the conjuror cannot prevent the air of the room from dispersing them by their own lightness.

We are next presented with the private study of a Doctor in Divinity, in which the sixth volume of Dr. Warton's edition of Pope's works is lettered *Rochester* instead of *Pope*. He strives hard, in laboured terms, to persuade the spectators that the scene-painter only is in fault; but the letters are too plain to be mistaken.

The scene then changes to a view of the coasts of Brittany and Normandy, with the images of Pantagruel and Panurge † in the ship, when they met nine sail *spooming* before the wind, full of Dominicans, Jesuits, Capuchins, Austins, Bernardins, Cordeliers, Carmelites, and the d--v-l and all of holy monks and friars who were going *to council* at the castle of W——. He shews you how Panurge played the good fellow *after the storm was over*, and would fain have sung with Friar *John* ‡ the *Contra Hostium Insidias*, as matter of breviary.

---

* See the motto to the Progress of Satire; concerning " *the addle-headed publick*," or the English Nation; and HIS OWN " *Scales of Truth and Sense.*"

† Rabelais, b. 4. chap. 18, &c.

‡ Q. Whether an ancestor of *John* Milner, of Winchester?

breviary. The Progressionist then comes forward himself, and gives you to understand that *his own* name is *William* Dreadnought, and swears, " by the pavilion of Mars, that he fears nothing but danger."

One of the last scenes exhibits Samuel Johnson in a *desert* island, and Junius (from the neighbourhood of *Stow*) in a mask ; and between the two, uprises " *Jack the Giant-killer* in a coat of darkness." In the back-ground a figure of St. John in the wilderness, in chiaro oscuro, with an inscription from the Bible *.

The Progressionist having thus for some time re-called the publick attention to the objects of his pane-gyrick, by such a judicious exhibition, suddenly quits his character of Raree-show man, and the language of the Fantocini. He next commences *verse-maker*, and having snuffed up a sufficient quantity of the fatal blossoms on the celebrated tree near Helicon, † *whose scent alone is death*, he rhymes lustily and furiously, and not without great danger to himself. He tells us *how* Satire was born and bred, and *how* she grew up, married and had children, and what were the names of the children, and who were their nurses. ‡. But in spite of all his lusty efforts, the language is still that of lullaby, and it is well, if we can recollect even the matters of fact. But as he himself recollects, that *the zeal* of a certain description of persons must always offend, but most of all in rhyme, he not unwisely divides his labours.

Verse-

---

* See the end of The Progressionist's Preface, 2d edit.

† Est etiam in magnis Heliconis montibus arbos,
Floris odore hominem tetro consueta necare.
Lucret. l. 6. v. 786.

‡ See " The Progress of Satire," from p. 1. to p. 28; that is, " *the whole of the verses.*"

" Verse-man or prose-man, term him which you will,
His head and heart come flowing through his quill;
His *foes* will wish his life a longer date;
But scarcely will *his friends* lament his fate."

The Progressionist then suddenly drives to Westminster-hall, and casts a longing lingering look upon the benches in the different courts, particularly in the King's Bench. Gowns, briefs, demurrers, replications, issues, and libels dance before his eyes in legal confusion; and his language is the unnatural mixture of law, nonsense, verse, and absurdity. It is in short any thing but the common *parlance* of Parnassus, and the courts above. He should take a little instruction from ". *The Pleader's Guide;*" which the friends of wit and good sense have long wished to see compleated. He toils and groans, and would fain give Mr. Barsister Erskine a retaining fee against the Author of the P. of L. " who, (as he declares) " holds barristers in such supreme contempt." It would, however, be difficult to prove this. He speaks indeed of the dulness of lawyers in state-affairs; but as to their dignity, brightness, integrity, and intelligence in their own department he does not so much as hint at them. But, I hear, general dulness is implied in the charge. I make no doubt if some literary Charles Surface were to ask the Progressionist, like *Moses* in the play, if it were not so; he would say with the little Israelite, " O *yesh*, I *vill* take my oath of that." Really from the specimen he has given, you might also take him for Moses in another point, when Sir Oliver enquires after the family library. "I don't think, says Charles, that MOSES *can direct you there.*"—No, no, he replies, *I naiver meddlesh vith books,*" Now The Progressionist certainly does *meddle* with books; but as to understanding their contents, or the plain sense of a single argument in law, prose, or verse, " *dat ish quaite out of hish* way."

3   Whether

Whether logick originally begat law, or law engendered logick, I know not; but there is often some pleasant confusion between them. Yet I would advise the Progressionist to speak with more respect of Duncan's Elements, than he does of Blackstone. It is plain, that he has been formerly engaged in an *academick* hunt after truth, and has endeavoured, with very great diligence, to distinguish a curve from a strait line: but all his industry has been in vain. If Eton and Oxford united their great masters in philology and philosophy, in the cultivation of the Progressionist's understanding; I will say with Cicero, " Invideo sane Magistris, qui illum, tantâ mercede, nihil sapere docuerunt." I am sure he will never make an honest livelihood by his logick, his law, or his verse. He gravely tells us, that the irrefragable argument of whips and bludgeons is against the King's peace; but that *an action for damages* lies against the Author of the P. of L. Poor man! I am sure none but his own bookseller will ever sue the Progressionist for damages. I believe he is like Ebenezer Broadbrim, in Foote's Devil on Two Sticks, and would willingly " send for *a sinful man in the flesh*, called an Attorney, to prepare a parchment, and carry the Author of the Pursuits to judgment before the *men clothed in lambskin* at Westminster." I think however the cause of the P. of L. might be safely entrusted to Lord Kenyon. His Lordship exercises the talent of classical quotation with too curious a felicity, to be very angry at the application of Horace, *except in a translation.* You remember the discourse between Trebatius and the Poet too well, to trouble you with the passage. In my opinion, in these times, the Plaintiff against the Pursuits, (like the Progressionist by the publick) would be hissed in Court, my Lords the Judges would laugh, and the Defendant be dismissed.

The Progressionist tells us, with great effect, of the approbation which has been given to his *Essay* by many of the best judges,

judges, and *by the publick in general.* He says, " he scorns to quote the private conversations of any man in favour of *his work.*" It is most certainly true, that Mr. Bryant, Sir George Baker, Mr. Gifford, and Mr. Antony Storer, have expressed very favourable opinions of " the Pursuits of Literature." *Two* of these *four* gentlemen the Progressionist could also name, as his panegyrists. Prudence and gratitude however induce him to decline it. It seems he has some regard for the character of *the two.* But he cannot stir a step without shewing his literary lineage, and hereditary right to the broad honours of the Dunciad. He is not indeed witty himself, but he has half Falstaff's merit ; he is, and will continue to be, the cause of wit and pleasantry in other men. There is an amiable modesty in with-holding the names of the *two* panegyrists, while the names of above *two* hundred and twenty *two* thousand, or more, are alluded to, namely, *the Publick in general,* who have applauded the Progressionist's little pamphlet. I will supply him with a sentence for the next edition, very much to his purpose. It is conceived in the following words.

" I, THE PROGRESSIONIST, do here return my most humble thanks, *to the utmost of my poor capacity,* and with extreme gratitude, to his Majesty, and both Houses of Parliament, to the Lords of the King's Most Honourable Privy Council, to the Reverend the Judges English, Welch, Scotch, and Irish; to the Clergy, Gentry, and Yeomanry, the Provisional Cavalry, Fencibles, and Volunteers ; and in particular, to my worthy friends in Westminster Hall, the Inns of Court, Moorfields, and all other halls and fields; *for their generous and universal acceptance of* THIS MY DIVINE TREATISE."[*]

I am indeed willing to believe, that not an Empyrick in the country has his study filled with so many attestations to

his

* Tale of a Tub, sect. 10.

his extraordinary merit. He need only take his *patients* before my Lord Mayor, to swear to the truth, and then seal every copy of his Essay with his own name and seal, with directions *how* to use it. But, like other quacks, he records only the cures.

In the last page of his *Postcript*, he assumes a more awful appearance. The Bird, to whose quill he is so much indebted, believes that he frightens passengers by lifting up his bill, and hissing. This is quite in character. He absolutely threatens the Author of the Pursuits " *with a continued Commentary*" on his work. " Such a Commentary, says he, I had sketched, and had *some thoughts* of publishing." He reminds his reader of Colly Cibber, and the furious Mr. John Dennis ; and if he should go on in this manner, it may perhaps be necessary to give some new account of " The strange and deplorable phrenzy of the Progressionist." Nay, should the two well-known lines be produced,

" Some have at first for wits, then poets past ;
Turn'd criticks next, and prov'd plain fools at last :

There is great reason to think, he would fling down the book, like Mr. John Dennis, in a terrible rage, and cry out, " By G—, he means me.'"

But it seems, his Commentary is reserved. I make no doubt it will be penned by the light of Mr. Chalmers's *critical* lamp ; or of the modern invention, which consumes it's own smoke. I believe Pope might as soon have dreaded a Commentary (for he too was threatened with a Commentary) from the pen of Matthew Concanen, *who was bred to the law*, or have been affected by the scurrilities of such men in the British and London Journals of his time.

But

But The Progressionist tells the Publick, *who have applauded* HIS WORK, that he has actually begun to sketch the Commentary. Here again is another palpable imitation of one of his Predecessors. He reminds me of Mr. Giles Jacob, *who was bred to the law*, like Mr. Matthew Concanen. He also *told the Publick*, that he diverted himself with poetry, between the intervals of his more laborious studies. He again *told the Publick*, that " *He* (Mr. Giles Jacob) has by him a poem of his own writing, *not yet finished*, which begins thus, &c." The plagiarism of Dunces is natural. But the imitation of the Progressionist is defective in one point; he has not told the Publick, *how* his Commentary begins. If " The Progress of Satire" may be considered only as the beginning, I would advise him, not even to advance so far as the celebrated Canto of the Bear and Fiddle, but to break off at an earlier period. .

But you must now prepare yourself. I am to announce the fatal catastrophe ; *the death and demise* of the Author of the Pursuits of Literature, declared by the Progressionist. Hear his words. " I perceive *my Adversary* sinking without a blow. We now scarcely ever hear of the Pursuits of Literature. The Author HAS HAD HIS DAY! and will be more *remembered* hereafter, (if he is remembered) IN THE WORKS of *his Antagonists*, than by his own !!!".

So sunk the stone of David into the front of the Philistine: so falls the Author of the Pursuits of Literature by the hand of the Progressionist! MORTALITATEM EXPLEVIT!

As his friend I must lament him. I will report him, and his cause to the unsatisfied. I know he loved his country, and would fain have done her some service. I heard him say, " She has my dying voice."

As

As the election lights on me, as his Apologist, I must rise from this scene of death, and say a few words. Since the Author of the P. of L. " HAS HAD HIS DAY," *and is no more*; I will request a few minutes in his behalf. The Progressionist yet lives, and posterity will wonder at his labours, in proportion to the admiration of the present age.

Many are the sayings of the wise and eminent, concerning the love of fame, and of honourable estimation. Tacitus and Milton have declared it to be the last infirmity of noble minds. Mr. Pennant has improved upon the text, and first taught us to anticipate the pleasure of dissolution. But the desire of life and reputation increased with the supposed extinction. The sensible warm motion of the ingenious Naturalist soon chose to resume it's functions. The Pæonian herbs from *Hindostan* have convinced the publick that he had only suffered a suspended animation; and it would be kind if he would inform us all, but authors in particular, what dreams attended him in this sleep of death.* The Progressionist, full of his own ideas, has no desire of becoming a *kneaded clod*; but waits patiently for his destiny.

Yet if I were in his situation, I should take the celebrated Peter Porcupine,† for my example. I may here observe, that America has not a more active, zealous, and useful citizen, or Great Britain a warmer friend, than honest Peter. In his literary features he is rather roughly stamped; but he understands the time. He can descant upon the deformity of
d
it,

* See the Life of *the late* Mr. Pennant, written by Himself. Since his departure from the world, he has published a history of *Hindostan*, in 2 vols. 4to.

† Willia Cobbet.

it, and hold a looking glass to the world, wherein they may see strange sights. There is a vigour, a simplicity, and an upright intention in all his works, which speak to the heart. When Nature and honesty are working at the root, the plants will be sound and healthy. *Læta et fortia surgunt, quippe solo Natura subest!* I offer, with pleasure, this passing tribute to a bold, sensible, industrious, spirited, and most deserving man.

I wish the Progressionist would profit by his modesty, and imitate it. Let him say fairly for once with Peter; " I should never look upon my family with a dry eye, if I did not hope to outlive my works.*

But though the Author of the P. of L. " HAS HAD HIS DAY," *and is no more*; yet I still think we hear of his work, and other countries hear of it too. It seems as if they would not willingly let it die. In the very day of turbulence, terror, and rebellion, Ireland thought proper to adopt and *naturalize* it. Literary leisure still found a place with loyalty in her best subjects. May the times of refreshing and restitution soon arrive, CUSTODE RERUM CÆSARE ! May the words of a poet be soon realized by the great and good CORNWALLIS, in that deluded, unhappy, and distracted kingdom.

> Janum clausit, et ordinem
> Rectum, et vaganti fræna licentiæ
> Injecit, amovitque culpas,
> Et veteres revocavit artes !

I am

* See the Republican Judge, or the American Liberty of the Press, &c. by William Cobbet, or Peter Porcupine, p. 49. Printed for Wright, Piccadilly. This pamphlet should be read.

I am also pleased to record, that beyond the Atlantick, in that country which has resisted, and is at this instant resisting, with a temperate, collected, firm, and reflecting wisdom and spirit, the tyranny, the arrogance, and the shameless insidious corruption of the Ministers of France; this work on the Pursuits of Literature is *now* circulating. The inhabitants of the United States find in it the true principles of practicable government, and the exposure of pretended patriots. They find the principles of religion recommended and enforced, without bigotry and superstition, or the indifference of an accommodating philosophy. Whatever is important to man, to social order, and to the bonds of all good government, is shewn by reason, by precept, and by example. They find the men, the measures, and the doctrines marked, which conduce to that end.

I now speak only of the work, as the Author himself *is no more;* and even the Progressionist may adopt the sentiments and expressions of his favourite Horace:

Qui prægravat artes
Infra se positas, *extinctus amabitur idem.*

It is indeed singular and surprising, when we are told, that " *the very purpose* of my *deceased* friend's work is to exalt, or depress the fame of contemporary writers at his sovereign will and pleasure."* Such is the assertion of the Progressionist. The kindred malevolence of his *Impartial* Brother informs us in terms much stronger, and with still more effrontery, that " The Pursuits of Literature is an *indiscriminate abuse* levelled against genius and ability of *every* description;" and that it is "An endeavour to depreciate the

d 2
abilities,

* Progress of Satire.

abilities, the learning, and the morals of THE BEST,
THE WISEST, AND THE GREATEST OF THE SONS" (a)
of Great Britain.

An appeal to the work itself is the best answer. If you
turn to the book, you will not be less disgusted, than indignant at such a charge. The incubation of heated dullness
upon malignity could alone generate such an abortion. For
my own part, I wish you would once again have recourse to
the pages of the Pursuits of Literature, which, as we are told,
is' " An *indiscriminate abuse* levelled against genius, and
ability of *every* description ;" and in which, as it would
seem, *nothing* is to be found in praise of living contemporary writers.

Is the panegyrick on Mr. Bryant, *nothing?* Are the
recorded and repeated eulogies on Mr. Burke, living and
dead, nothing? Is the praise so liberally given to Mr.
Roscoe, nothing? Is the feeling encomium on Mr.
Melmoth, nothing? Is the solemn and dignified recommendation of *parts* of Mr. King's work, nothing? Is the
tribute, so justly deserved, to the philosophick genius
of Mr. Atwood; nothing? Is the character of Mr. Pitt's
eloquence, firmness, and ability, nothing? Is the honourable testimony to Bishop Hurd's merit, " the laureat
wreath of Worcester," nothing? Is the record of Bishop
Watson's literary services, professional labours, and
sacred eloquence, nothing? Is the memorial of Count
Rumford's active and unceasing benevolence, nothing?
Is the generous and just praise of Mr. Gifford, a rival
poet in the same province, nothing? Are the poets
Beattie, Cowper, and Cumberland; the ingenuity and
deep researches of Mr. Maurice; the classical and judicious

(a) Impartial Strictures, &c. p. 26 and 27.

cious labours of that polite scholar Mr. Lumisden; the amiable mildness of the very learned Mr. Cracherode; the scientifick skill and unwearied perseverance of Mr. Samuel Lysons; the honourable, virtuous, efficient, and constitutional labours of Mr. Reeves; or the pious patriotism of Mr. Bowdler, passed over in silence and without honour? Are the professional exertions of that excellent, humane, and learned lawyer, Sir John Scott; or the dignity, knowledge, and temperate eloquence of the Rt. Hon. Mr. Addington, forgotten or disregarded? Are the erudition and medical skill of the venerable Dr. Heberden, Dr. Glynn, Sir George Baker, Dr. Milman, and Dr. Littlehales; the philosophical researches of Mr. Abernethy; or the rising genius, and talents of Mr. Westall; unnoticed? Is the glory of Architecture, Mr. Wyatt, or the fancy of Mr. Soane, without remembrance? Is the respect paid to the learned diligence of Mr. Isaac Reed; to the polite manners, and extensive parliamentary investigations of Mr. Hatsell; and to the correct understanding of Mr. Planta, to be considered as nothing? Is the tribute to the liberality, the abilities, and generous exertions of Sir Joseph Banks, nothing? Are the testimonies to the erudition, piety, and talents of Dr. Paley, Mr. Wilberforce, Dr. Hey, Dr. Blaney, Dr. Vincent, and Mr. Gisborne, nothing? Are all the just honours offered to Dr. Douglas, the Bishop of Salisbury; to Dr. Sutton, the Bishop of Norwich; to Dr. Yorke, the Bishop of Ely; and Dr. Porteous, the Bishop of London; to be considered as nothing? Are they all dead? Is their virtue all defunct? or are they not still among the *living* ornaments of their Country?

Surely this is a voluntary offering to *living*, contemporary merit. I consider it, Sir, as a libation from

that

that Pierian vase, which the Theban once described, as sparkling with the choicest dew of the vine. In this at least the Author of the Pursuits of Literature has approved himself, as the herald of *living* genius, truth, and virtue.

But must we say, that " the *abilities*, the *learning*, and the *morals*, of THE BEST, THE WISEST, and THE GREATEST of the Sons" of Great Britain, are depreciated, because such persons as I shall recite, without one word of comment, from the book before me, are not mentioned with particular honour or commendation? Must we consider THEM (however good, wise, or great they may be,) as " *the best, the wisest, and the greatest of the Sons*" of Great Britain? Are we to ftile Horne Tooke, Dr. Priestley, Lord Stanhope, Dr. Parr, Mr. Porson, Dr. Darwin, Peter Pindar, Mr. Lewis, Mr. Knight, Mr. Jerningham, Mr. Boscawen, Mr. George Steevens, Mr. Ritson, Mr. Ireland, Mr. Tierney, Gilbert Wakefield, Dr. Geddes, CHARLES JAMES FOX, Richard Brinsley Sheridan, Mr. *Barrister* Erskine, the Duke of Bedford, Lord Lauderdale, Lord Lansdown, Mr. Jofeph Jekyll, William Godwin, Thomas Paine, Thomas Holcroft, or John Thelwall, as absolutely " THE BEST, THE " WISEST, AND THE GREATEST OF THE SONS" OF GREAT BRITAIN?

If ever contemptible sophistry and gross falsehood were to be found in a charge, they are found in this charge. Upon my word, Sir, it is either egregious trifling in the Progressionist, and his *Impartial* Brother to talk in this manner; or it is wilful, wicked, shameless, and scandalous misrepresentation. It betrays a corrupted heart, and an irritated head. There is besides

such

such a stupidity and dulness in the mode of the attack, which all the " urticæ marinæ" or sea-nettles, so *lovingly* recommended by one of the Commentators on Shak-speare, could not excite into action. I would ask with Junius, " Is the union of *Blifil* and *Black George* no longer a Romance ?" (a)

I think the declaration of the Author of the P. of L. may be *now* fully justified. It may be deduced in all its parts ; and the work itself proved to have been begun, conducted, and compleated upon publick principle alone. The words of it's Author may now appear with new force, and with truth not to be resisted. " The work was written " upon *no* private motive whatsoever ; but simply and solely " as the conduct of the persons mentioned or alluded to, or " the manner of their compositions, or the principles of " their writings, tend to influence and affect the learning, " the government, the religion, the publick morality, the " publick happiness, and the publick security of this " Nation." (b)

· The author of the Pursuits of Literature is said by the Progressionist " to have disdained *(while he was yet living)* to name any of *his adversaries*, or to reply in detail to any of their accusations." I think he was right. He is said also, to have corrected some mistakes pointed out by the Progressionist, and not to have acknowledged *the kindness*. The confusion in this man's mind is equal to it's

d 4

irritation.

(a) Junius. Letter 57.

(b) P. of L. Preface to the First Dialogue, page 42. 7th edit.

irritation. I presume, before an obligation is personally acknowledged, a favour must be received. If indeed I could believe, that he had ever attended for a moment to *such* a Critick as the Progressionist, I think he must have remembered an allegory preserved by Pausanias, (*a*) and beautifully restored to it's original meaning by the celebrated Dean of St. Patrick's. It is this. " The " Nauplians in Argia learned the art of *Pruning* their " vines, by observing, that when AN ASS had browzed " upon one of them, *it thrived the better*, and bore fairer " fruit." (*b*)

The Progressionist absolutely condemns the poetry of the Pursuits of Literature. This is unfortunate; but he is positive in his assertion. From *such* a judge, (for whom, I suppose, Cremona and Mantua might formerly have contended) it is difficult to appeal. He and his *Impartial* Brother produce thirty or forty lines, out of near sixteen hundred, some of which might certainly be improved, and they exult in their discovery. That author indeed appealed to the lovers of Dryden and Pope; and (*if he were yet living*) I am convinced he would continue to do so. Read his *poem* again, and I think you will be persuaded that he acted wisely. You recollect, that Dryden, in his latter days, once addressed Congreve in these pathetick lines.

> Be kind to my *remains;* and oh, defend
> Against your judgement, your *departed* friend ;

Let

(*a*) Τα λεγομενα ες τον Ονον, ὡς επιφαγων αμπελυ κλημα, αφθονωτερον ες το μελλον απεφηνε τον καρπον. Pausan. Corinth. lib. 2, c. 28. p. 201, Ed. Khunii.

(*b*) Tale of a Tub, sect 3.

Let not th' insulting foe my fame pursue,
But shade those laurels which *descend* to you."

But all which I shall offer in the defence of the Author of the P. of L. shall be strictly according to my judgment, and my knowledge of him. For my own part, if I knew him right in his *poetical* education and character, I will speak of him, *as he was.*

From his very childhood he grew up in silence and in solitude ; neither seduced, nor diverted from his purpose; in a quiet independance; not embarrassed by difficulty, or depressed by neglect; constant in thought ; waiting patiently for his hour; of the world not unknowing, though unknown. Much and often would he muse on other times ; and dwell with the bards and sages, whose names are written in the books of fame and eternity. His studies and his meditations were an habitual poetry. To those who obferved the mantle he would sometimes wear in his *youth*, it seemed

Inwrought with figures dim, and *on the edge*
Like to that sanguine flower, *inscribed with woe.*

But he never blamed his fate. Most of all, he reverenced the lyre; and sought out those who could strike the strings most cunningly and sweetly. One such he found. He looked abroad through all the realms of Nature ; through her scenes of majesty, of softness, or of terror; the wilds of solitude, the stormy promontory, the cultivated prospect, the expanse of forests, the living lake, the torrent, or the cataract. By the shores of the interminable ocean, on the cliffs, and on the ragged rocks, he found and felt the power of inspiration. But still his fancy wandered chiefly in the mild retreats of the elder poetry, the banks of Mæander,
and

\

and the Mincio. The scenes of ancient Greece and Latium were the hermit haunts of his imagination. In the valley of Tempe, by the hill of Hymettus, and the grove of Plato, he first heard, and learned

> The secret power
> Of harmony, in tones and numbers hit
> By voice, or hand; and various measur'd verse,
> Æolian charms, and Dorian lyrick odes,
> And His, who gave them breath, but higher sung.

Sometimes reclined on the verge of Castalia, he would drink of the *original* fountain, whose murmurs were familiar to him. Last of all, in the moments of divine and of serene delight, he would ascend the chariot of the Muses, and fix his eye, but not without *superior* guidance, upon the central heaven. Such, indeed, is the right of Poets, whose interest is that of their country ; whose gain is not lucre, but the hope of an honourable acceptance.

I speak as if I could myself take a part in these ennobling labours, and august contemplations. But other cares await me. I feel myself dragged back once more to darkness, and the Progressionist. The descent to Avernus is said to be easy, but I choose Homer, Virgil, or Dante for my guides and companions in such a region.

Recall then for a moment all that I have advanced. Consider and estimate the temper, the conduct, the sentiments, the scurrility, and what the penury of language constrains me to call, the *arguments* of the Progressionist. He has lavished upon the Author of the Pursuits of Literature every opprobrious and brutal term, which even *his own* language could supply. He has called in sophistry and falsehood to assist him in misrepresenting his words, his actions, and his intentions. And now—will you give me credit

when

when I repeat it?—He gives at last three solitary lines to
the praise of a passage or two, which it seems, are spirited
and eloquent, in behalf of publick order, morality, and
religion. If I had been the Author of the P. of L. I
would have returned such impudent panegyrick upon his
hands, with the contempt he deserves, and has incurred.
Tollat sua munera cerdo. Let the cobling donor take his
gift back again. Pope is still more to the occasion:

> Of all mad creatures, if the learn'd are right,
> It is *the slaver* kills, and not the bite.

To conceive, Sir, that such men *can* confer praise, is an
insult to any understanding. The publick do not wait to
discover what is eloquent and spirited, from such wooden
oracles. The State will acknowledge it's best friends, and
Literature it's best defenders, without their assistance or
direction. Such men have neither part nor lot in the region of the Muses. In the temple of immortality their
voice cannot be heard. Even the names they would fain
present to the guardians of that temple, would be rejected
from the unworthiness of the votaries. The Swans would
drop their beaks, and the stream flow backward.

I would not have stooped to notice this man, and his
Impartial Brother, for *their own* sakes. Writers of their
description are quite innocent, when they are quite angry.
But there is a respect due to the English Nation, which the
Progressionist terms " *the addle-headed Publick,*" and which,
I maintain, has honourably received a work dedicated to
their service. If I knew the names of either of these
writers, I would not embalm and preserve them in this
Apology for my *deceased* friend. The Progressionist
may be suffered to sink in *his own* verse and prose. I
would leave *Sir Fretful* between Sneer and Dangle. But
as

as to the deliberate defender of Mr. Lewis's " MONK" in the face of an insulted kingdom, I would consign him to the vindictive malice of the Cloyster, and all it's impurity; or to the more wretched drudgery of palliating ribaldry, and blasphemy. *Such* are the men, Sir, who declare themselves the enemies of the Poem on the Pursuits of Literature. But the spirit of it's *departed* Author may have yet some consolation.

Non *illá* manes jacuere favillâ,
Nec cinis *exiguus* talem compescuit umbram.

Whoever indeed stands forward at such a perilous period as the present, with boldness, confidence, and an honest intention in the publick service, with a name or without a name, known or unknown, is surely worthy of some regard, and I should think, of kindness. But when a gentleman (without *any* interest, but that of every other subject in the country,) has devoted his time, fortune, and ability in the hope of being useful, it is but a common cause to rescue *his memory* from the gripe of injustice, and the fangs of malignity. When he has defended THE TRIPLE FORTRESS of Religion, Morality, and Literature, from it's foundation to the topmost battlements, must he be left on the field without the common honours of a common soldier ? Because a few trumpery Poetasters, half-critics, jugglers in science, or indecent Commentators are held forth and consigned to ridicule or contempt, as they have respectively deserved, must this work on the Pursuits of Literature be degraded and depreciated? I trust not. The Publick will never suffer such impotence and dulness, such Under-conjurors and Journeymen Astrologers, the Sidrophels and Whacums of
the

the day, to read *backwards* for them the great page of Literature, and declare the interpretation of it. When the Sun is high in the heaven, who asks for subsidiary light ?

Literature indeed, at this hour, can hardly be divided from the principles of political safety. Satire also has a character, which she was never before called upon to affume. *Sensum cælesti demissum traxit ab arce!* She must *now* co-operate with the other guardians, and watchful powers of the state in her degree.

Such AN UNION is now demanded of the minds, the talents, and fortunes, of the souls and bodies, of all the inhabitants of Great Britain, as never before entered into the hearts of Englishmen to conceive. We must be preserved from the tyranny and power of France; from all her principles, and from all her arms, open or concealed, mental, moral, or political. I have pride and satisfaction in seeing, and feeling that we are all *so* convinced. We know we must die, or defend ourselves from THE MONSTROUS REPUBLICK.

> Instat terribilis vivis; morientibus hæres;
> Nulla quies : oritur prædâ cessante libido ;
> Divitibusque dies, et nox metuenda maritis ;
> Emicat ad nutum stricto mucrone minister !

If we consider it from the commencement, it has threatened, devoted, and given over all it's victims to desolation, wretchedness, plunder, and final death. BLOOD is the cement of the Republick of France.

Some victims have bled for principle, others for example, some for funeral pomp, and some for a civick feast. Blood must flow. Each Faction has delivered over it's predecessors to death. The Priests of Reason hold their rites in the field of Mars. First indeed, they soothe awhile their savageness with song and festival. But these are the

3   preludes

preludes of sanguinary cruelty; the stops and pauses of their war-symphonies. With their laurel and cypress branches bound together and dipped in blood, they advance to the altar, and perform their abhorred lustration. The Manes of all that is brave, and all that is ferocious, are invoked in their democratick incantations to Reason and her Republick.

Sævis opus est, et fortibus umbris;
Ipsa facit manes; HOMINUM MORS OMNIS IN USU EST.

On the blood of their murdered Monarch they have sworn hatred to tyranny; and they have established a Directory. On the blood of innocence and virginity they have sworn to restore, and to protect the female dignity; and they have annulled the bond of marriage, and the charities of consanguinity. On the blood of their Generals streaming on the scaffold, and on the blood of armies partially devoted by other Generals in the day of battle, they have sworn to give honour, and *encouragement* to the Defenders of the Republick. Such are their decrees; such are their oaths registered in blood. All is contradiction with them, yet all is in action. Principles of the moment, principles of reflection, principles of desolation, principles of safety, all have had their hour; all have risen and fallen. Banishment and deportation have now superseded the axe of the guillotine, and the sabre of ruffian massacre. How long?—All changes with them: all, but the fixed lust of plunder, and aggrandisement, and the rooted hatred to Christian Religion. To every government, and to every establishment in Europe they apply but one axiom, " WHATEVER IS, IS WRONG!"

Whoever strives to resist such an adversary, upon principle and reflection, with eloquence, or wisdom, or learning, in the robes of state, or in the vestments of religion or law, with arms in his grasp, or with well-directed

opulence

opulence, by counsel, by precept, or by example, must
be numbered among THE FRIENDS OF MAN.

I am most serious in my words, and earnest in my thoughts. I
have been instructed by these great events, to consider all
actions as of some weight, and that nothing is *now* to be neglected, as wholly unimportant. If the efforts of the united
genius, learning, poetry, and eloquence of a country can be
directed with strength and discretion, in their proper and natural courses, we may yet have confidence. Enterprises of
great pith and moment will succeed, and a righteous security
may be established. Consider for a moment what is the hope
of bad men. The Orator of Athens has declared, "Their
hope of safety is placed IN THE EXCESS OF THEIR
WICKEDNESS, AND INIQUITY ALONE*." The haunts,
and caves, and tenements, and sculking huts of sophistry,
anarchy, rebellion, democracy, and Jacobinism, will at
length be fully revealed, and *finally* levelled and ruined.
When the fountains of hallowed fire are once opened, and
flowing with liquid purity in the silence of the night, the
objects which darkness would conceal, are not only discovered, but destroyed.

The force of France is indeed formidable; but HER
PRINCIPLES, wherever they take root, and grow, and bear,
are *alone* invincible. If we think otherwise, I fear, we deceive
ourselves, and the truth is not *with* us. France invites
every European government to suicide. Her high Priest†
told her long ago, that no Government could perish but by
it's own hand, and by it's own consent to die. The Government of Great Britain has given no such consent. Her
King,

---

* Εν τη της πονηριας υπερβολη την ελπιδα της σωτηριας
εχει. Demosthenes Orat. 1. Contra Aristogiton. pag. 483. Ed.
Benenati Gr. 1570.

† Voltaire.

King, her Nobles, her Commons, her Senators, her Statesmen, her Lawyers, her Artists, her Merchants, her Citizens, her Peasants, all maintain and declare with *one* voice, and with arms in their hands, " GREAT BRITAIN HAS GIVEN NO " SUCH CONSENT." She has not lifted up her arms against herself : she is willing and desirous to live. She has humbled herself before GOD the Judge of all, through the Great Mediator of humanity. She knows her strength, and has felt her infirmity ; she is earnest for her preservation from her foes within and without ; and having done all, and still committing herself, and her cause, TO HIM who judgeth righteously, She hopes yet to stand.

Whether the end of all things may be at hand ; and what the decrees of Eternal Power, Wisdom, Justice, and Goodness may intend in the last resort, we acknowledge to be inscrutable. But we trust, it cannot be deemed an unwarrantable presumption, to suggest or to affirm, that, if the attributes of God are true ; if man is *his* creature, and governed by *his* laws ; the opposers of this overbearing, desolating, impious, and UNIVERSAL Tyranny must be justified BEFORE HIM. As to us, the inhabitants of Great Britain, if we would exist at all, we must be preserved AS WE ARE. Our Constitution is not lost ; and the ramparts we have raised around it, will maintain it entire. Our liberties are supported equally against arbitrary power, and against the engines of licentiousness and democracy. UPON US the destiny of Europe, and perhaps of the whole civilized world, ultimately depends. It seems placed in our hands : a fearful and an awful charge.

Omnia Fata laborant,
Si quidquam mutare velis ; UNOQUE SUB ICTU
STAT GENUS HUMANUM!

I am sure words on this subject cannot be thought out of season, or out of place, while terrors are yet gathering

around

around us. Circumstances have instructed us all, not to regard any thing as common, which is designed for the publick service.

In consideration *therefore* of the importance of every *single* effort, and of the tendency of individual zeal and labour in the common cause, I have written this letter, and now deliver it to the publick. I have stood forth as the apologist and defender of the principles, the justice, the severity, and the composition of the Poem and Notes on " The Pursuits of Literature." My business has been not to produce what is excellent in the work, but to shew the futility and falshood of the objections to it. I know not whether it called for any defence ; but it is not uncommon for some persons to suffer themselves to be misled by super-ficial and malevolent writers and observers, when they have a specious appearance.

The numerous appeals, in the notes to " The Pursuits of " Literature," to various authors in languages not univer-sally understood, or partially studied, have diminished some portion of its general effect. I have designed to remove this inconvenience by the present attempt. If any person shall hereafter be enabled to understand the force of Grecian or Roman wisdom better than he did before; or if one English reader, and a lover of his country, shall be induced to peruse the work, who without this translation, would not have attended to it at all; I shall not look upon my labour as useless, or unrewarded.

I have prefixed to the Title-page a few lines from Pindar, of some signification. You will consider them, as if *the departed* Author of the Pursuits of Literature did himself address you by me. The paraphrase and the meaning of them *in a very extended sense,* is this. " The Time is now

e   arrived

arrived, in which all persons should fully understand whatever is of importance sacred or civil. There should be no ambiguity; all should be laid open, and justly comprehended. Though without authority, and in a very private station, I will consider myself in some measure, as sent forth in the publick service. I have declared, recommended, enforced, and appealed to the wisdom, the eloquence, the doctrines, and the experience of our forefathers in every age, and in every country. I have shewn what is that heroick virtue, and dignified deportment which are required of my countrymen in this revolutionary age ; that they consist not in patience, but in action ; and that the sword, the voice, and the pen must be united in the common cause for the common salvation. I will preserve this integrity to the last: I WILL SPEAK THE TRUTH."

I am, &c. &c. &c.

SEPTEMBER 1798.

THE END.

TRANSLATION

OF THE

GREEK AND LATIN PASSAGES

QUOTED IN

THE PREFATORY EPISTLE.

TRANSLATION,

&c. &c.

~~~~~~~~

MOTTO to the TITLE-PAGE of the TRANSLATION.

Νοῆ—

σαι καιρος αριστος.

Εγω ΙΔΙΟΣ ΕΝ ΚΟΙΝΩ σταλεις,

Μητιν τε γαρυων παλαιγονων,

Πολεμοντ' εν ἡρωϊαις αρεταισιν

Ου ψευσομαι. *Pind. Olymp. O.* 13.

" This is the season for the right underſtanding of the subject which is before us. I, as a private man ſent forth, in some meaſure, in the publick ſervice, will speak the truth; while I am declaring to you the whole political or sacred counsel and wisdom of our ancestors, and all their heroick virtues displayed in war."

~~~~~~~~~~~~~~~

P. 1.

Post resides annos, longo velut excita somno,
  Romanis fruitur Musa *(Britanna)* choris:
Sed magis intento studium censore laborat,
  Quòd legitur medio conspiciturque foro.
Illi conciliat gratas impensiùs aures,
  Vel meritum belli, vel *Stilichonis* amor.

" After many years of inactivity, roused, as it were, out of a long slumber, the Muse (of *Britain*) wakes and expatiates among the *Roman* choirs. But her compositions are subjected to a more severe censure, in proportion to their celebrity and the general attention they have excited. The merit however of the cause itself, and of the warfare in which she is

engaged,

engaged, joined to the predilection for *Stilicho*, ensures the affection and favour of the nation."

P. 3.

Δει μεν, μη της πολλης των εξηγητων μιμημενης, ξηρον και ελλιπη τον τοπον διαλειπειν· μηδε ωσπερ ετερης, αμηχανον οσην απεραντολογιαν επεισαγειν. Αλλα δει αυτο μονον το προχειμενον Συγγραμμα προστησαμενης, υπ' οψιν αγειν τοις σχολαζησι την Προθεσιν, διερευνημενης το ειδος, την υλην, τα δογματα συνηρημενως, την δι' ολη τη Συγγραμματος διηκησαν των λογων υποθεσιν. Ουτω γαρ αν τοις ακηησι γενοιτο καταφανες το παν βηλημα ΤΟΝ ΔΙΑΛΟΓΩΝ.

Ex PROCLI *Commentariis in Platonis* Πολιτειαν.
edit. Gr. *Basil.* 1534, pag. 349.

" It is not adviseable, after the example of many Commentators, to treat these topics in a dry and barren manner, or to leave them wholly untouched ; nor like others, to introduce a mere babble of words, and endless difquisition. But it is necessary, to set the whole composition fairly before the reader; and to place in a clear point of view, to those persons who have leisure, the full subject of it. To consider and investigate the species, the matter, the principles, taken together, and the great purpose which pervades the whole. By this method the compleat design, scope, and intent of THE DIALOGUES may be made manifest to those who will attend to it."

P. 6.

Ne incognita pro cognitis habeamus.

Cicero de Offic. l. 1.

" Not to mistake what is unknown, for what is known."

P. 19.

P. 19.

Gaudet monstris, mentisque tumultu. *Lucan.*

" He delights in what is strange or monstrous, and in all the tumult and confusion of the mind."

P. 27.

Hos mirabantur Athenæ
Torrentes, pleni et moderantes fræna theatri.

Juvenal. Sat. 10.

" Athens looked with astonishment at the torrent of their eloquence, while they wielded at will the passions of the full assembly."

P. 28.

Expende Annibalem. *Juvenal. Sat.* 10.

" Let us weigh Hannibal."

P. 30.

Periere la·ebræ
Tot scelerum: POPULO VENIA EST EREPTA NOCENTI;
Agnovere suos! *Lucan. l.* 4. v. 192.

" The retreats and fkulking places of their accumulated crimes are destroyed: THE GUILTY NATION has no longer any plea left. They know their own."

P. 33.

De Republica graviter querens, de homine nihil dixit.

Cicero.

" He complained deeply for the sake of the State; of the man himself he said nothing."

P. 35.

Cujuslibet rei simulator et dissimulator. *Sallust. B. Catil.*

" He

" He could, with equal ſkill, pretend not to be, what he was; and to be, what he was not."

P. 38.

Quando aliquid prohibetur, prohibetur et omne, per quod devenitur ad illud.

" When any thing is prohibited to be done; whatever tends or leads to it, as the means of compassing it, is forbidden at the same time."

P. 39.

Id cinerem, aut manes credis curare sepultos ?

Virg. Æn. 4.

" Do you conceive that dust and ashes, or the buried Manes can have any concern for this?"

P. 43.

Est etiam in magnis Heliconis montibus arbos,
Floris odore hominem tetro consueta necare.

Lucret. 1. 6. v. 786.

" There is a particular tree, which grows in the great mountains of Helicon, whose scent is able to destroy the life of man."

P. 45.

Jnvideo sane Magistris, qui illum tantâ mercede nihil sapere docuerunt.

Cicero.

" His Instructors are indeed enviable, who at ſuch a considerable expence, taught him to be so foolish."

P. 48.

Mortalitatem explevit.

Tacit. A. 3.

" He has filled up the measure of mortality."

P. 50.

P. 50.

Læta et fortia surgunt,

Quippe solo natura subest.   *Virg. G.* 2.

" They rise up lusty and vigorous, for Nature is working at the root, and the soil is wholesome."

P. 50.

Janum clausit, et ordinem

Rectum, et vaganti fræna licentiæ

Injecit, amovitque culpas,

    Et veteres revocavit artes.   *Hor.*

" He closed the temple of Janus, established a just order, and curbed the licentiousness of the time. He re-moved the causes of offence, and called back the ancient arts which had disappeared.

P. 51.

Qui prægravat artes

Infra se positas, extinctus amabitur idem.

    Hor. Ep. ad August..

" The man who, from his real or supposed merit, is hated by his contemporaries, becomes an object of affection, when he is no more."   .

P. 60.

Non illâ manes jacuere favillâ,

Nec cinis exiguus talem compescuit umbram.

    Luc. l. 9.

" His Manes rested not under the embers of *that* pile ; nor could the sprinkling of a few insignificant ashes quench the ardour of a spirit like his."

P. 61.

P. 61.

Sensum cælesti demissum traxit ab arce.

Juv. Sat. 15,

" She hath derived her origin, and the spring of action
from the regions above.

P. 61.

Instat terribilis vivis ; morientibus hæres ;
Nulla quies : oritur prædâ cessante libido ;
Divitibusque diés, et nox metuenda maritis :
Emicat ad nutum stricto mucrone minister.

" She (*a*) is an object of terror and dismay to all the living ;
and she claims the inheritance of those who are ready to
perish. With her there is no pause. When plunder ceases,
lust awakes and rages : the rich tremble by day, and the
married, by night. At her nod Satellites, with their swords
unsheathed, start forth prepared for action.

P. 62.

Sævis opus est, et fortibus umbris ;
Ipsa facit manes : hominum mors omnis in usu est.

Luc. l. 6.

" She (*a*) requires in her service the spirits of the cruel and
of the brave. She herself creates them. She finds her
account in death under every form."

P. 64.

Omnia Fata laborant,
Si quidquam mutare velis ; unoque sub ictu
Stat genus humanum !

Lucan.

(*a*) Applied to the Republick of France.

" Every

" The fates and fortunes of all around totter and shake, if you attempt to change what exists. The whole human race stands or falls in the issue of this one conflict!"

THE END OF THE PASSAGES QUOTED IN THE
PREFATORY EPISTLE.

A
TRANSLATION
OF THE PASSAGES FROM
GREEK, LATIN, ITALIAN,
AND
FRENCH WRITERS,
QUOTED IN THE
NOTES AND PREFACES
TO
THE PURSUITS OF LITERATURE,
A POEM
IN
FOUR DIALOGUES.

ADVERTISEMENT.

The Pages of the *Seventh* Edition of the P. of L. are referred to in the following Tranflation. But as the Paffages are placed in the order in which they occur in the Notes to each Dialogue, the Tranflations may be confidered as adapted to any preceding Edition of the Poem.

A

TRANSLATION

OF THE

GREEK AND LATIN PASSAGES, &c.

IN THE

PURSUITS OF LITERATURE.

~~~~~~

Ὑμεις, ω παντα εν πᾶσι φυσει και παιδεια χρηστοι, και μετριοι, και φιλανθρωποι, και της Βασιλειας αξιοι, τυτοις τοις λογοις επινευσατε.

Athenagoræ Atheniensis Legatio Imperatoribus Antonino et Commodo.

Ad fin. Op. Justin. Martyr. edit. Paris, 1636. p. 39.

"Ye, who from your natural disposition, as well as from your education, are in all things good and kindly affectioned, moderate, and worthy of the kingdom which you uphold, be favourable to this Work."

———

P. 1.

Δια δυσφημιας και ευφημιας.

" Through evil report and good report."

B   P. 2.

P. 2.

‗Ex phrasi, ex ore, ex locutione, aliisque compluribus, mihi persuasi hoc opus maximâ saltem ex parte esse Hieronymi Aleandri. Nam mihi genius illius ex domestico convictu adeo cognitus perspectusque est, ut ipse sibi non possit esse notior.

Erasmi.Epist. 370. c. 1755. op. fol. edit. opt. Lugduni.

" From his phraseology, his manner of speaking, his peculiar diction, and other circumstances, I am convinced that the whole work, or the greater part of it, is the composition of Hieronymus Aleander. From my constant, familiar, domestick intercourse with him, I am as intimately acquainted with his genius and disposition, as he himself can be."

MOTTO TO THE INTRODUCTORY LETTER.

P. 3.

Nel cerchio accolto,
Mormorò potentissime parole ;
Girò tre volte *all' Oriente* il volto,
Tre volte ai regni *ove dechina il Sole* ;
" Onde tanto indugiar ? FORSE ATTENDETE
" VOCI ANCOR PIÙ POTENTI, O PIÙ SECRETE?

Tasso. B. 13.

" Retired within the magical circle, he murmured words of mightiest power. Thrice he turned his countenance to the East, and thrice to the realms where the Sun declines: " Whence (he cries) is this delay ? Do ye wait for words " more secret than these, or of greater potency?"

PASSAGES IN THE INTODUCTORY LETTER.

P. 4.

" Quid de me alii loquantur, ipsi videant; sed loquentur tamen." *Cicero Somn. Scipionis.*

" As to what some persons may say of me, let them look to their own words; but nevertheless they will talk."

P. 5.

P. 5.

Vitæ est avidus, quisquis non vult,
MUNDO SECUM PEREUNTE, mori.   *Senec. Tragèd.*

" He is greedy of life, who is not willing to die, when
the world is perishing around him."

P. 7.

" Των άιρεσιωνκαταλυσον τα φρυαγματα."
*Liturgia Sancti Gregorii Alexand. Liturg. Oriental. Col-
lect. v. 1. p. 107.   Ed. Paris* 1716.

" Destroy the insolence, and high language of these here-
sies, and make them of none effect."

P. 7.

Αγαθυς αγαθοις αντεξεταξειν.
*Dion. Halicarn. Ep. ad Cn, Pomp. Epist. de Platone;
pag. 757. sect. 1. vol. 6.   Ed. Reische,* 1777.

" To examine the excellent with the excellent, and compare their several merits with each other."

P. 8.

(Αρχιλοχυ) φωνημα και οφρυοεσσαν αοιδην
Πυργωσας; στιβαρη πρωτος εν ευεπιη.
Anthol. p. 393.   *Ed. Brodæi;*

" The first who strengthened the exalted strains of Archi-
lochus, with a rampart of firm and solid words."

P 8.

Magnificabo Apostolatum meum;
" I will magnify my office."

P. 10.

Της φρονησεως συννυν και πεπυκνωμενον;
Basil. Archiepisc. Cæsareæ Op. v. 2. p. 698. ed. 1618,

" The compact and condensed power of the understanding."

P. 12.

Ego, si risi, quòd ineptus.

Pastillos Rufillus olet— ..

Lividus et mordax videar ?   ,   *Hor.*

" If I smile at the perfumes with which Rufillus is scented, or at any similar piece of folly, must I of necessity be stigmatised as a man of an envious and malicious disposition?"

P. 14.

Ει μεν δη Ἑταρον γε κελευεις μ' αυτον ἑλεσθαι,

Πως αν επειτ' ΟΔΥΣΗΟΣ Εγω ΘΕΙΟΙΟ λαθοιμην ;

Ὁυ περι μεν προφρων κραδιη και θυμος αγηνωρ

Εν παντεσσι πονοισι ;   *Hom. Il.* 10. v. 242.

" If indeed you require me to chuse a companion, how can I forget the divine Ulysses ? His heart, his affections, and his spirit are tried, ready, and prepared for every enterprise."

P. 14.

Donum

Fatalis virgæ, longo post tempore visum.

                                Virg. Æn. 6.

" The present of the fatal branch, now seen again after a long period."

P. 16.

Semel Causam dixi (vel iterum dicturus) quo semper omnia agere solitus sum, ACCUSATORIO SPIRITU.

                                Liv. l. 2. fect. 61.

" I have once spoken in this great Cause (prepared to repeat my words, if required) with that spirit which I am ever wont to assume, the spirit of an accuser."

P. 17.

Sævi spiracula Ditis.   *Virg. Æn. 7.*

" The mouths of the cavern which leads to cruel Tartarus."

P. 17.

Tibi nullum periculum esse perspicio, quod quidem sejunctum sit ab omnium interitu.

Cic. Epist. ad Fam. l. 6. e. 1.

" For my own part, I can see no danger to which you are personally exposed, separate and apart from the destruction of us all."

P. 18.

Senza levarmi a volo, avend'io l'ale,
Per dar forse di me non bassi esempi.

Petrarc: Part 2. Son. 86.

" Without attempting some adventurous flight, when I had pinions to support me; that I might present no ignoble example of myself."

P. 19.

Le Roi et ses Ministres peutêtre se feroient lire ces Memoires, qui assurèment ne sont pas ceux d'un ignorant.

Gil Blas.

" The King and his Ministers might perhaps peruse these memoirs, which most assuredly are not the composition of an uninformed man."

P. 20.

Αλυτοι απορίαι.

" Difficulties of hard solution."

                    P. 21.

P. 21.

Altius his nihil est; hæc sunt fastigia mundi;
Publica naturæ domus his contenta tenetur
Finibus. *Manil. Astron.* lib. 1.

" Nothing can be more exalted than speculations like these;
they are the very heights of the world. The great publick
mansion of Nature herself is contained within these boundaries."

P. 21.

Αυται ἁι ΤΟΥ ΘΕΟΜΑΧΟΥ φωναι επι κακιας ιστχϋι μεγα-
λαυχυμενυ, και τας προς τυ Υψιστυ τοις αγγελοις παραδοθεισας
τῶν εθνῶν ὁροθεσιας διαρπασαι και συγχειν απειλυντος, προνομευσειν
τε την οικυμενην, και παν το τῶν ανθρωπων γενος διεκφεισειν και
μεταστησειν της προτερον ευταξιας απαυθαδιαζομενυ.

Eufeb. Demonfl. Evang. l. 4. f. 9.

" These are the vauntings of Him who fighteth against
God; who glorieth in the strength of his wickedness; who
threateneth utterly to destroy and confound the boundaries
of nations, (once delivered by The Most High to his an-
gels and messengers;) and to make the whole Earth one scene
of plunder and devastation; who boasteth that he will shake
all the sons of men, and subvert and change the state of
every ancient ordinance, institution, and regular government."

P. 25.

" Facere aliquid ad veram pietatem feu doctrinam, Græcâ
potius quam aliâ linguâ loqui."

Casaub. Exercit. 16. *ad Annal. Eccles. Baronii.*

" (It cannot be supposed) that speaking or writing in the
Greek language, in preference to any other, can have any
peculiar efficacy in promoting the interests of true piety or
learning."

P. 26.

P. 26.

Frons læta parum, et dejecto lumina vultu.

Virg. Æn. 6.

" His brow was not brightened with chearfulness; and his countenance was dejected."

P. 26.

Aspro concento, orribile armonia,

D'alte querele, d'ululi, e di strida,

Istranamente concordar s'udia.

Ariosto, O. F, cant. 14.

" The strains were harsh; it was the harmony of horror: shrieks, and groans, and lamentations loud and deep, were heard to agree in strangest consonance."

P. 27.

Svegliata fra gli spirti eletti,

Ove nel suo Fattor l'alma s'interna. *Petrarch.*

" Awakened, as from slumber, among the spirits of the elect, where the soul enjoys a more intimate communion with her Maker."

P. 27.

Ωσπερ απ⁚ των ευωδεστατων λειμωνων αυρα τις ἡδεια απ' αυτης φερεται. *Dionys. Halic. Ep. ad Cn. Pomp.* sect. 2.

" A gale of odorous sweets is wafted around, as from meadows of freshness and of choicest fragrance."

P. 28.

Capita argumentorum contra morofos quosdam et indoctos.

Erafmus.

" The heads of arguments and objections against certain persons of morose, peevish natures, and without erudition."

P. 28.

P. 28.

Che tempo è ormai, ch'ai capi voti o macri
Di senno, si soccorri con l' ampolla.

Ariosto O. F. cant. 38.

" For it is now high time to offer some assistance from the celestial vessel (called the ampolla) to those heads, which are either empty, or scantily provided with sense."

P. 29.

Mendici, mimi, balatrones.   *Hor.*

" Beggars, players, and varlets of every description."

P. 29.

Τρισσοχαρηνος ιδειν, ολοον τερας, υτι δακτον,

Ταρταροπαις Εκατη.   *Orph. Argon.* v. 974.

" Hecate, with her triple head, a fatal and tremendous prodigy, the child of Tartarus."

P. 29.

Και δι' Ενυω, και τριγεννητος Θεα.   *Lycophron,* v. 519.

" The divine Bellona, and the Tritonian goddess, Minerva."

P. 30.

Γυμνωθη ρακεων πολυμητις Οδυσσευς,

Αλτο δ' επι μεγαν υδον! εχων Ϲιον ηδε Φαρετρην

Ιων εμπλειην, ταχεας δ' εγχευατ' οιστυς

Αυτη προσθε ποδων.   *Hom, Odys.* 22. v. 1.

" Ulysses stripped himself of his sordid garments, and leaped upon the great threshold of the mansion. His bow and quiver, full of arrows, were in his hand, and he scattered the shafts of destruction before his feet."

ſ   P. 30.

P. 30,

Συνδικον Μοισᾶν κτεανον.   *Pind. Pyth.* 1.

" The lawful possession and right of the Mufes."

P. 32.

Pensa, che questo dì mai non raggiorna.

                                             Dante. Parad.

Pause ; and reflect, that a day like this may never dawn
again.

P. 32.

Quos orbe sub omni
Jam vix septenâ numerat sapientia famâ.

" Wisdom herself can scarcely number seven persons,
from among all the sons of men, whom she can honour with
such a name."

P, 34.

Grave virus munditias pepulit.

                                             Hor. Ep, ad August.

" The virulence of the infection has corrupted and
destroyed all that is sound, beautiful, and healthy."

P. 37.

Non tenues ignavo pollice chordas
Pulso, sed Aurunci residens in margine templi,
Audax magnorum trumulis adcanto magistrûm.

                                             Statii. Sylv.

" I strike no feeble chords with an idle, unavailing impulse ; but holding my residence by the *Auruncian* temple,
(where fleeps the spirit of *Lucilius*) I bend before the tombs
of mightiest masters, and raise my voice with boldness."

END OF THE INTRODUCTORY LETTER.

TRANSLATION

TRANSLATION

OF THE

PASSAGES IN THE NOTES

TO THE

FIRST DIALOGUE

OF THE

PURSUITS OF LITERATURE.

~~~~~~~~

P. 39.

Audaci quicunque afflate Cratino,
Iratum Eupolidem prægrandi cum sene palles,
Aspice et hæc, si forte aliquid decoctius audis ;
Inde vaporatâ lector mihi ferveat aure.

Pers. Sat. 1.

" Whoever thou art, who feelest thyself inspired with the
spirit of the fearless Cratinus; who turnest pale over the page
of the indignant Eupolis, and of the venerable, dignified
master of the sock * ; look also upon these my labours,
if by chance you should discover something matured
and perfected by study. May my readers approach them
with an ear purified *with incense from their altars.*"

————

P. 42.

Apollineæ bellum puerile pharetræ.   *Statius.*
" The childish war of Apollo's quiver."

* Aristophanes.

P. 43.

P. 43.

Talia dum çelebro subitam civilis Erinnys
Tarpeio de monté facem, Phlegræaque movit
Prælia ; sacrilegis lucent *Capitolia* tædis,
Et *Senonum* furias Latiæ sumpsere Cohortes.

Stat. Sylv. l. 5. c. 3.

" While I am recording these events, the Fury of civil
Discord hath shaken her torch over the *Tarpeian* rock, and
kindled wars fiercer than those on the plains of Phlegra.
Behold, THE CAPITOL is blazing with sacrilegious fires, and
the Roman Legions have assumed the maddening spirit of
the Gauls."

P. 44.

Sol occubuit : nox nulla secuta est.

" The fun set ; but no night ensued."

P. 47.

Quæ tibi, quæ tali reddam pro carmine dona ?

Virg. Eclog.

" What remuneration can I offer you for a poem like
this ?"

P. 47.

Phyllidas, Hypsipilas, vatum et plorabile si quid.

Pers. Sat. 1.

" The tales of Phillis and Hypsipile, and all the lamentable
stuff of sing-song poetasters."

P. 48

Unus

Sceptra potitus, eâdem aliis sopitu' quiete est.

Lucret. L. 3.

" Having obtained and enjoyed the sovereignty, he closed
his eyes in the fame common sleep of mortality."

P. 49.

P. 49.

Deficiens crumena.

" A purse under a consumption."

P. 50.

" Sine vi non ulla dabit præcepta.

Virg. Georg. 4.

" He will utter no oracular precepts but upon compulsion."

P. 50.

Utrum chimæra bombinans in vacuo possit comedere secundas intentiones ?

" Whether a chimæra buzzing in a vacuum, has the power of eating up or devouring second designs, thoughts, or intentions ?*

P. 52.

Stupet hic vitio, et fibris increvit opimum
. Pingue, caret *culpâ*, nescit quid perdat, et alto
Demersus summâ rurfum non bullit in undâ.

Pers. Sat. 3.

" He is become insensible by long habits of vice, and the heart of the man is waxed fat and gross; he is placed beyond the imputation of guilt, he has nothing to lose, and is plunged so deep, that he cannot rise even to bubble on the surface of the stream."

---

* A Germanick question, to ridicule the abfurdities of metaphysicks run mad. See a similar collection in the seventh chapter of the Memoirs of Martinus Scriblerus ; for instance : " An præter *Esse reale* actualis Essentiæ sit aliud *esse necessa-* " *rium* quo res actualiter existat ?—In English thus : " Whe- " ther, besides the real being of actual being, there be any " other being necessary to cause a thing to be."

P. 52.

P. 52.

Non hæc in fædera. *Virg. Æ. 4.*

" Not into such alliances and leagues as these."

P. 55.

Piger scribendi ferre laborem,
Scribendi rectè, nam ut multum, nil moror.

Horat. l. 1, s. 4.

" Too careless or too idle to undergo the toil of writing,
I mean, of writing well; for as to the quantity of his
compofitions, it is out of the question."

P. 56.

Une boutique de verbiage.

" A mere word-shop."

P. 56.

De Causis corruptæ Eloquentiæ:

" A treatise on the Causes why Eloquence has been so
much corrupted."

P. 56.

Abundat dulcibus vitiis. *Quintil.* l. 10. c. 1.

" He abounds with luscious faults."

P. 57.

Ου γαρ εν μεσοισι κειται
Δωρα δυσμαχητα Μοισᾶν
Τω 'πιτυχοντι φερειν.

" The gifts of the Mufes are not offered to every one
who paffes by, as common favours ; they muft be fought after,
and obtained with difficulty."

P. 58.

Mugitus labyrinthi. *Juv. Sat.* 1.
" The bellowing of the labyrinth."—N.B. Put for any common topick of ordinary poets or writers.

P. 58.

. La nudrita :
Damigella Trivulzia al sacro speco.

Ariosto O. F. Cant. 46. st. 4.
" Trivulzia, brought up and nourished in the sacred cavern."

P. 59.

Per più fiate gli occhi ci fofpinfe
Quella lettura, e fcolorocci il viso;
Ma solo un punto fu quel che ci vinse.
Quando leggemmo, cominciai, Ahi lasso,
Quanti dolci pensier, quanto desio
Menò costoro al doloroso passo!"

Dante Inf. c. 5.
" That work often affected us, and our cheeks turned pale as we were reading it; but there was one circumstance which quite subdued us. As we were proceeding, I exclaimed,
" Alas! what softness of sentiment, what extasy of rapture,
" conducted these wretched souls to the paths of sorrow."

P. 62.

Omnes
Admonet, et magnâ testatur voce per umbras,
Difcite justitiam moniti, et non temnere Divos.

Virg. Æn. 6.
" He gives admonition to all, and cries with a loud voice through the shades; Give ear unto me, and be warned; revere justice, and despise not the power of the Gods."

P. 63.

P. 63.

Sunt adhuc curæ hominibus fides et officium; sunt qui
defunctorum quoque amicos agant.

Plin. Epist.

" The offices of kindness and *fidelity* are yet cultivated
among men : some are still to be found who will perform the
duties of friendship to the departed."

P. 64.

Agri, edificia, loca, possessiones, (cœlum et mare præter-
miserunt,. cætera complexi sunt) publicè data, ASSIGNATA,
vendita !" *Cic. de Leg. Agrar. Or.* 3.

" Lands, edifices, estates, possessions of every species, all
have been seized within their grasp ; the heaven above, and
the sea excepted, all have been declared publick property, by
gift, by *assignment*, by auction."

P. 64.

Si vous voulez une REVOLUTION, il faut commencer par
décatholiciser la France. *Mirabeau.*

" If you are in earnest for a *Revolution*, you must *begin*
by annihilating the Catholick religion in France."

P. 66.

Quantis suspiriis et gemitibus fiat, ut quantulacunque ex
parte possit intelligi DEUS! *Augustin:*

" (They feel) by what prostration of soul, by what prayers
and strong conflicts of the spirit, even the slightest and most
imperfect knowledge of GOD is to be obtained !"

P. 67.

Auctor nominis ejus CHRISTUS, qui, Tiberio imperitante
per

per Procuratorem Pontium Pilatum supplicio affectus erat.

Tacit. Annal. l. 15. f. 44.

" The founder of that denomination of worship was
CHRIST, who, in the reign of Tiberius, suffered the punishment
of death under the Procurator Pontius Pilate."

P. 67.

Non est qui judicat verè ; confidunt in nihilo, loquuntur
vanitates ; conceperunt laborem, pepererunt iniquitatem.

" There is not one who judgeth with true judgment ; no,
not one : their trust is in nothing ; they talk words of vanity ;
they have conceived mischief, and brought forth iniquity."

P. 68.

I, Lictor, colliga manus.   *Liv.* 1.

" Go, Lictor, and bind his hands."

P. 68.

Græcè

Discumbunt ; nec velari PICTURA jubetur ;
Forsitan expectes ut Gaditana canoro
Incipiat prurire choro.   JUV.

" Their entertainments are in the Greek fashion ; and the
pictured emblem appears without a veil : you might expect to
see the dancing-girls (from the East) displaying their attitudes
before the guests."

P. 69.

Σοφια πρωτον ἁγνη εστιν, επειτα ειρηνικη.

" Wisdom is first pure, then peaceable."

P. 70.

Si sic omnia !   *Juv.*

" Would he had always written so !"

P. 67.

P. 70.

Bella femina che ride,
Vuol dir, borsa che piange.　　　　　　*Ital. Comed.*

" The smiles of a pretty girl are the tears of the purse."

Italian Proverb.

P. 71.

Composuit octo volumina, inepté magis quam ineleganter.

Sueton. Claud. Sect. 41.

" He composed eight volumes, not without elegance,
but without sufficient discernment."

P. 72.

Propera *stomachum* laxare saginis ;
Et tua servatum consume in sæcula rhombum.

Juv. Sat. 4.

" Prepare your *stomach* for these delicacies ; and feast
upon the fish which has been preserved for your times."

P. 74.

Corpus fine pectore.　　　　　　　　　　*Hor.*

" A body without a foul."

P. 74.

Vitæ summa brevis.　　　　　　　　　　*Hor.*

" The short span of life."

P. 74.

Magno conatu magnas nugas.　　　　　　*Terent.*

" Great efforts for great trifles."

P. 76.

Quousque fruſtra pascetis ignigenos istos ?

Apulei. Metam. l. 7.

" How long will ye idly support these sons of fire ?"

C　　　　　　　　　　　　　　　P. 77.

P. 77.

Nè pour la digestion.

" Born for nothing but to eat and digest."

P. 80.

Grande munus

Cecropio repetat cothurno.

" May he re-affume the weight and dignity of the tragick bufkin."

P. 81.

Ces propos, diras tu, sont bons dans la satire,

Pour ègayer d' abord un lecteur qui veut rire :

Mais il faut les prouver ; en forme : j'y consens.

Repons moi donc, Docteur, et mets toi sur les bancs ;

Qu' eft ce qu' un Commentateur ?

Boileau, Sat. 8.

" These subjects, you may say, are certainly pleasant in a Satire, to enliven and amuse a reader who loves to laugh. But I want the proof; let me have it in regular form. I agree with you; well, Doctor, answer me, and take your seat quietly, as in the schools. *What is a Commentator ?*"

P. 84.

Non more probo ; cum carmina lumbum

Intrant, et tremulo scalpuntur ubi intima versu.

Pers. Sat. 1.

" The manner is neither good nor respectable ; when the verses, or the subject of them, enter the very marrow, and the effeminate, lascivious accents provoke and irritate the inmost sensations."

P. 85.

P. 85.

Pauca suo Gallo, quæ vel legat ipsa Lycoris.

Virg. Ecl. 10.

" Such effusions of verse and fancy, as even Lycoris herself might read."

P. 85.

Hoc defuit unum

Fabricio. *Juv. Sat.* 4.

" This was the only point in which *Fabricius* was deficient."

P. 87.

Carminaque Aonidum, justamque probaverat iram.

Ovid. Metam. l. 6. v. 2.

" (Minerva) approved the strains of the Muses, and their honest indignation."

P. 88.

Παρφασις, ἥ τ' εκλεψε νοον πυκα περ φρονεοντων. *Hom. Il.*

" Such is the power of insinuating flattery ; it steals away the understanding of the best and the wisest.

P. 92

Videre CANES ; primusque Melampus,
Pamphagus et Dorceus, velox cum fratre Lycisca,
Ichnobatesque sagax, et villis Asbolus atris,
Nebrophonosque valens, et trux cum Lælape Theron,
Labros et Agriodos, et acutæ vocis Hylactor,
Quosque referre mora est. Ea turba, cupidine prædæ,
Quà via difficilis, quàque est via nulla, sequuntur.
Heu famulos fugit IPSE suos : clamare libebat,
ACTÆON *Ego fum* ; dominum cognoscite vestrum ;
Vellet abesse quidem, sed adest.

Ovid Metam. l. 3.

THE

" THE DOGS descried him: first rushed forth Melampus, Pamphagus, and Dorceus, and the swift-footed Lycisca, with her brother, the quick-scented Ichnobates; and Asbolus, black and shaggy, and the powerful Nebrophonos, Lælaps, and the fierce Theron, Labros, and Agriodos, and the shrill-toned Hylactor, and others which I cannot name. The whole pack, eager for their prey, follow in full cry, where the path is rough and difficult, and even where no path at all is to be traced. Alas! he flies from his own attendants. Fain would he have cried out, I AM ACTÆON; behold in me your lord and master.—He wished to be away from them: but in vain. *He is left in their power.*"

P. 94.

Αυτον και Θεραποντα.   *Homer.*

" Himself, and his faithful attendant." Or, " The knight and his squire."

P. 95.

Mihi sit propositum in tabernâ mori;
Vinum sit appositum morientis ori;
Ut dicant, cum venerint angelorum chori,
Deus sit propitius huic potatori."

Drinking Song, by Walter de Mapes, * *Archdeacon of Oxford, in the* 11*th century.*

" My resolution is to die in a tavern; may wine be placed before my lips as I am expiring; that the angelick choirs, when they appear, may say, " Heaven be propitious to this jovial drinker!"

P. 96.

------

* Quoted by Mr. Warton, in his second Dissertation, prefixed to his History of English Poetry.

I

P. 96.

Illum pro literato plerique laudandum duxerunt, quum ille, næniis quibusdam anilibus occupatus, inter Milesias Punicas Apuleii sui, et ludicra literaria consenesceret.

Julius Capitolinus in Vitâ Clodii Albini ad Constantium Augustum.

" Many were inclined to consider him as a deep scholar, engaged as he was with old-wives fables and trifles, and passing a learned old age among the Milesian Tales of his own Apuleius, and the child's-play of literature."

P. 96.

Utilium sagax rerum,   *Hor. A. P.*

" Subtle and sagacious in useful discoveries."

P. 97.

Altum Saganæ caliendrum.

Hor. l. 1. sat. 8.

" The towering head-dress of the Sorceress Sagana."

P. 98.

Κατακαυχᾶται Ελεος κρισεως.

" Mercy rejoiceth against judgment."

P. 99.

Cuicunque veterum fortiter opposuerim;   *Quintil.*

" I would confidently put it in competition with any of the ancients."

P. 99.

Νεκυων αμενηνα καρηνα.   *Hom. Odys.*

" Phantoms of the dead, without strength or substance."

C 3   P. 100.

P. 100.

Ecce pro Clericis multum allegavi;
Nec non pro Presbyteris multum comprobavi;
Pater noster pro me, quoniam peccavi,
Dicat quisque Presbyter cum suâ Suavi.

Drinking Song (as above) by Walter de Mapes, in the 11th century.

" See what allegations I have made in favour of Priests and Presbyters; and so may every grateful *Clerk*, with his sweetheart, say a Paternoster for me and my sins!"

P. 100.

" Si quis dixerit Episcopum aliquâ infirmitate laborare, anathema esto."

Decree of the Council of Constance.

" If any one presume to say, that a Bishop may have his failings, let him be accursed."

P. 101.

" Hic liber est conglutinatus ex tam multis libris, quot unus pinguis Cocus oves, boves, sues, grues, auseres, passeres, coquere, aut unus fumosus calefactor centum magna hypocausta ex illis calefacere possit."

Epist. Obscurorum Virorum.

" This book* is *conglutinated*, or made up, of as many books as would serve *one fat cook* for fuel, to dress sheep, oxen, swine, pigs, ducks, turkeys, and geese, without number; or as many as would be sufficient for *one High-Dryer* to heat a hundred stoves." From a book, intitled, " The Epistles of *Obscure* Men."

* *i. e.* The Notes on the Edition of Shakspeare, by Johnson and Steevens, &c. &c. &c.

END OF DIALOGUE THE FIRST.

PASSAGES IN THE NOTES

TO THE

SECOND DIALOGUE.

OF THE

PURSUITS OF LITERATURE.

~~~~~~~

P. 103.

Ετ' αϐλητος και ανητατος οξει χαλκω,
Δινευω κατα μεσσον, αγοι δε με Παλλας Αθηνη
Χειρος ελϐσ', αυταρ ϐελεων απερυκοι ερωην.

Hom. Il. 4. v. 540.

" Yet untouched and without a wound, I pass through the thickest of the ranks; and may Minerva lead me by the hand, and defend me from the *missile* weapons of the enemy."

P. 105.

Ανειρυσας
Και φασγανϐ ζωστηρα, και ξιφος πατρος,
Κρημνων ενερθεν αιγιλιψ ϐοιζϐμενων,
Παλιν (δοκευω.) *Lycophron, Cassand.* 1321.

" Drawing forth the belt and the paternal sword, buried deep under the cliffs and rocks sounding with storms, I again take my stand of observation*."

P. 106.

Flebit, et insignis totâ cantabitur urbe. *Hor.* Sat. 1. l. 2.

He

---

* This dark allusion of Lycophron is to a legend concerning Theseus. See Plutarch in the Life of Theseus. If I recollect right, there is a picture, in Lord Exeter's collection at *Burleigh*, on this subject.

C 4

" He shall regret it, and become the burthen of some popular song."

P. 110.

Dechirans à l'envi leur propre Rèpublique,
Lions contre Lions, parens contre parens,
Combattent follement POUR LE CHOIX DES TYRANS.

                Boileau, sat. 8. v. 132.

" Tearing in pieces their own Republic, we see them, lions opposed to lions, relations to relations, madly and foolishly fighting with each other FOR THE CHOICE OF TYRANTS."

P. 111.

Καταιθει γαιαν ορχηστης Αρης,
Στρομβω τον αιματηρον εξαρχων νομον.
Απασα δε χθων πρ'υμματων δηϊϡμενη
Κειται, πεφρικαν δ', ωστε λἠϊϡ γυαι,
Λογχαις αποστιλϭοντες. Οιμωγη δε μοι
Εν ωσ: πυργων εξ ακρων ινδαλλεται,
Προς αιθερος κυρϡϡα νηνεμϡς ἑϭρας,
Γοω γυναικων, και καταρῥαγαις πεπλων,
Αλλην επ' αλλη συμφορϡν δεϭϡγμενων.

            Lycophron Cassandra. v. 249.

" The God of battle kindles the flames of war in the land, and sounds the sanguinary blast from his trumpet. The kingdom all around presents one scene of devastation, and the fields are bristled with spears, waving thick as the ears of corn. Lamentations, wafted through the silent regions of the air, are heard from the pinnacles of the towers, with the rending of veils, and the shrieks of women, waiting for misery upon misery, and calamity upon calamity."

P. 113.

P. 113.

Glomerare sub antro
Fumiferam noctem, commixtis igne tenebris.

Virg. Æn. 8. v. 254.

" To gather together, in the recesses of the cavern, a thick night, palled in the dunnest smoke of hell *, while the darkness is mixed with fire !"

***

P. 113.

Ubi passim
Palantes error recto de tramite pellit.   *Hor.* l. 2. sat. 3.

" Where error drives them in endless deviations, from the right path."

***

P. 117.

Dogmatizer en vers, et rimer par chapitres.

Boileau, s. 8. v. 116.

" To deliver dogmas or sentences in verse, and to rhyme " chapter by chapter."

***

P. 119.

Vitreo bibit ille Priapo.   *Juv.* s. 2. v. 95.

" He drinks from his glass goblet, shaped like a Priapus."

***

P. 120.

Historia quoquo modo scripta delectat.   *Plin. Epist.*

" History is always pleasing, write it as you will."

***

P. 120.

Sed tamen in pretio.   *Hor. A. P.*

" But still it has a value."

P. 121.

* Expressions from Shakespeare's Macbeth.

P. 121.

Amoretti alati.

" Little Cupids with little wings."

P. 123.

Υπνε αγωγα ἁπασι τα ξυνηθεα. Ναυτικω μεν ἡ εν ακατω
καταχλισις, και εν θαλασση περιφορα, και αιγιαλων ηχος, και
κυματων κτυπος, ανεμων τε ϐομϐος, κτλ.

Aretæus, de Morbis Acutis. c. 1. p. 7. Edit. *Boerhaave.*

" All things which are habitual, such as motions to which
" we are accustomed, are favourable to sleep. For a sailor
" you will recommend the reclining on ship-board, a voyage
" at open sea, the sounding of the shore, and the noise of the
" winds, and the roaring of the waves, &c. &c. &c."

P. 123.

Apollineo nomina digna choro.

" Names worthy to be inscribed in the choir of Apollo."

P. 124.

Il cantar, che nell' anima si sente ;

Il più ne sente l'alma, il men l'orecchio.

" That musick, which is felt internally ; it is not the ear, but
" the soul itself, which is affected."

P. 126.

Felix curarum ! cui non Heliconia cordi

Serta, nec imbelles Parnassi e vertice laurus;

Sed viget ingenium, et magnos accinctus in usus,

Fert animus quascunque vices. *Statius. Sylv.*

" Happy and fortunate in his cares and engagements ! For
him the garlands of Helicon, and the *idle* laurels which bloom
on the brow of Parnassus, *have no charms !* But the powers of

his

his understanding are vigorous, and his mind, from long experience, is bound up to bear the vicissitudes of the world."

P. 126.

Ingenium illustre altioribus studiis juvenis admodum dedit; non, ut plerique, ut nomine magnifico segne otium velaret, sed quo firmior adversus fortuita Rempublicam capesseret.

Tacit. Hist. l. 4. c. 5.

" In early youth he devoted all the powers of his illustrious mind to the higher philosophy; not, as the manner of some is, to shelter sloth under the covert of a splendid name, but, by a steady and deliberate firmness against the accidents of life, to prepare himself for the administration of the state."

P. 126.

" Opum contemptor, recti pervicax, constans adversus metus." *Tacit. ib.*

" Superior to *avarice*, of a persevering *rectitude of principle*, and unmoved by fear."

P. 126.

Magnum est vectigal Parsimonia. *Cic.*
" Œconomy is a great possession."

P. 127.

Mæcenatis Rana, ob collationem pecuniarum, in magno terrore erat." *Plin. Nat. Hist.* l. 37. c. 1.

" The frog of Mæcenas (i. e. his seal bearing the figure of that animal) was an object of great terror, as the instrument of levying money."

P. 128.

Οικεια ξυνεσει, φυσεως μεν δυναμει, μελετη; δε βραχυτητι, κρατιστο; δη ητο; αυτοσχεδιαζειν τα δεοντα. *Thucyd.* l. 1. s. 138.

" His

" His sagacity was peculiarly his own; gifted by nature with intuitive skill, he had moreover such promptitude of counsel, as gave him a decided superiority in advancing all that was necessary upon any subject, and on the spur of the occasion.

P. 130.

Informatum fulmen.

" An unfinished thunder-bolt."

P. 130.

Tres imbris torti radios, tres nubis aquosæ
Addiderant, rutili tres ignis et alitis Austri;
Fulgores nunc terrificos, sonitumque metumque
Miscebant operi, flammisque sequacibus iras.

Virg. Æn. 8. 429.

Mr. BURKE himself has *thus* translated this passage in part 5, chapter 5, of his treatise on the Sublime and Beautiful, as an example that words may affect without raising distinct images. " *Three rays of twisted showers, three of watery*
" *clouds, three of fire, and three of the winged South wind;*
" *then mixed they in the work terrifick lightnings, and*
" *sound, and fear, and anger, with pursuing flames,*"

P. 131,

Cum tot abortivis fæcundam Julia vulvam
Solveret, et patruo similes effunderet offas.

Juv. Sat. 2. v. 32.

" Since the teeming womb of Julia has produced so many crude births, or rather abortions, which confess their incestuous sires."

P. 132.

Ανα̂ῤῥηγνυμενης εκ βαθρων γης, αυτε τε γυμνεμενε Ταρταρε.

Longin. de Subl. sect. 9.

" While

" While the earth is burst asunder from its foundations, and the very depths of Tartarus disclosed and laid bare to view."

P. 133.

Quando ullum invenient parem?　　　　　　*Hor.*

" When shall'they look upon his like again ?"

P. 133.

Monumenta rerum posteris quærentibus tradidit.　Frequentabunt ejus domum optimi Juvenes, et veram viam, velut ex oraculo, petent.　Hos ille formabit; ut vetus gubernator, littora et portus, et quid secundis flatibus, quid adversis ratis poscat, docebit, et communi ductus officio, et amore quodam operis.　　　　　*Quintil.* l. 12. c. xi. s. 1.

" He has delivered down to all posterity, who may enquire after them, the monuments and records of these transactions. Young men of character and ability will be desirous of *his* company and conversation, and will learn from him, as from an oracular decision, the path which it is their interest, or duty, to follow. He will instruct them, and will form their minds. Like an experienced pilot, he will shew them what is necessary to direct and preserve the vessel, when the gale is prosperous, or when the storm is raging.　He will be led to this by a sense of duty and of common good, and even by the pleasure he finds in the office itself."

P. 134.

Magno discrimine causam
Protegere affectus ? te consule, dic tibi, quis sis,
Orator vehemens, an Curtius, an Matho, truccæ
Noscende est mensura tuæ.　　　　*Juv. Sat.* 11. v, 32.

" Are you about to undertake the management of a cause of great importance ? First consult your own self : say fairly and honestly, who and what you are ; an orator of power and strength,

strength, or Curtius, or Matho. Understand well the measure of your eloquence and ability."

P. 135.

Hunc ne pro Cephalo raperes, Aurora, timebam.

Ovid. Epist. Sapph. Phaoni.

" I was apprehensive that you, Aurora, might seize upon him, for your own Cephalus."

P. 136.

Virus lunare. *Lucan.* l. 6.

" Drops of infection distilling from the moon."

N. B. Shakspeare, in his Macbeth, alludes to this piece of ancient witchcraft.

" On the corner *of the moon*
Hangs *a vaporous drop* profound;
I'll catch it, ere it fall to ground."

P. 139.

Της Φυσεως γραμματευς ην, τον καλαμον αποβρεχων εις Νην.
Suidas.

" He was the Scribe, or Secretary of Nature, dipping his pen into mind."

P. 141.

Nunc non e manibus illis,
Nunc non e tumulo fortunatâque favillâ,
Nascentur violæ. *Pers. Sat.* 1. v. 38.

" Will not violets spring from the spot where his manes repose, from his tomb and favoured ashes?"

P. 142.

Ad quæ
Discutienda valent sterilis mala robora ficus.

Juv. S. 10. v. 144.

" The shoots of a wild fig-tree are sufficient to burst them asunder."

ásunder."—N. B. Juvénal alludes to the wild fig-tree stretching its roots deep under ground, and then shooting out with strength sufficient to break the stones of sepulchres.

P. 143.

Rite maturos aperire partus.   *Hor.*

" To bring forth the matured birth in due form."

P. 144.

Oro miserere laborum
Tantorum, miserere animi non digna ferentis.

Virg. Æn. 2.

" Consider, I beseech you, all that I have undergone ; have compassion on a mind which has suffered most unworthily."

P. 145.

Nomen in exemplum sero servabimus ævo.

Milton ad Patrem.

" We will preserve his name for an example to late posterity."

P. 146.

Ιατρικωτατος, φιλοδωρος και αδωροδοκητος, φιλοπτωχος, γενναιος, νεων διορθωτης, οσιος, δικαιος, ευσεβης, εις ακρον της παιδειας εληλακως.

" A *Physician* of consummate skill ; generous, liberal, not to be corrupted ; a friend to the poor and needy ; *a gentleman in principle;* a regulator and conductor of youth ; a man of sanctity, justice, and piety ; whose attainments have reached the utmost heights of erudition."

P. 148.

Nudus agas ; minus est insania turpis.   *Juv. Sat. 2.*
" Plead then quite naked ; madness is less to be censured."

3   —N. B.

—N. B. Juvenal alludes to the indecent summer dresses of the Roman advocates in the courts of law."

P. 150.

Quel d'amor travagliato Sacripante. *Ariosto. O. F. c. 1.*

" I speak of the *love-lorn* Sacripante."

P. 150.

Συνετοισι.

(This note is addressed) " To the intelligent."

P. 150.

Della commodità che quì m' è data,
Io povero Medor, &c. *Ariosto, O. F. c. 23. s. 108.*

" I, poor Medoro, in gratitude for the *favourable* reception I found in this place," &c. &c. *

P. 150.

Era scritto in Arabico, che il conte
Intendea così ben come Latino. *Ariosto, O F. ib.*

" It was written in the *Arabick* language, which the noble Earl understood *as well* as he did Latin."

P. 151.

Nè sono a Ferraù, nè a Sacripante
(O sia Carliglio) per donar più rima ;
Da lor mi leva il Principe d'Anglante, &c.

Ib. Cant. 12. s. 96.

" I cannot allot any more of my verses to Ferraù, or Sacripante (or even to *Carlisle*) ; the Prince of Anglante calls my attention from them ; &c."

---

* Part of the inscription on the entrance of the cave or grotto, where Angelica and Medoro were accustomed to meet.

P. 152.

P. 151.

Οι θεοι οικτειραντες ανθρωπων (fome MSS. add πολιτικων) επιπονον πεφυκος γενος, τας Μησας, και Απολλωνα, και Διονυσον ξυνεορταστας; εδοσαν. *Plato de Legibus*, lib. 2.

" The Gods in compassion to the race of men * born to toil and trouble, gave the Muses, and Apollo, and *Bacchus* as companions of their festivals."

P. 151.

Εκλυσις,—εκβολη,—ψαλμος αντιφθογγος.

N. B. These are Greek musical terms, and technical words, which it would be needless to explain, and indeed would answer no purpose. Dr. Burney's History of Musick will, I believe, give their explanation at large.

P. 156.

Di Patrii, quorum semper sub numine *Troja* est,
Non tamen omnino Teucros delere paratis,
Cum tales animos Juvenum, et tam certa tulistis
Pectora. *Vir. Æn.* 9. v. 247.

" O ye Gods of my country, tutelary Deities of *Troy,* ye cannot surely have resolved to extirpate the sons of Teucer, since ye have inspired the breasts of our youth with such loyalty of zeal, and with such determined bravery."

END OF THE SECOND DIALOGUE.

D PASSAGES

---

* Some manuscripts read here, " politicians."

3

PASSAGES

IN THE

THIRD DIALOGUE

OF THE

PURSUITS OF LITERATURE.

~~~~~~

P. 159.

Εκλαγξαν δ' αρ' οϊστοι απ' ωμων χωομενοιο,
Αυτη κινηθεντος· όδ' ηϊε Νυκτι εοικως.
Εζετ' επειτ' απανευθε νεων, μετα δ' ιον ἑηκε,
Δεινη δε κλαγγη γενετ' αργυρεοιο βιοιο.
Ουρηας μεν πρωτον επωχετο, και Κυνας αργης,
Αυταρ επειτ' Αυτοισι βελος εχεπευκες αφιεις
Βαλλ'· αιει δε πυραι νεκυων καιοντο θαμειαι.

Hom. Il. 1.

" The arrows rattled in his quiver, as he moved along in
all the fierceness of his wrath. His march was like the Night.
He took his station at a distance from the ships, and sent forth
a shaft; and the sounding of the silver bow was terrible;
His first attack was on the animals, the mules and *dogs*; but
after that, he smote THE ARMY ITSELF with many a deadly
arrow, and the funeral piles of the slain blazed frequent
through the camp."

————

P. 161.

Ταυτα παιθ' ὑπερ Ὑμων, ὑπερ της Αληθειας, ὑπερ της
ὑμετερας

ὑμετερας Πολιτειας, και των Νομων, και της Σωτηριας, και
της Ευσεβειας, και της Δοξης, και της Ελευθεριας, ὑπερ των
κοινῇ πασι Συμφεροντων, ακριβολογυμαι και διεξερχομαι.

Demosthenes, Περι Στεφανυ.

· " I present these considerations as the result of accurate
and solemn investigation ; they are offered in behalf of YOU
ALL; in the cause of Truth, your Constitution, and your
Laws ; for your common Salvation, your Religion, your
Honour, and your Liberty."

P. 163.

Απαυγασαι Όιος Εφεδρος·
Ουρεος εξ ὑπατυ σκοπιην εχει, ός κε Σε ῥεια
Βυσσοθεν εξερυσειε !

Callimachus, Hymn. ad Delum. v. 125.

" Look upon " the great Vision * of that guarded
mount," see what a power holds his watchful residence on
the summit of the cliff, a power able to overthrow you from
your foundations !" N. B. The poet is speaking of Mars
personified on the higheſt mountain of Delos.

P. 163.

Τειχεα μεν και λᾶες ὑπαι ῥιπης γε πεσοιεν
Στρυμονιυ Βορεαο· θεος δ' αει αστυφελικτος !
Δηλε φιλη, τοιος Σε ζοηθοος αμφιζεζηκει.

Callim. Ib. v. 25.

" Ramparts, and walls of stone may be shaken and fall at
the blast of Strymonian Boreas ; but THE GOD is immoveable !
Such is the power who surrounds and protects thee, O my
beloved Delos."

D 2　　　　　　　　, P. 162.

* An expression adapted from the Lycidas of Milton.

P. 163.

L' alpestro monte, ond' è tronco Peloro.

Dante Purgat. c. 14.

" The Alpine mountain, whence Pelorus is torn."

P. 164.

Quæ cum magna modis multis miranda videtur
Gentibus humanis Regio, visendaque fertur,
Rebus opima bonis, multâ munita virûm vi,
Nil *tamen* hoc *habuisse* Viro præclarius in se,
Nec sanctum magis, et mirum carumque videtur."

Lucret. l. 1. v. 728.

" A Region, long the subject of speculation and wonder
to all the surrounding nations ; a kingdom which abounds in
every production which is valuable, and which is defended
by the *internal, consolidated* strength of her own natives;
yet she appears to have possessed no greater object of love
and veneration, or more illustrious than THIS MAN."

P. 164.

Animo vidit; ingenio complexus est; eloquentiâ
illuminavit."   *Paterculus concerning Cicero.*

" These subjects he saw by the power of his mind; he
comprehended them by his understanding; and by his eloquence
he cast a brightness upon them."

P. 166.

La piova maladetta, fredda e greve,
Regola, e qualità (estrana) e nuova,
Grandine grossa, ed acqua tinta e neve,
Per l' aer tenebroso si riversa!

Dante Infern. cant. 6.

" It

" It was a storm of accursed quality ; of rain, cold, heavy, and frequent, with hail stones and sleet, and thick discoloured snow, pouring down in torrents through the darkened regions of the air."

P. 167.

Ευδεις !—αλλ' 8 Σειο λελασμενοι εσμεν, Αχιλλευ!

Ου μεν Ση ζωοντος ακηδεες, 8δε θανοντος.　　　Hom. Il.

" Thou sleepest the sleep of death !—But we are not unmindful of thee, O Achilles ; in life and in death thou art equally the object of our regard and veneration."

P. 168,

Οικον 'αμερον αστοις,

Ξενοισι δε θεραποντα, γνωσομαι

Ταν ολΒιαν Κορινθον,

Προθυρον Ποτειδᾶνος, αγλαοκ8ρον.

Εν τᾶ γαρ Ευνομια ναιει, κασιγνη-
ται τε, Δικα πολιων

Ασφαλες Βαθρον, και ομο-
τροπος Ειρανα, ταμιαι

Ανδρασι πλ8τ8, χρυσεαι

Παιδες ευΒ8λ8 Θεμιτος.

Εθελοντι δ' αλεξειν ύΒριν, κορ8
Ματερα θρασυμυθον.

Εν δε Μοισ' άδυπνοος,

Εν δ' Αρης ανθει νεων

Ουλιαις αιχμαισιν ανδρων.

Pind. Olymp. Od. 13.

" I record the praises of *Corinth*, a state mild to its own citizens, hospitable to strangers, famed for opulence, the sacred residence of Neptune, whose youth are renowned for courage and ability.　There dwells Eunomia, the goddess of

D 3

wel .

well-ordered governments, and her sisters, Justice, the unshaken basis of every state, and Peace, of like manners; the dispensers and arbiters of wealth, the golden daughters of Themis, whose counsel never deceives. It is their wish and purpose to chase away injury, the bold-tongued parent of satiety and insolence.

Here too the Muse breathes out her sweetest, softest inspirations; and Mars himself flourishes anew in the prowess of her youthful heroes."

P. 168,

Hæc Ego non credam Venusinâ digna lucernâ?

Hæc Ego non agitem? *Juv. Sat.* 1. 51.

" Shall I not rouse myself at such a call, and attack them? Shall I not hold up the torch of Satire to works like these?"

P. 170.

Μη φιλοχωρειν εν Πολει μηδενος αυτοις αγαθυ μεταδιδυση.

Dion. Halicarn. l. 5, 63.

" Not to be interested, or take any part in the welfare of a State, which never allowed them to share any advantage."

P. 170.

Ουδεν οἱ Ρωμαιοι ταπεινωθεντες, ὁ παθειν εικος ην της μεγαντε πολεμον αναιρυμενυς, και πασας απεγνωκοτας Συμμαχικας ελπιδας, αλλα ταις οικειαις δυναμεσι πιστευσαντες μοναις, πολλω προθυμοτεροι προς τον Αγωνα εγινοντο, ὡς δια την αναγκην ανδρες αγαθοι παρα της κινδυνης εσομενοι, και εαν κατα νυν πραξωσι, ταις ιδιαις αρεταις κατορθωσαντες τον Πολεμον, υδενι κοινωσαμενοι της δοξης.

Dion. Halicarn. Ant. Rom. Hist. l. 5. s. 62.

" The

" The *Romans* were nothing humbled, as might have been expected, engaged as they were in an arduous war, and deserted by all their Allies. But on the contrary, with a firm reliance on their *internal* powers alone, they rushed forward to the contest with still greater alacrity, and with a courage, inspired by danger and necessity. They were bold and confident of their ability (under the guidance of good counsel,) to carry on the war with effect by their own native courage and virtues, without any to participate their glory and success."

P. 171.

Ferro Argolicas fœdare latebras. *Virg. Æn.* 2.

" To pierce with the sword the inmost concealments of *the Greeks.*"

P. 172.

Tu ne cede malis; sed contra audentior ito,
Quam tua te Fortuna sinet. *Virg. Æn.* 6.

" Suffer not your spirit to be subdued by misfortunes; but on the contrary, steer right onward, with a courage greater than your fate seems to allow."

P. 173.

Ματαιολογων φημα προσεπτατο Ελλαδα μυσοπολων, σοφας επιφθονον τεχνας ονειδος.

Athenæi Deipnosophist. l. 14. p. 617. *Ed. Casaub.*

" The fame of some vain pretenders to poetry has been noised about *Greece,* to the disgrace of a learned and distinguished art."

P. 175.

PLACE DE LA TRADUCTION.

par Monsieur Peltier.

" JEAN NORBURY, Docteur en Théologie, Chanoine et
" Associé à Eton. Agé *soixante et huit* ans.

" ETIENNE WESTON, Bachelier en Théologie, Abbé,
" Voyageur, Versificateur, *ci devant* Recteur. Agè *cin-*
" *quante ans.*

" CHARLES COOTE, * Docteur en Théologie, Doien
" Irlandois. Agé *cinquante et deux ans*, selon la Registre.

" EDOUARD TEW, Bachelier en Théologie, Chanoine
" et Associé, à Eton. Agé *cinquante et sept ans.*

" GUILLOTINÉS *à la Grecque,* 25 *Floreal,* Quintidi, 1796.
Extrait du Registre de la Guillotine Literaire."

N. B. *Ils sont montés sur l' échaffaut avec assez de
courage ; a dix heures et un quart du matin leurs têtés sont
tombés.*"

Extrait

---

* P. S. J'ai reçue une lettre trés obligeante de la part de
Monsieur *Peltier*, dont j'ai *la plus* haute considération, qui
m'a informé, qu'il y a une petite méprise dans le Registre,
au sujet de Monsieur LE DOCTEUR COOTE, Traducteur
celebre. Qu'il n'étoit pas Doien Irlandois, et par consequent, grand théológien, mais Docteur en Droit Civil en
Angleterre, *très instruit dans la grammaire Grecque.*
Monsieur PELTIER, avec le zele le plus édifiant pour la
verité, et avec beaucoup d'onction, m'a prié de corriger le
Registre et la poésie là dessus ; et m'a informé, que Monsieur
NARES, Auteur trés aimable en son genre, et editeur de
l'ouvrage périodique, (*The British Critick*) la voulût aussi
avec beaucoup d'empressement. Malheureusement, c'est
impossible ; et j'ai répondû très franchement : " Mon cher
Peltier, quand une fois la tête doctorale est tombée ; eh !
que faire ?" (Nov. 1797.)

Extrait du Rapport fait AU CONSEIL DES ANCIENS, par l'Executeur de la haute Justice Litéraire.

Communication to the author of the P. of L. by Monsieur Peltier, editor of " The Picture of Paris, &c. &c."

" PLACE OF TRANSLATION.

" JOHN NORBURY, Doctor in Divinity, Canon and " Fellow of Eton College. *Aged* SIXTY-EIGHT *years.*

" STEPHEN WESTON, Bachelor in Divinity ; an Abbé, a " Traveller, and a maker of verses ; *formerly* Rector of a " parish. *Aged* FIFTY *years.*

" CHARLES COOTE,* Doctor in Divinity, a Dean in " Ireland. *Aged* FIFTY-TWO *years*, according to the " Register.

" EDWARD TEW, Bachelor in Divinity, Canon and " Fellow of Eton College. *Aged* FIFTY SEVEN *years.*

" GUILLOTINED *after the Greek fashion,* 25th " *of Floreal ;* 5th *day of the Decade,* 1796." *Extract from the Register of* THE LITERARY GUILLOTINE.

N. B. *They ascended the scaffold with great resolution ; at a quarter past ten in the morning their heads fell.*

" Extract from the Report made to THE COUNCIL OF ANCIENTS, by the Executive Minister of Literary Justice."

P. 176.

---

* P. S. " I have received a letter from Monsieur Peltier, for whom I entertain *the highest consideration*, who has informed me, that there is a little mistake concerning DR. COOTE, the celebrated translator. He says, that Dr. Coote was not an Irish Dean, (and consequently a great Theologian,) but a Doctor in the Civil Law in England, *deeply versed in the Greek grammar.* Mr. Peltier, with a zeal for truth of the most edifying nature, and with great devotion of mind,

has

P. 176.

Αρχετε, Σικελικαι τω πενθεος, αρχετε Μωσαι.

       Moschi Epitaph. in Bion.

" Begin, ye Sicilian Muses, begin the strain of woe."

P. 178.

Je trouve dans le libraire *Elmsley*, un conseiller sage, instruit, et discret.

Mr. Gibbon to Mr. Deyverdun. Letters Miscell. Works,
             vol. 2. 4to. p. 596.

" I find in *Elmsley*, the bookseller, an adviser of much wisdom, knowledge, and discretion."

P. 179.

Εστιν ὃ το ὁπωσὃν τινα ΟΜΟΣΑΙ *μεγα, το δε πὃ, και πως, και εφ' ὡν καιρων, και τινος ἑνεκα.*

       Longin. de Subl. sect. 16.

" An oath is not sublime of itself; but the place, the manner, the occasion, and the circumstance of introducing it, make it so."

P. 182.

Λοξων ες διεξοδὃς επων.   *Lycoph. Cassand* v. 14.

" Into all the meandrings of verbal obliquity."

---

has requested me to correct the Register and the Poetry in this particular; and has also signified to me, that the Rev. MR. NARES, a very amiable author in his way, and editor of the periodical work called *The British Critick,* was very eager and solicitous on the same account. Unfortunately, it is wholly out of my power; and I returned an answer with great frankness; " My dear Peltier, when once a doctor's " head is off, what can be done ?" (Nov. 1797.)

               P. 182.

P. 182.

Εταιρα χρυσια ει φοροιη, δημοσια εστω.

" If a courtezan wears ornaments of gold, let them be confiscated, or *let her* person *be publick.*"*

P. 183.

Μηδε τα Κυπρια προπαροξυτονως επιγραφεσθαι τα ποιηματα.

Photii Biblioth. pag. 984. edit. 1653.

" The Cyprian verses are not marked with the accent on the ante-penultima."

P. 183.

Ex libris deprehendi hominem ardentis ingenii, variæ lectionis, et multæ memoriæ; alicubi tamen majore copiâ quam delectu, ac dictione tumultuosâ magis quam compositâ.

Erafmi Ep. 1248.

" From his writings I discovered him to be a man of a glowing genius, extensive reading, and comprehensive memory; but in general more copious, than choice; and his style and phraseology rather confused, than clear and chastised."

P. 184.

" Figuram animi magis quam corporis complectantur.

Tacit. Vit. Agric.

" Let them rather present us with the features of his mind than of his body."

P. 185.

Si tibi *Mistillus* cocus, Æmiliane, vocatur,
Dicetur quare non *T'arat'alla* mihi?

Mart. Ep. lib. 1.

If

---

* The construction depends upon the mode of placing the accent on the word δημοσια.

" If your Cook's name is *Mystyllus*, why may I not call him also *T'arat'alla*." *

P. 187.

Pleno jure—and usufructuario.

" Not of absolute right, but only † usufructuary."

P. 187.

Supera ut convexa *revisant*,
Rursus et incipiant *in corpora velle reverti*. ‡

Virg. Æn. 6.

" That they may *revisit* the superior regions, and again manifest an inclination to return to their *corporeal, visible forms*."

P. 188.

Τῇ νυν, και σοι τυτο, Γερον, κειμηλιον εστω. *Hom. Il.* 22.

" Take this reward as a prize, thou venerable *old man*, and preserve it for a memorial of thy skill."

P. 188.

Melioribus olim auspiciis.

" Once under more favourable expectations."

P. 189.

Hoc Juvenem egregium præstanti munere dono.

Virg. Æn. 5.

---

* The words *Mystyllus* and *T'arat'alla*, are a play upon two Greek words, which cannot be explained in English.

† Terms in the Roman law.

‡ This was an Eton allusion to Dr. Norbury's series of old clothes, re-appearing, after having been locked up for many months. It is hardly possible to translate the spirit of it in English.

" I present

" I present the illustrious youth with this distinguished, mark of my regard, and of his merit."

P. 190.

'Οτε γεγονα Ανηρ, κατηργηκα τα τυ Νηπιυ..

" When I became *a man,* I put away childish things."

P. 191.

Sic liceat magnas Graiorum implere catervas.   *Hor.*

" In this manner we may attempt to fill up the measure of Grecian literature."

P. 191.

Tunc cum ad canitiem—tunc, tunc, ignoscere—NOLO.'
                                    Pers. Sat. 1.

" What? when the hair is absolutely grey with years— do you ask me to overlook such folly?—No; no; no;."

P. 194.

Spiritus intus alit; totamque infusa per artus
Mens agitat molem, et magno se corpore miscet.
                                    Virg. Æn. 6.

" The spirit feeds it within; and the soul, by infusion into every member, agitates the mass, and blends itself intimately WITH THE WHOLE BODY."

P. 195.

Dixerat Anchises; natumque unàque Sibyllam
Conventus trahit in medios, turbamque sonantem;
Et tumulum capit, unde omnes longo ordine possit,
Advestos legere, et venientum discere vultus.
                                    Virg. Æn. 6. (1796.)

" Anchises finished his speech, and led his son Æneas and
                                                    the

the Sibyll into the midst of the Convention, and the buzzing
crowd. He then chose a rising ground, that he might
observe the whole company as they came successively in
review before him, and mark with discrimination their
countenances, as they passed by."

P. 197.

Decernunt quodcunque volunt de Corpore nostro.

Juv. Sat. 13.

" They do what they will with our whole body."

P. 197.

Per Solis radios, Tarpeiaque fulmina jurant,
Quicquid habent telorum armamentaria Cœli."

Juv. Sat. 13.

" They swear by the light of the sun, and by the
thunderbolts of their TARPEIAN JOVE; by every instrument
of warfare in the celestial regions."

P. 198.

Ejectos littore, egenos
Excepi, et regni DEMENS in parte locavi.

Virg. Æn. 4.

" I received them outcasts from their own coasts, in exile,
and in poverty; and in an hour of madness, folly,
or inconsiderateness, I *almost incorporated* them in the
kingdom."

P. 203.

Hæc limina VICTOR
Alcides subiit,

Virg. Æn. 8.

" Through this threshold the Conqueror Alcides himself
passed.

P. 63.

·P. 205.

Te quoque dignum

Finge Deo! *Virg. Æn.* 8.

" Render yourself worthy of the Deity."

P. 205.

Tanquam portum at sabbathum humanarum contem-
plationum." *Bacon de Augm. Scient. ap. init.* l. 3.

" The haven, as it were, and the sabbath of all the
contemplations of man."

P. 209.

Vineta cædit sua. *Hor. Ep. ad Aug.*

" He prunes his own vineyards."

P. 215.

Naturäi

Perturbatur ibi totum sic corpus, et omnes
Commutantur ibi POSITURÆ PRINCIPIORUM.

Lucret. l. 4. v. 670.

" The whole body and frame of Nature is thus thrown into
confusion and disturbance, and the position of every principle
is made to change its place."

P. 217.

Γενομενος εν αγωνια εκτενεστερον προσηυχετο.

" Being in an agony he prayed more earnestly."

P. 217,

Ηδη γαρ μοι σκοτος αγνοιας απαντα, και απατη μελαινα,
και απειρος πλανη, και ατελης φαντασια, και ακαταληπτος
αγνοια. Ταυτα τοινυν διεξηλθον, βυλομενος δειξαι την εν τοις
δογμασιν υσαν αυτων εναντιοτητα, και ως εις απειρον αυτοις
και αοριστον προεισιν ἡ ζητησις των πραγματων, και το τελος
αυτων

αυτων ατεκμαρτον και αχρηστον, εργω μηδενι προδηλω και
λογω σαφει βεβαιωμενον. ·

‑Hermiæ Διασυρμος (sive Irrisio) των εξω Φιλοσοφων.—
Sub fin. Ed. Paris: Justin. Martyris Op. 1636.

" In my opinion, the whole of their systems present to us
nothing but the gross darkness of ignorance, and the blackness
of deceit, with errors wide and infinite; mere fancies, and
crude conceptions, and ignorance which sets all comprehension
at defiance. I have therefore submitted to examine them,
from a desire to point out the contradictions which prevail in
their writings, and to shew that they lead into discussions
incapable either of limit or of definition; and further to
convince you, that the end and result of them all is
unsatisfactory and productive of no advantage whatsoever;
without any support from matter of fact, or from the
evidence of reason.

P. 218.

Notis et Commentariis perpetuis Doctoris Guillotini."
" With the unceasing perpetual notes and commentaries
of Doctor *Guillotine*."

P. 218.

'Ο πανυ.
" A man of supreme eminence."

P. 218.

Melliti verborum globuli.
Petron. Arbit. Satyricon. c. 1.
" The honeyed globules of language."

P. 218.

Ut magis sit hasce contortiones orationis, quam signorum
ortus obitusque, perdiscere.

" It

" It is far easier to comprehend the doctrine of the rising
and setting of the stars, than to understand these strange
contortions and excentricities of speech."

P. 219.

Λυχνυς εχοντες και μινυριζοντες μελη
Αρχαιομελησιδωνοφρυνιχηρατα.   *Aristoph. Vespæ,* ✝. 219.

" Holding lights in their hands, and trilling out melodies,
and verses " between ancient and modern." (a)

P. 219.

Salva res est ; philosophatur quoque jam ;
Quod erat ei nomen ? Thesaurochrysonicochrysides.
                                      Plaut. Captiv. A. 2. S. 2.

" The matter is all safe ; he actually is setting up for a
philosopher ; pray what was his name ? (b) a strange one."

. P. 219.

Convenisse Neptuno majestatique ejus, ut longiore tempore
satus ex eo grandesceret.
                                      Aul. Gell. lib. 3. c. 16.

" It was suitable to the majesty of Neptune, that the
offspring of his godship should acquire a more ample form,
the time of his gestation being protracted."

P. 220.

(a) It is impossible to render the original Greek word in
English, which is compounded ludicrously. An explanation
could serve no purpose whatsoever.

(b) The name in the original Latin cannot be translated
with any effect, for the reason given in the last remark on
Aristophanes.

·E

P. 220.

Επει ουκ αποφωλιοι ευναι

Αθανατων.   *Hom.*

" For the embraces of the immortals are not ineffectual."

P. 220.

Εν ταις αγαθαις χωραις, προς το μη φυλλομανειν, επινεμουσι και επιχειρουσι τον σιτον.

Theophrast. Hist. Plaut. l. 8. c. 7.

" In rich and good soils they thin and lop the corn while it is growing, to prevent its being rank and luxuriant."

P. 221.

In nullum reipublicæ usum *ambitiofâ loquelâ* inclaruit.

Tacit. Ann. l. 4. s. 20.

" He became celebrated for an affected style, and ambitious *wordiness*, without any advantage whatsoever to the state."

P. 227.

Sint hic etiam sua præmia laudi.   *Virg. Æn.* 1.

" Let merit ever here obtain its reward."

P. 229.

Musarum spondet chorus, et Romanus Apollo.

Sulpiciæ Sat. v. ult.

" The whole Pierian choir and the Roman Phœbus himself answer for him."

P. 231.

Huic Musæ indulgent omnes, hunc poscit Apollo.

Vida A. P. l. 1. v. 327.

" To him every Muse is propitious, and Apollo claims him for his own."

P. 232.

P. 232.

Ὀθι τ' Ηὺς ηριγενεη; —

Οικια, και χοροι εισι, και αντολαι Ηελιοιο.

Hom. Odys. l. 12. v. 3.

" Those regions where Aurora has fixed her palace, and
holds her festal solemnities, and whence the Sun himself
" begins his state."*

END OF THE THIRD DIALOGUE.

PASSAGES IN THE PREFACE AND NOTES

TO THE

FOURTH DIALOGUE

OF THE

PURSUITS OF LITERATURE.

Ουδ' αλαοσκοπιην ειχε κρειων Ενοσιχθων·

Και γαρ ὁ θαυμαζων ἡστο Πτολεμοντε Μαχηντε,

Υψε επ' ακροτατης κορυφης Σαμε ὑληεσσης

Θρηϊκιης· ενθεν γαρ εφαινετο πασα μεν Ιδη,

Φαινετο δε Πριαμοιο πολις, και νηες Αχαιων·

Αυτικα δ' εξ ορεος κατεβησατο παιπαλοεντος.

ΤΡΙΣ μεν ορεξατ' ιων, ΤΟ ΔΕ ΤΕΤΡΑΤΟΝ ἱκετο τεκμωρ,

Αιγας, ενθα δε ὁι κλυτα δωματα ΒΕΝΘΕΣΙ ΛΙΜΝΗΣ

Χρυσεα, μαρμαιροντα τετευχαται, αφθιτα αιει.

Hom. Il. 13. v. 10.

' Neptune, who shakes the earth, was not idle in his
observation, as he was seated on the loftiest summit of the
wood-crowned Samos, lost in wonder at the contest and the
war. From that eminence appeared all Ida, with the city of
Priam, and the ships of the Grecians. He then descended
from the craggy mountain. *Three* steps he advanced in his

E 2   march

* An expression from the Allegro of Milton.

march, and at *the fourth* he reached his destination at Ægæ; where his imperial palace, emblazed with gold and gems, was erected in the depths of the abyss, unperishable, enduring for ever."

P. 237.

L'ombra sua torna, ch'era dipartita!   *Dante Inf.* c. 4.

" His shade, which had left us for a season, is now on his return."*

P. 240.

O proceres, censore opus est, an Haruspice nobis ?

" O ye chiefs of the land, does this require a censor to punish it, or an augur to explain the prodigy ? Do ye call for the arm of the law, or the lustration of religion ?

P. 242.

Ημεις, οις ιερα και ταφοι προγονων υπαρχυσιν εν τη Πατριδι, και διατριβαι, και συνηθειαι μεθ' υμων ελευθεροι, και γαμοι κατα τυς νομυς, και κηδεσται, και τεκνα, αξιοι της υμετερας πιστεως.   *Æschines de Falsa Legatione*, sect. 11.

" In this our country we have our religious rites, and the sepulchres of our forefathers. Here we enjoy the freedom of intercourse, society, and conversation; the blessings of lawful marriage, relations, and children, and the charities of life. All these we enjoy in common with you ; and from these obligations we hold ourselves worthy of your trust and confidence."

P. 243.

At vos Trojugenæ vobis ignoscitis, et quæ
Turpia cerdoni Volesos Brutosque decebunt.

Juv. Sat. 8. v. 181.

" But ye, who boast yourself of *Trojan* ancestry, find

excuses

---

* Dante is speaking of the shade of Virgil in the Inferno.

excuses for one another; and such actions, as would disgrace the meanest mechanick, are esteemed honourable in men of rank and dignity."

P. 243.

Το γαρ γερας εστι θανοντων.   *Hom:*

" For this is the tribute which we pay to the departed."

P. 246.

Tanquam in pistrinum aliquod detrudi et compingi videtur.

" He seems to be confined, and shut up as in a kind of workhouse."

P. 248.

Quales et quantos viros!

" Men indeed of eminence and of high attainments."

P. 248.

Idoneus quidem meâ sententiâ, præsertim quum et Ipse eum audiverit, et scribat de mortuo; ex quo. nulla suspicio est amicitiæ causa eum esse mentitum.

         Cicero de Clar. Orat. sect. 15.

" In my opinion a competent judge, and for this reason; he was accustomed to hear him speak often, and he did not publish his sentiments on his works till the orator himself was no more. From this circumstance there is no reason to think that he has gone beyond the truth from the partiality of friendship."

P. 249.

Si trapassammo per sozza mistura

Dell' ombre, e della pioggia, a passi lenti;

Toccando un poco la vita futura.

" Thus with slow and wandering steps we passed through *the palpable obscure,* through the solid temperament of

darkness

darkness, mixed with drizzling rain. Our talk was of the
life to come."

P. 251.—(8th Edit.)

Episcopatus non est artificium transigendæ vitæ.

Augustini Epist. 58.

"The office of a Bishop was not devised merely to pass
away life, (but it is an office of duty, labour, and attention.")

P. 251. (8th Edit.)

Ὅτι δη τονδε μετιοντες τον τροπον, φρονηματι την ψυχην 'εις
ουρανον μετεγηνεγμενοι, δια τινες Θεοι, τον των παντων εφορωσι
βιον· ὑπερ τε παντος γενεσ ἱερωμενοι τω επι παντων Θεω,
ψυχης· διαθεσει κεκαθαρμενης, ορθοις δογμασιν αληθες ευσεβειας,
και τοις κατ' αρετην εργοις τε και λογοις, 'οις το Θειον
εξιλεωμενοι, την ὑπερ σφων 'αυτων, και των σφισιν ὁμογενων
αποτελωσιν ἱερουργιαν. *Euseb. Demonstrat: Evang.* l. 1. s. 8.

" They, who have thus fashioned their manners, godlike
Beings, carried up by devout aspirations to the heavenly
regions, superintend the lives of all around them. They are
set apart and sanctified unto GOD HIMSELF, who is above
all, for the sake of the whole human race; by a spirit
and disposition purified from every stain, by the unerring
doctrines of true and unfeigned piety, and by words and works
according unto righteousness. By these and such actions they
offer up a propitiation to the Deity for themselves, and for
those of the same common nature, and compleat their
hallowed ministry in full consummation."

P. 251. (8th Edit.)

Saltem daretur in sacris literis tranquillè consenescere.

Erasmi Epist.

"May the evening of my life pass in tranquillity, and in
the study of the sacred Scriptures."

P. 250.

P. 250.

Quibus occupatus et obsessus animus quantulum loci bonis artibus relinquit. *Dial. de Oratoribus;* Sec. 29.

" The mind busied and beset with (political) considerations, finds but few intervals for the polite literature."

P. 251.

Corpora lentè augescunt, cito extinguuntur.

Tacit. Vit. Agric. sub init.

" Bodies are slow of growth, but their dissolution is rapid."

P. 251.

Que ma vue à Colbert inspiroit l'allegresse.

Boileau Ep. 10.

" My presence gave chearfulness to the minister." (Colbert)*.

P. 251.

Την μεν αιτιαν επιφερόντες τοις τον Δημον καταλυθσιν. Απεθανον τινες ιδιας εχθρας ενεκα, και αλλοι χρηματων σφισιν οφειλομενων ὑπο των λαβοντων. *Thucyd.* l. 3. s. 81.

" They endeavoured to impute to them the charge of being enemies to the people. Some were destroyed from private malice, and others because they were the creditors of their murderers."

P. 252.

Trunco, non frondibus, efficit umbram. *Lucan.* l. 1.

" The aged tree casts a shadow with its trunk, not with its foliage."

E 4   P. 252.

---

* Boileau is speaking of the great Colbert, and those who honoured him with *their* friendship.—Such times are now passed for ever in France, and perhaps in England.

P. 252.

Ἐυ μεταφορειν εστιν ευ θεωρειν.   *Aristot.*

" To manage metaphors with discretion, is the mark of a just and comprehensive mind."

P. 252.

Των Μεταφορων ευδοκιμησι μαλιστα ἁι κατα αναλογιαν.

Aristot. Rhetor. l. 3. c. 10. sect. 3.

" The metaphors which are drawn from analogy, generally meet with the greatest approbation.

P. 253.

Ὁι εν ταις πολεσιν πρωτταντες μετ' ονοματος ἑκαστοι ευπρεπες, πληθες Ἰσονομιας πολιτικης, και Αριστοκρατιας σωφρονος προτιμησει, τα μεν κοινα λογω θεραπευοντες αθλα εποιϟντο, παντι δε τροπω αγωνιζομενοι αλληλων περιγιγνεσθαι. Και η μετα ψηφϟ αδικϟ καταγνωσεως, η χειρι κτωμενοι το κρατειν, ετοιμοι ησαν την αυτικα φιλονεικιαν εμπιμπλαναι.

Thucyd. l. 3. sect. 82.

" The chiefs of the factions had each of them a specious name and pretext. Some held forth a political equality among the citizens, and some, a plan of a more temperate aristocracy. Their speeches had a reference to the common prize of contest, power and sovereignty ; and every art was used by the antagonists to defeat each other. Having obtained their ends either by unjust sentences, or by acts of violence, they were prepared to fill up the measure of their crimes and iniquity."

P. 254.

Απροσιχτων ερωτων οξυτεραι μανια..   *Pind. Nem. Od.* 11.

" The rage after desires hard to be attained, is increased by the difficulty."

P. 254.

Tristis FELICIBUS UMBRIS
Vultus erat ; vidi Decios, natumque patremque
,Lustrales bellis animas, flentemque Camillum.
Abruptis Catilina minax fractisque catenis
Exultat, Mariique truces nudique Cethegi :
Vidi ego lætantes, popularia nomina, Drusos,
Legibus immodicos, ausosque ingentia Gracchos.
Æternis chalybum nodis, et carcere Ditis
Constrictæ plausere manus, CAMPOSQUE PIORUM
POSCIT TURBA NOCENS !

Lucan. Pharsal. l. 6. v. 784.

The shades of the happy spirits in Elysium had a gloom
on their appearance. I saw the Decii, the parent and the
son, souls which might well expiate the guilt of war ; and
Camillus himself in tears. Catiline stands in frantick
exultation with his chains burst and broken asunder, and by
him the Marii, terrible of aspect, and the bare, naked Cethegi.
I saw the Drusi, names of popular celebrity, Tribunes,
extravagant in their proposals of laws and decrees ; and
the Gracchi, gigantick in their enterprises. Bound in the
dungeons of Pluto, they rattled their adamantine iron
chains in sign of applause ; and the guilty inhabitants of
Tartarus seemed to claim for themselves the mansions of
the just and good."

———

P. 257.

" Fare ogni cosa *di nuovo* in quello stato ; nelle Città
fare *nuovi governi con nuovi nomi*, con nuova autorità, con
nuovi nomini, fare i poveri ricchi, disfare delle vecchie
città, cambiare gli abitatori da un luogo ad un altro, e in
somma, non lasciare cosa niuna intatta, e che non vi sia
nè grado, nè ordine, nè stato, nè richezza, che chi la tiene
non riconosca da te. *Machiavel. Discorsi,* lib. 1. cap. 6.

" To

" To create all things anew in that state; to make new offices of government with new names, with new authority, with new men; to make the poor rich; to dismantle ancient cities; to transport the inhabitants of one place to another; and briefly, to leave no one thing or condition of life untouched, and not to suffer the existence of any one species of rank, or order, or state, or possession, without an acknowledgement of YOUR having granted it, and that the occupier holds it OF YOU."

P. 258.

Nisi Bellum Gallicum exoriatur.

Lex de Vacatione.

" Except in the case of a *Gallick* war."————The law concerning exemptions from military service.

P. 258.

Ου μην αλλα μεγαν ἡ τε χωρα παρειχε φοβον, δια την γειτνιασιν, ὁμορω και προσοικω πολεμω συνοισομενοις και το παλαιον αξιωμα των Γαλατων, ἡς μαλιστα Ρωμαιοι δεισαι δοκꙋσιν. ατε δη και την Πολιν ὑπ' αυτων αποβαλοντες, εξ εκεινꙋ δε θεμενοι Νομον, ατελεις ειναι της στρατειας της Ιερεας, πλην ει μη Γαλατικος επελθοι Πολεμος. Εδηλꙋ δε και τον φοβον αυτων ἡ τε Παρασκευη. Μυριαδες γαρ εν ὁπλοις ἁμα τοσαυται Ρωμαιων ꙋτε προτερον, ꙋτε ὑστερον γενεσθαι λεγονται.

Plutarch. Vit. Marcelli, p. 244. vol. 2. *Ed. Bryan.*

" Moreover the country itself, from its vicinity, and the ancient renown and valour of *the Gauls*, was an object of considerable terror to the Romans who were about to undertake a war so near home, and upon their own borders. In particular, as the Gauls had once taken their city. On this account they made a special law, that the priests should enjoy an exemption from all military service, except in the case

case of a Gallick war. The very preparation itself proved the 'nature of their apprehension. For it is not recorded, that the Romans ever had so many *myriads* in arms at one time, either before or since that period."

P. 259.

Ut oportet, Bello Gallico, ut majorum jura moresque præscribunt, Nemo est, Civis Romanus, qui sibi ullâ excusatione utendum putet."

Cicero pro Fonteio, Sect. 16. sub fin.

" There is not a man, worthy of being a Roman citizen, who would think of availing himself of any indulgence, or exemption from service, in the time of a *Gallick* war, according to the laws and customs of our ancestors."

N. B. The object of that oration of Cicero was to inculcate this doctrine; " Gallis fidem non habendam, hominibus " levibus, perfidis, et in ipsos Deos immortales impiis :" *i. e.* " That no trust or confidence whatsoever should be " placed in the Gauls, a nation fickle, perfidious, without " faith, and impious against the Gods themselves."

P. 259.

Vocem adyti dignam templo.

" A voice from the interior shrine, worthy of the temple."

P. 259.

Ουτε τεω σπενδεσκε Θεων, ει μη Διι Πατρι.

Hom. Il. 6. c. 227.

" He poured no libation from this cup, to any of the gods, save to Jove alone."

P. 263.

In sua templa furit, nullâque exire vetante
Materiâ, magnamque cadens, magnamque revertens

Dat

Dat stragem late, sparsosque recolligit ignes.

Lucan. l. 1.

" The thunderbolt rages against it's *own* temples, and without any matter to obstruct it, both in it's fall and in it's return, spreads devastation far and wide, and collects again it's scattered fires."

P. 263.

Talibus ex adyto dictis Cumæa Sybyllo
Horrendas canit ambages, antroque remugit
Obscuris vera involvens.   *Virg. Æn. 6.*

" In words like these the Sibyll utters her tremendous oracles of dubious import, and sounds them forth from the cavern, blending truth with obscurity.

P. 264.

Europæ hæc Vindex Genio decora alta Britanno.

Inscription at Blenheim Palace.

" The avenger of Europe dedicates these lofty trophies to the Genius of Britain !

P. 265.

Προς το αιδιον εϐλεπεν.   *Plato.*

" He looked to that which is eternal and incorruptible."

P. 266.

Conditur omne

Stellarum vulgus, fugiunt sine nomine signa.

Manil. Astron. l. 1. 477.

" All the company of the stars hide themselves, and the constellations pass away without a name."

P. 267.

Τη μεν εμπειριᾳ πολεμικος, τη φυσει φιλοπολεμος· τω δε αλλω τροπω σωφρων, φιλανθρωπος, Ελληνικης παιδειας
και

και λογων, αχρι τε τιμᾶν και θαυμαζειν τες κατορθεντας, εραστης.

Plutarch. Vit. Marcelli. p. 242. vol. 2. *Edit. Bryan.*

" He was an experienced warrior, and his nature inclined him to military pursuits. But as to the other habits of his life, he was temperate and collected, of a philanthropick disposition, and so attached to Greek literature and Greek writing, as to make the professors of them the objects of his praise, and even of his veneration."

P. 270.

Primâ vel voce Canentis
Concedunt, carmenque timent audire secundum:

Lucan. l. 6. v. 527.

" They yield to the first notes of the enchanter, and tremble to wait for the second invocation."

P. 272.

Exequiale sacrum, carmenque *minoribus umbris*
Utile.   *Stat. Theb.* l. 6. v. 123.

" That funereal dirge, that strain which appeases *the minor shades.*"

P. 275.

Ουκ ἡσυχος
Δαφνηφαγων φοιβαζεν εκ λαιμων οπα.

Lycophron. Cassand. v. 8.

" He could not rest; but nourished, as he was, with the laurel of Apollo, poured forth his oracular strains."

P. 277.

Hic Cimbros et summa pericula rerum
Excipit, et solus trepidantem protegit urbem.

Juv. Sat. 8. v. 249.

" He sustained the attacks of the Cimbri, and met the

I   last

last extremities of the state, and by his single prowess
supported the city in all its terrors."

P. 278.

Ταυτά παντα λογισμω λαβων, ήσυχιαν εχων και τα αυτη
πραττων, διον εν χειμωνι κονιορτη και ζαλης ύπο πνευματος φερομενη
ύπο τειχιον ύποστας, όρων της αλλης καταπιμπλαμενη; ανομιας,
αγαπα ει πη αυτος καθαρος αδικιας τε και αγοσιων εργων, τον τε
ενθαδε βιον βιωσεται, και την απαλλαγην αυτη μετα καλης
ελπιδος ίλεως τε και ευμενης απαλλαξεται.

Plato de Republica, l. 6. p. 496. Op. vol. 2. Edit.
Serrani.

Such a man, taking all these things into his consideration,
living in quietness and tranquillity, (like one who takes
shelter when the storm is raging,) occupied wholly in his
own concerns, and seeing the world around him filled with
all manner of iniquity, is contented to pass the time
of his sojourning here in peace; pure himself from all
unrighteousness and the works of unholiness, and with calm
confidence expects his dismission and departure in all the
fulness of hope."

P. 282.

Questi erano gli scherzi d'una penna poetica, non gli
sentimenti d'un animo catolico.

" These were only the sportive fancies of a poetical pen,
not the serious opinions of a *catholick* mind.

P. 283.

Les Romains eurent aussi leurs Allegories sur le double
soleil successif de l'anneé; ils l'appliquerent à leur Remus
& Romulus. Les noms sont allegoriques, et tous relatifs à
l'année.

*Mr. Gebelin's Primitive World analyzed and compared
with the modern.* Vol. 4. p. 264.

" The

" The Romans had also their allegories upon the *double*
sun in its succession at different times of the year. They
applied them to their *Remus* and *Romulus*. The names are
allegorical, and all of them *relate to the year*.

P 284.

Ils en firent la fête des *Lemures* pour des *Remures*, &c.
Ib. p. 263.

" They changed the festival of the *Lemures* into *Remures*."

P. 284.

Nous avons *vu* dans le chapitre precedent, que *Romulus*
étoit LE SOLEIL ; que tout le *prouvoit*. *Ib*.

We have *seen* in the preceding chapter that *Romulus* was
THE SUN ; that every argument *proved* it !"

The proof is this. " Le nom de sa mere, celui de son
pere, son frere, la mort de son frere, (REMUS) son propre
nom, &c. &c. *Q. E. D. Ib*.

" The name of his mother, that of his father, his brother,
the death of his brother (Remus), his own name, &c."

Q. E. D.

P. 284.

Ce qu'exprimoient à cet ègard les Grecs par l'Apothéose
d'Hercule, les Romains l'exprimerent par l'Apothéose de
Romulus. *Ibid*.

" What the Greeks meant to express by the Apotheosis
of Hercules, the Romans expressed by the Apotheosis of
their Romulus."

P. 284.

Quirinus (nom de Romulus) la traduction litérale de
Melcarthe, ou *Melicerte*, que portoit *Hercule* chez les Tyriens,
EST UNE AUTRE PREUVE, qu'on regardoit *Romulus* comme
le Soleil." *Gebelin Ib*. p. 269.

3   " Quirinus

" Quirinus (a name of Romulus), being the literal translation of *Melcarthe*, or *Melicerta*, among the Tyrians, ·IS ANOTHER PROOF, that they considered *Romulus* AS THE SUN."

P. 284.

Deliramenta doctrinæ.

" The wild speculations of learned men."

P. 285.

Si CAPTIVOS *aspiceres*, Molossi, Thessali, Macedones, Bruttius, Apulius ; *si* POMPAS, aurum, purpuræ, signa, tabulæ, Tarentinæque deliciæ.   *Flori Hist.* l. 1. c. 18.

" If you regard *the captive* nations, behold the Molossi, the inhabitants of Thessaly, and Macedonia, the Bruttians and those of Apulia ; if you consider the splendid ornaments · of other countries, look at the gold, the purple, the statues, the pictures, and all the luxuries of Tarentum."

P. 287.

Negatas artifex sequi voces.   *Prolog. ad Pers. Sat.*

" He attempts to express the language which nature has denied him."

P. 287.

Attaquer Chapelain ? ah, c'est un si bon homme ;
Il est vrai, s'il m'eut crû, qu'il n'eut point fait des vers;
Il se tue à rimer.   Que n'écrit il en prose ?
Voila ce qui l'on dit ; *et que dis je antre chose?*

Boileau Sat. 9.

" What ? attack poor Chapelain ? ah, no ; he is such a very good sort of man. To be sure, if he had taken my · advice, he would never have made verses. He absolutely exhausts and *kills himself with rhyming.* Why does he not write

write prose?—This is what the world in general says of him; and do I sáy any thing else?

P. 283.

Ego si risi, lividus et mordax videar ?   *Hor.*

" If I indulge myself in a smile at such trifling follies, must I of necessity be an envious and malicious tempered man? Surely not."

P. 288.

Munus Apolline dignum.   *Hor. Ep. ad August.*

" An offering worthy of Apollo. *

P. 289.

Criticus, assuetus urere, secare, inclementer omnis generis libros tractare, apices, syllabas, voces, dictiones confodere et stylo exigere, non continebit iste ab integro (REIPUBLICÆ NOSTRÆ) statu crudeles ungues ? &c. &c.

Orat. P. Burmanni Lugd. Bat. 1720.

" A mere critick, whose whole business is to torture, hack, and abuse without mercy, every book of every description ; to stab, or reduce with his pen, all commas, syllables, points, words, and sentences; will not such a man withhold his unrelenting talons, from attempting to destroy the good order and government of such a kingdom as this ?"

P. 290.

Πτιλον το μεγα Κομπολακυθυ πεσεν:

Aristoph. Acharn. sub fin.

" The principal feather of the vain-glorious bird is plucked and fallen."

P. 294.

* Horace is speaking of the Palatine library, erected at Rome by Augustus.

F

P. 294.

Πασαν Ποιητικης ἑξιν διαλαμπυσαν.

Procli Comment. in Πολιτειαν *Platonis*, p. 403. Edit. fol.

Basil. 1534.

" The very form, substance, and image of Poetry in all its brightness."

P. 294.

Ὁταν ενθυσιαζων και ταις Μυσαις κατοχος; ων, κατα την πρωτην ενεργει και ενθεον Ποιητικην.   *Procl. ut sup.*

" When feeling the power of enthusiasm, and fully subdued by the influence of the Muses, he calls forth into action all the primal, original, and divine energies of poetry."

P. 295.

Την των Ποιητων μανιαν κινυμενην τε και κινυσαν, και πληρυμενην ανωθεν, και εις αλλα διαπορθμευυσαν την εκειθεν ελλαμψιν.

Procli Comment. ut sup. in τρεις Ιδεας της Ποιητικης? pag. 401.

" The enthusiasm of poets, when it is roused and set in motion, and communicates the impulse to others ; when it receives it's fulness from above, and diffuses to all around the light imparted from heaven."

P. 295.

Κληιζω Μυσας ξυνην οπα γηρυσασθαι,
Παμφωνοις ιαχαισι παναρμονιαισι τ' ερωαις,
Ὁιον επ' Αιακιδη στησαι χορον εκληιξαν
Αθανατων μανιαισιν, ὁμηρειαισι τ' αοιδαις.
Αλλα γε Μυσαων ἱερος χορος απυσωμεν,
Εις-ἑν αποπνειοντες αοιδης τερματα πασης.

Υμμι

3

Ὑμμι και εν μεσσαισιν Εγω Φοιβος ζαθυχαιτης.

Porphyr. in Vita Plotini; Oper. Plotin: Ed. Ficini.

Basil. MDXXC.

" I call upon the Muses to send forth their united voices, full and symphonious, in all the varied power of harmony; such as they are recorded to have celebrated in choral bands at the tomb of Achiiles, in Homerick strains and immortal inspiration. Let us therefore, the sacred Pierian choir, join and breathe in one all the fulness of the song; and I, Apollo with the clustering locks, seated in the midst of you, will myself preside."

P. 296.

Οργᾳ ἡ φυσις τυ υιυ συ προς τα μαθηματα.

Marcellini Vit. Thucyd. p. 8. Edit. *Hudsoni Oxon.*

" The disposition of your son has a strong impulse to learning and the sciences."

P. 296.

Legere si desideras,
Vaces oportet, Eutyche, a negotiis,
Ut liber animus sentiat vim carminis.
Ego, quem Pierio mater enixa est jugo,
In quo tonanti sancta Mnemosyne Jovi,
Fœcunda novies, artium peperit chorum; .
Quamvis in ipsâ pene natus sim scholâ,
Curamque habendi penitus corde eraserim,
Et laude invitâ in hanc vitam incubuerim,
Fastidiosè tamen in cætum recipior.
Rem me professum dicet aliquis jam gravem;
Sed literatæ cum sim propior Græciæ,
Cur somno inerti deseram Patriæ decus?

Phædrus. l. 3. *Prolog.*

" If you are desirous to read and study works like these,

F 2

you

you must be free from the cares and anxieties of business, that your mind may be at full liberty to comprehend the force of poetry. As to myself, though I was produced on the very mountain of the Muses, where the consecrated Mnemosyne, with her nine offspring, bore to Jove the whole choir of the arts: though I was born in their very school; though I have obliterated from my soul the very traces of the love of money and possessions; though I have adopted and exercised the profession, against even the appearance of success; yet it is with reluctance that I am received and enrolled in the assembly. I may be told, I have undertaken a work of weight and dignity: but, allied as I am to all the literature of Greece, why, from indolence and sloth, should I abandon the honour of my native country?"

P. 296.

Neque enim Aonium nemus advena lustro,
Nec mea nunc primis albescunt tempora vittis.

Stat. Achill. l. 1. v. 10.

" I wander not through the Aonian grove with the steps of a stranger; nor are my brows now, for the first time, encircled with the fillets of the Muses."

P. 297.

Helas! je n'ai point vû ce séjour enchanté,
Ces beaux lieux ou Virgile a tant de fois chanté;
Mais j'en jure et Virgile et ses accords sublimes,
J'irai; de l'Apennin je franchirai les cimes,
J'irai, plein de son nom, plein de ses vers sacrés,
Les lire aux mèmes lieux qui les ont inspirés.

De Lisle. Les Jardins. L. 1.

" Alas! I have never visited that abode of enchantment, those scenes of beauty and delight, where Virgil hath so often sung. But I swear by the poet and his sublime strains, I

I   will

will visit them; I will pass the summits of the Apennines; I will repair thither, full of his great, name, full of his consecrated verses, and repeat them among the very scenes themselves which inspired the bard."

P. 302.

Et meæ, si quid loquar audiendum,
Vocis accedet bona pars.   *Hor. Od.*

" And, if any opinion of mine is worthy of attention, I will give it freely in his favour."

P. 302.

Sic gemmas vaginæ in fronte solebat
Ponere zelotypo Juvenis prælatus Hiarbæ.

Juv. Sat.

" In this manner did Æneas place the gems of honour in the very front of the scabbard."

P. 303.

Στεντορι εισαμενος μεγαλητορι χαλκεοφωνω,
'Ος τοσον αυδησασκ' ὁσον αλλοι πεντηκοντα.   *Hom.*

" Like Stentor, with a heart of courage, and a voice of brass, whose speech was equal to that of *fifty* men united."

P. 303.

Vicinas alii Veneres, Charitumque choreas
Carmine concelebrent; nos Veri dogma severum,
Triste sonant pulsæ nostrâ testudine chordæ.

" Let others celebrate in song the charms of many a neighbouring Venus, and the dances where the Graces preside; it is our province to record the austere doctrines and decrees of truth. The chords of our lyre sound in deeper and more solemn tones."

F 3   P. 304.

P. 304.

Ὅιον ὁ τω ᾽πολλωνος εσεισατο δαφνιδος ὅρπηξ!
Ὅια δ᾽ ὑλον το μελαθρον! ἑκας, ἑκας ὁστις αλιτρος·
Και δη πυ τα θυρετρα καλω ποδι Φοιϐος αρασσει.

" How is the branch of Apollo's own laurel shaken!
how is the whole temple convulsed! Hence, avaunt, ye
profane. Apollo himself approaches; and the sound of his
steps in the threshold is propitious!"

P. 304.
De lodice parandâ
Attonitus Doctor.   *Juv. Sat.* 7.
" A *house-wife* doctor, or schoolmaster."

P. 306.
O nondum cognita divùm
Munera! virtutis custos et amica pudori,
Luxuriæ frænum, vitæ tutela!   *Prudentius.*

" O ye gifts of the gods not yet fully understood! All-
hail, Frugality, thou guardian and friend of virtue and
modesty; thou curb of luxury, and tutelar genius of life
itself!"

P. 308.

In quâ Ego nactus, ut mihi videbar, locum resecandæ
libidinis et coercendæ Juventutis, vehemens fui, atque
omnes profudi vires animi atque ingenii mei, non odio
adductus alicujus, sed spe reipublicæ corrigendæ et sanandæ
civitatis. Afflicta est Respublica!
         Cic. Epist. ad Attic. l. 1. *Ep:* 18.

" Being, as I thought, in possession of the vantage ground,
with the opportunity of cutting up by the roots, or of curbing
the headstrong impetuosity of youth, I was earnest in my
endeavour, and exerted every faculty of my courage and
understanding,

understanding, not from dislike or hatred to any one, but from an honest hope of correcting the errors, and healing the disorders of the state. The Republick is sorely smitten and afflicted!

P. 308.

Salve, magna parens doctrinæ, *Etonia* tellus,
Magna Virûm!

" Hail to thee, Eton, Thou great nursing mother of learning and of men!"

P. 308.

Mussat tacito Doctrina timore.

" Learning is struck dumb with apprehension."

P. 309.

Academia degli Arcadi, et degli Buffi caricati.

" An academy of Arcadians and Italian *Buffos* or comedians."

P. 309.

Uni quippe vacat, studiisque odiisque carenti
Newtoni lugere genus.

" I have leisure, without prejudice or partiality, to drop a tear on the degenerate race and kindred of NEWTON."

P. 310.

Stupet äere primo :

Quæ loca? qui fluctus? ubi Pelion? omnia versa,
Aut ignota videt; dubitatque agnoscere matrem,

Statius. Achill. l. 1.

" Achilles stands astonished as he first breathes that air. He aſks, what places are these? what waves he hears? where is his beloved Pelion? he finds all things either

overthrown

overthrown and altered, or strange to his view; and he even hesitates to acknowledge his own mother."

P. 311.

Γενος εχλεκτον, λαος εις περιποιησιν, Cασιλειον Ιερατευμα.

" A chosen generation, a peculiar people, a royal priesthood."

P. 312.

Jam Thebæ juxta, et tenebrosa vorago.

Stat. Theb. l. 6.

" The scenes of Thebes are not far off; and the gulph of darkness is yawning before us."

P. 316.

Quis gremio Enceladi doctique Palæmonis affert,
Quantum grammaticus meruit labor ?

Juv. Sat. 7.

" Who confers the tribute of reward on Enceladus and the learned *Palæmon*, in proportion to the labours and fatigue of publick instruction?"

P. 316.

Status dicitur *a stando*, quià quando quis habet *unam bonam Præbendam*, tum dicimus, Is bene stat."

Epistolæ Obscurorum Virorum.

" The word " *state*" (or condition of life) is derived from " to stand," because when a man is in possession of *one good prebend, we say, he stands well in the world.*" *

P. 317.

Recorderis Marescottum nostrum *tria* se sacræ arti nostræ
(Medica

The Latin words are ludicrous.

(Medicæ scilicet) debere professum, quibus caruisset, si propositum a parentibus sacerdotium suscepisset; scilicet, sanitatem athleticam ætatis anno 82mo, *centum aureorum millia*, atque intimam innumerorum illustrium amicitiam.

Sammarthani Elogia, p. 83. et 84.

" You remember our friend Marescottus used to say, that he was indebted to our sacred art (of medicine) for three things, which he never should have enjoyed, if he had taken upon him the order of priesthood, as his parents proposed to him. The advantages were these: a strong athletick habit of body to his eighty-second year; a *hundred thoufand pounds*; and an intimate acquaintance and friendship with men of rank and eminence."

P. 317.

Siccat inæquales calices Conviva Sacerdos.

" The Priest is invited, but *not* to an *equality* in the glasses.

P. 317.

Ipse capillato diffusum consule potat." *Juv.*

" My Lord himself drinks of the most costly vintage matured by years and good keeping."

P. 318.

È ben cosa certa, che PAOLO, come quello che era d'animo grande e de vasti pensieri, teneva per sicuro di poter rimediare à tutti i disordini *per la sola sua autorità pontificale*, nè riputava di aver bisogno in ciò di Principe alcuno; solito di non parlar mai con gli Ambasciadori, se non intonandogli nelle orecchie, che EGLI ERA SOPRA TUTTI GLI PRINCIPI; che non voleva che alcuno d'essi domesticasse seco, *che poteva mutar regni*, che era Successor di chi ha deposto Rè et Imperadori.

Sarpi Istor. di Concil. Trident. lib. 5.

" It is

" It is a certain fact, that Pope PAUL the Fourth, who
was a man of a great mind, and of immeasurable thoughts
and designs, was convinced, that he could HIMSELF rectify
all the disorders of the state, by his pontifical authority alone.
He never conceived the necessity of having recourse to any
prince in these affairs. It was his custom, never even to
converse with the ambassadors, without thundering in their ears,
that HE himself was above all Princes and Potentates ; that
he would not suffer any one of them to live in habits of
familiarity with HIM ; that HE could change and dispose of
kingdoms ; that HE was the direct successor of HIM, who
had cast down and deposed kings and emperors."

P. 319.

Ubi Papa, ibi Roma! in sæcula sæculorum.

" Wherever the Pope resides, there is Rome ! for ever
and ever, till time shall be no more !

P. 321.

Crimine ab uno
Disce omnes.   *Virg. Æn.*

" From one single offence, learn the nature of them all."

P. 321.

A. D. 1544. Merindoliani et Caprarienses, &c.
existentesque *Reliquiæ Albigensium* sequentem fidei suæ
confessionem obtulerunt Francisco I. Regi Galliæ, quam
a majoribus quasi per manus acceperunt, abhinc anno post
Christi Incarnat. 1200, &c.

Sandii Histor. Ecclesiast. p.,425.

" In the year 1544, the Merindoliani and the Caprarians,
&c. the poor existing remnant of the *Albigenses,* presented
to Francis the First, King of France, the following Confession
of

of Faith, which they had received by uninterrupted tradition from their ancestors, from the year of Christ, 1200, &c."

P. 322.

Σφιγγος μελαινης γηρυν εκμιμουμενος.

Lycopron. Cassandra, v. 7.

" In imitation of the oracular voice of the obscure Sphinx."

P. 324.

O magnâ sacer et superbus umbrâ.

Stat. Sylv. l. 2. Carm. 7.

" Hail to thee, in awful concealment, and conscious pride ; great is the shadow of thy name !"

N. B. Junius's motto to his Letters is, " Stat *nominis umbra*." Lucan. — " *There is only the shadow of the name.*"

P. 326.

State super vias antiquas.

" Stand firm upon the old paths."

P. 327.

Cur non omnia ?

" Why are they not all so ?

P. 328.

" Quis rapiet ad se quod erit commune omnium ?

" Who will be eager to appropriate to himself what is generally expressed ?

P. 328.

Qui se fera connoitre mal à propos ?

" Who will make himself known out of season, and without necessity ?"

P. 328.

P. 328.

Unde Doctoris titulo gloriantur, nisi ut doceant?

Erasmi Epist. ad Cardinalem Lovanium. 1520.

" Why do they glory in the title of *Doctor*, but to instruct and teach others?"

———

P. 330.

Εγραφη απο Ρωμης, ότε εκ δευτερѧ παρεστη Παυλος τѡ Καισαρι Νερωνι.

" The epistle was written from Rome, when Paul stood before Cæsar Nero for the second time."

———

P. 332.

Negotium Ædilibus dedit, ne quem posthac in foro paterentur, nisi positis lacernis, togatum consistere.

Sueton. Octav. cap. 40.

" He gave it in strict charge to the Ædiles, not to suffer any Roman who wore the toga or gown, to remain in the forum, except he laid aside the *Lacerna* * or *Pænula*."

———

P. 332.

Multo stillaret Pænula nimbo.   *Juv. Sat.* 5.

" When the pænula, or cloak, was dripping with the rain."

———

P. 333.

Εν συναρμογᾱ αδιαλυτѡ κατα λογον αριστον.

. *Plat. Timæi Locri. de anima mundi Plat. Op.* Edit.

Serrani, vol. 3 p. 95.

" In

———

* The Lacerna was a garment worn over the toga or gown, in bad weather; but chiefly on a journey. The old Scholiast on the first satire of Persius, v. 68. calls the Lacerna and Pænula both, *Pallia.* The pallium was a long open manteau,

" In an indissoluble connection and agreement according
to the rules of the best reason."

P. 333.

O Vecchi, ch'avete *bifogno* di moglie," &c.

      Opera. Scola de' Maritati.

" O ye old fellows, who feel that you *have need* of a
wife, &c. &c."   *School for Husbands.*

P. 335.

Cum reserata viget genitabilis aura Favonî,
Doctores primum aërii te, Diva, tuumque
Significant initum, &c. &c. &c.   *Lucret.* l. 1.

" When the genial breeze of Favonius begins to blow,
the ætherial race first declare the power of thy impulse,
thou goddess of soft desire," &c. &c.

P. 336.

Longa est injuria, longæ
Ambages.   *Virg. Æn.* 1.

" The account of the injurious transaction is rather long,
and the particulars of it tedious."

P. 336.

O Fortunati, quorum *pia* tecta resurgunt !
Æneas ait, et fastigia suspicit urbis.

                Virg. Æn. 1.

" Hail, fortunate and favoured people, whose *temples* and
palaces are rising again under such auspices !"—Such were
the words of Æneas, as he was surveying the pinnacles of
the city."

338.

P. 338.

" Fortunæ majoris honos, erectus et acer.

Claudian.

" A man who reflects honour on his distinguished situation, and opulent fortune; of an erect and independant spirit."

P. 338.

Carbonem pro Thesauro. *Proverb.*

" A coal instead of a treasure."

P. 339.

Oceano libemus, ait. *Virg.*

" Let us pour forth our libations to the Ocean."

P. 339.

Privatis majora focis. *Juv.*

" Too expensive for a private man's purse."

P. 339.

D'ou ce visage enfin, plus pâle qu'un rentier,
A' l'aspect d'un arrêt qui retranche un quartier ?
Qui vous a pû plonger dans cet humeur chagrine ?
A-t-on par quelqu' 'édit réformé la Cuisine ?

Boileau, Sat. 3.

" Whence is that look, paler than a stock-holder at the sight of a decree, which cuts off a quarter of his income? Who, or what, has plunged you so deeply in chagrine and melancholy ? Is there any edict in force *for the reformation of the kitchen ?*"

P. 340.

Prens moi le bon parti ; laisse là tous les livres ;
Exerce-toi, mon fils, dans ces hautes sciences.
Prens, an lieu d'un Platon, ce Guidon des finances.

Boileau, sat. 8.

" Be

" Be advised, my son; choose what is useful; lay aside all your books and your studies. Be conversant in these sublime sciences; fling away your Plato, and take this *Guide* to the knowledge of finance."

P. 340.

Fame rabidâ tria guttura pandens.   *Virg. Æn.* 6.

" Opening his *triple* throat raging with hunger."

P. 340.

Vitâ cedat, uti conviva satur.   *Hor.*

" May he take leave of life, as a guest satisfied with his entertainment."

P. 342.

Rendono un alto suon, che a quel s'accorda
Con che i vicin cadendo il Nilo assorda.

Ariosto, O. F. l. 16.

" They send forth a sound, loud and deep as the Nile, when he deafens the neighbouring shores with all his cataracts."

343.

Soyez plutôt maçon, si c'est votre talent,
Ouvrier estimé dans un art necessaire,
Qu'écrivain du commun, et pöete vulgaire.

Boileau, A. P. ch. 4.

" Better be a mechanick, a builder, a mason, if such is your talent, a workman of character in some necessary art or trade, than an ordinary writer, or a common maker of verses."

P. 344.

P. 344.

Par classes et par titres,
Dogmatizer en vers, et rimer par chapitres.

Boileau, sat. 8.

" By divisions of subjects, and heads of sections, to dogmatize in verse, and rhyme chapter by chapter."

P. 345.

Ταυτα ὑμων της ἡδυπαθειας; τα αρχετυπα, αὑται της ὑβρεως ἁι θεολογιαι, αὑται των συμπορνευοντων ὑμιν Θεων ἁι διδασκαλιαι.—Πανισκοι, και γυμναι κοραι, και μοριων εντασεις ταις γραφαις απογυμνωμεναι. — ʿΗταιρηκεν ὑμιν τα ωτα, πεπορνευκασιν ὁι οφθαλμοι, ἁι οψεις μεμοιχευκασι. Ω βιασαμενοι τον ανθρωπον, και το ενθεον τυ πλασματος ελεγχει απαρξαντες !—κτλ.

Clement. Alexandrini Λογος προτρεπτικος, seu *Admonitio ad Gentes.* p. 30, &c. Edit. 1616.

" These are the archetypes, the exemplars of your soft and delicate life; these are the shameful and scandalous tenets of your theology; these are the doctrines of your fornicating gods.—As to pictures or images; you have the little figures of Pan, and naked girls, and obscene protrusions in forms gross and palpable. Your very ears are impure; your eyes have committed fornication; your countenance is adulterous. Shame! shame! ye have done violence to the nature of man, and by your corruptions ye have debased all that is divine in his composition."

P. 346.

Αλλο τε μοι ενδειν ηθως περιμνημονευσαι τυδε τυ Ανθρωπυ ὑδ' ὁτιην οιμαι· ἁπαντα γαρ αυτυ τα της ψυχης παθη ὑτος αν αξιοχρεως σημηναι διαρκως ειη. Επει ὁστις αλογησας την ὑπερ των πεπραγμενων αισχυνην, ὑκ απαξιοῖ τοις εντυγχανυσι βδελυρος

Εδελυρος φαινεσθαι, τυτω δη υδεμιά παρανομιας αταρπος
αβατος· αλλα την αναιδειαν αει τω μετωπω προβεβλημενος,
ραστα τε και υδενι πονω ες των πραξεων τας μιαρωτατας
χωρει.

Procopii Histor. Arcan. lib. 9. p. 46. Ed. fol. *Lug-*
duni 1623.

" I think this circumstance fully sufficient to mark
the morals of the man. This alone clearly displays the
nature of the affections and passions of his mind. For
when a man stands in no awe of the disgrace which
attends bad actions, and has no concern for his
character, there is no way of transgression in which that
man may not walk. With a countenance clothed in
shamelessness and audacity, he easily and naturally proceeds
from one bad action to the most profligate attempts."

P. 348.

Transeat in exemplum.
" May it pass into an example."

P. 351.

Perchè altrove non have
Dove voltare il viso,
Che gli é stato interciso,
Mostrar con altre imprese altra virtude.

" (He does this,) because he has no *other* object to engage
his attention; since he is cut off from every mode of action,
and cannot display any *other* courage and ability *(at prefent)*
in more arduous enterprizes."

P. 352.

Ut vellem his potius nugis tota illa dedisset
Tempora sævitiæ.
Juv. sat. 5.

G   " Would

" Would to heaven, he had given up to trifles like these,
all the times he devoted to savage and cruel purposes."

P. 354.

Περισσως εμμαινομενος.

" Wrought up to a high pitch of fury."

P. 354.

Triste ministerium! subjectam more parentum
Aversi tenuere facem.   *Virg. Æn. 6.*

" A melancholy office! after the manner of their ancestors,
they held the lighted torch to the funeral pile, and turned
aside their faces."

P. 354.

Η γλωσσα πυρ, ὁ κοσμος της αδικιας, ἡ σπιλασα ὁλον το
σωμα, ἡ φλογιζασα τον τροχον της γενεσεως, και φλογιζομενη
ὑπο της Γεεννης, ακατασχετον κακον, μεστη ια θανατηφορα.

" The tongue is a fire; a world of iniquity: it defileth
the whole body, setteth on fire the course of nature, and
is set on fire of hell; it is an unruly evil, full of deadly
poison."

P. 354.

Καλη αναστροφη — πραυτης σοφιας.

" A conversation and behaviour honest before men.—
The meekness and mildness of wisdom."

P. 355.

Αρνυμενος ἡντε ψυχην, και Νοστον Εταιρων,
Αλλ' αδ' ὡς ἑταρας ἐρρυσατο, ιεμενος περ.

                              Hom. Odys. l. 1.

" Endeavouring to secure his own existence and the return

of

of his companions; but in vain. He could not *secure his friends*, however anxious for their support."

P. 355.

Επει Τροιης ιερον πτολιεθρον επερσι.　　*Hor. Od.* l. 1. v. 2.

" Since he had brought the sacred citadel of Troy to destruction."

P. 355.

Αθρows την Βυλην, καθηρηκει. — Τυ δ' εργυ προιοντος μειζονως ετι εκφανηναι το επος τυ Γραχχυ — Ταχυ τε περιην ανεστραφθαι το κρατος της Πολιτειας!

Appian. de Bello Civil. l. 1. p. 363. *Ed. Steph.* 1592.

." He took away at once the power of the Senate. As the measures were proceeding, the words of Gracchus received still stronger confirmation.—The whole strength and power of the government *narrowly* escaped an utter subversion."

P. 356.

Errare Cives, si tum senatum aliquid in republicâ posse arbitrabantur."　　*Cicero Orat. pro Sext.* c. 12.

" (He said) the citizens were under a mistake, if they thought the senate had *now* any weight in the constitution."

P. 356.

Mirantur taciti, et dubio pro fulmine pendent!

Stat. Theb. l. 10.

" They stand in silent astonishment; and wait for the fall of the yet dubious thunderbolt."

P. 357.

Ut te, fortissime Teucrûm,
Accipio agnoscoque libens! ut verba parentis,
Et vocem Anchisæ magni mentemque recordor."

Virg. Æn. 8.

G 2　　　　　　　　" How

"How willingly do I receive and acknowledge thee, thou bravest, boldest of the Trojans! with what pleasure do I call to my remembrance the words, the voice, and the spirit of the great Anchises!"

P. 358.

Impudens liqui patrios penates.   *Hor.*

" I wandered from my own home, without a blush for my folly."

P. 358.

Mutemus Clypeos, Danaumque insignia nobis
Aptemus.   *Virg. Æn.* 2.

" Let us change shields, and adapt the devices of *the Greeks* to our own."

P. 360.

Ατυφв μοιρας φυσει μετεχον, Ζωον вρανιον εκειθεν δοθεν τοις τηδε εις επιμελειαν.

Themistii Orat. 1. p. 3. Ed. Fol. *Harduini.*

" A celestial *animal*, having nothing of pride or vanity in it's nature, sent down immediately from heaven, for the preservation and guardianship of men below."

P. 361.

Apud Græciam, quæ semper eloquentiæ princeps esse voluit, atque illas omnium doctrinarum inventrices Athenas, in quibus summa dicendi vis et inventa est et perfecta.

" In Greece, which ever was ambitious of the sovereignty in eloquence, and particularly in Athens, the parent of every science, in which the highest power and strength of speech was first cultivated and brought to perfection;" (no peroration was ever permitted!)

I

P. 361.

P. 361.

Epilogos illi mos civitatis abstulerat.

Quintil. lib. 10. c. 1.

On which Turnebus thus comments:

Non licebat Athenis affectum movere, ac ne epilogo quidem uti.

" The custom of the city precluded him from the use of the peroration."

On which Turnebus thus comments:

" It was not permitted to attempt to move the passions; and they denied an orator the epilogus or peroration."

P. 362.

Ει ανδραποδων η Πολις, αλλα μη των αρχειν ετερων αξιουντων, ωμολογειτο ειναι, ηκ αν, ω Ανδρες Αθηναιοι, τας υβρεις ηνεχεσθε τας; Τουτου, ας κατα την αγοραν υβριζεν, βοων εν ταις εκκλησιαις, επι του βηματος, δουλους και εκ δουλων καλων εαυτου βελτιους και εκ βελτιονων.

Demost. Orat. Κατα Ανδροτιωνος. Gr. Edit. Benenat. 1570.

p. 398.

" If the city, O Athenians, were indeed confessedly composed of slaves, *things* made over and bought, and not of MEN who consider themselves worthy of the rule and governance over others, ye would scarcely have endured the affronts and insulting language of this man; which he is daily pouring forth in the market place, in the assemblies, in the very tribunal itself; stigmatizing men better than himself, and far higher descended, as poltroons, and slaves, and the sons of slaves."

P. 364.

Illa se jactet in aula
Æolus!

" Let Æolus swagger in his own Hall!"

P. 364.

P. 364.

Proh dolor ! imperium Pelagi sævique tridentis
Cui nunc sorte datum ?   *Virg.*

" Oh heavy report ! to whom is the empire of the ocean,
and the unrelenting trident *now* consigned !"

P. 364.

Eunt tutis terrarum crimina velis !
Ex quo jura freti majestatemque repostam
Rupit Jäsoniâ Puppis Pagasæa rapinâ !

                              Stat. Achill. l. 1.

" *The crimes of the land* are wafted with impunity on the
sea : from the time when the ship, loaded with the plunder
of Jason, first disturbed the rights, the repose, and the
majesty of the ocean !"

P. 365.

Ρωμαϊκων ταγματων αλαλαγμος συμφερομενων, των
Στασιαστων πυρι και σιδηρω κεκυκλωμενων κραυγη. Ουτε
ηλικιας ην ελεος, υτ' εντροπη σεμνοτητος ! Λιμω μαραινομενοι
και μεμυκοτες εις οδυρμυς και κραυγην ευτονησαν. Συνηχει η τε
Πειραια, και τα περιξ ορη, βαρυτεραν ποιυντα την ορμην. Τυ
θορυβυ τα παθη φοβερωτατα.

Joseph. Hist. lib. 7. sect. 5. p. 1282. *Ed. Hudson. Oxon.*

" The war-cry of the Roman legions rushing to conquest,
and the shouts of the seditious, surrounded with fire and
sword, were heard aloud. There was no mercy for age ;
nor could dignity find any respect. Wasted and gaunt with
famine, they bellowed forth their groans and lamentations.
All the Peræa and the neighbouring hills resounded, and
made the tone deeper and deeper. The calamities and
sufferings were more formidable than the tumult itself."

P. 365.

P. 365.

Ουτω μεγαλοι οι λογοι, και εμβριθεις αι εννοιαι.
Ολον σωματιον δραματικον και εναγωνιον.

Longin. de Sublim. sect. 9.

" The composition and words are so sublime, and the
sentiments so weighty and full of matter. The whole body
of the narration is dramatick, and abounding with action."

P. 366.

Finis et ætas
Tota retro; seræ volumus decus addere morti.

Statius.

" The age and completion of all things is gone backward:
we will mark our late dissolution and death with honour
and renown! our death shall be delayed, and not without
honour."

P. 367.

Ils prennent leurs ordres sans le sçavoir.

" They take orders from them without being conscious
of it."

P. 367.

Ecce iterum Crispinus! et est mihi sæpe vocandus
In partes; monstrum nullâ virtute redemptum.

Juv. Sat. 4.

" Behold Crispinus again: I must often call upon him,
a monster whose faults are not compensated by a single
excellence."

P. 368.

Si tardius artus
Cessissent, potuit fulmen meruisse secundum.

Stat. Theb. l. 10.

G 4

" If

" If his limbs had not yielded so quickly to the stroke, he might have deserved a second thunderbolt."

P. 374.

Dat operam, ut cum ratione insaniat,

" He toils and labours with a desire of uniting reason with madness."

P. 375 and 376.

Gros paquet de toile verte et rouge—habits de drap tout uni, habits de velours un peu passés.   *Gil Blas.*

" (He opens) his large bundle of clothes, *green* and *red*; his suits of clothes all of one colour, and his second-hand velvet suits a little faded."

P. 376.

Vous êtes bien heureux, qu'on se soit addressé à MOI, plutot qu'a un autre.   Graces au ciel, j'exerce rondement ma profession : Je suis le seul Fripier qui ait de la morale.

Gil Blas.

" You are very fortunate in having applied TO ME, in preference to any other person.   Heaven be praised, I carry on my profession in a plain, honest manner.   I am the only *old-clothes-man* who has any *morality* about him."

P. 376.

Εξομεν δι ὁ τον Ανθρωπον τετον διαχριναι τε απο των αλλων Ζωων, και ειλιχρινως νοησαι δυνησομεθα.

Sext. Empirici Institut. Pyrrhon. l. 2. c. 5.

" We shall now have a criterion to distinguish THIS MAN from all other living beings, and be enabled thoroughly and distinctly to understand *the whole* of him."

P. 376.

P. 376.

Qui au travers de toute sa piété n'est pas Auteur
impunément, et qui a la satisfaction d'arracher les
Voluptueuses aux plaisirs, et d' affermir dans leur devoir des
Epouses ebranlées par des amans seducteurs.—(Though I
cannot say) qu'on trouve ses homélies et ses ouvrages
egalement forts et delicats.   *Gil Blas.*

" Who spite of all his piety certainly is not an author
with impunity, (or without paying for it), and who has
the satisfaction of reclaiming women of dissipation, and of
preserving spouses, shaken by seducing lovers, firm to their
duty. But it cannot be said, that all his *homilies*, and his
works, are equally strong and delicate.."

P. 377.

Avoir près de lui un homme *(comme moi)* qui ait de la
literature, et une bonne main, pour mettre au net ses
homélies.

" To have with him a man (like myself) who knows
something of literature, and writes a good hand, *to make a
fair copy of his homilies.*"

P. 378.

Doctor sanctissimus ille Gregorius, qui melleo prædicationis
imbre totam rigavit et inebriavit ecclesiam.

                              Johannes Salisburiensis.

" The most sacred Doctor Gregorius who bedewed, and
even *inebriated*, the church with the honey-heavy dew of his
preaching."

P. 377.

Nil habuit in tenementis.   *Law Latin.*
" He had nothing in the tenements."

P. 379.

P. 379.

Per verità, è un gran capriccio; ma in ciò segue il suo stile.

" In truth it is a great *capriccio* (or whimsical fancy); but in this he keeps up to his own style."

P. 382.

, Cumque superba foret Babylon spolianda trophæis
Ausoniis, umbràque erraret Crassus inultâ,
Bella geri placuit nullos habitura triumphos.

" And when the pride of Babylon was to be humbled and despoiled of Ausonian trophies; when the unappeased spirit of Crassus was ranging for revenge; they engaged in contests which never would admit of a triumph."

P. 383.

Pan etiam Arcadiâ dicat se judice victum.

Virg. Ecl.

" Pan would acknowledge himself vanquished, even by the decision of *Arcadia.*"

P. 384.

Hoc illis dico, qui me non intelligunt.

" I address this observation to those who do not understand me."

P. 386.

Temulentus videtur.

" He seems rather insolent and flushed."

P. 388.

In hos tota ruens.

" Rushing upon them with her whole force.'"

P. 388.

P. 388.

Te, Venus Regina, pio vocantum
Thure Wartoni et Stephani decoras
Transfer in ædes.

" O Venus, thou sovereign goddess, visit those temples where *Warton* and *Steevens* call upon thee in pious sacrifice."

P. 389.

Nobis non licet esse tam disertis,
Qui musas colimus severiores.   *Martial.*

" We who cultivate the muses of a more chastized spirit, cannot indulge ourselves in such licentious freedom of speech."

P. 391.

Ergo omnis furiis surrexit Etruria justis,
Regem ad supplicium præsenti marte reposcunt.

Virg. Æn. 8. 394.

" All Etruria rose up together with just resentment, and with instant arms demanded that the king should be brought to * *punishment.*"

P. 392.

Euse velut stricto Lucilius ardens
Infremuit.   *Juv. Sat.* 1.

" Lucilius, as with a drawn sword in hand, roused himself into ardent indignation."

P. 393.

Nos genera degustamus, non bibliothecas discutimus.

Quintil. l. 10. c. 1.

" We

---

* The modern democratick word for *murdering* kings and priests.

" We only touch slightly on the various kinds of books; it is not our business to digest whole libraries."

P. 393.

Αψ δ' ὁ παῖς προς κολπον εὐζωνοιο τιθηνης
Εκλινθη ιαχων.   *Hom. Il.* 6.

" The child, with a cry, shrunk back into the bosom of his nurse."

P. 393.

Τρις μεν ορεξατ' ιων, το δε τετρατον ἱκετο τεκμωρ
Αιγας.   *Hom. Il.* 13.

" He made three steps as he marched along; at *the fourth* he reached Ægæ, the boundary of his passage."

P. 394.

Δεινον απ' ακροτατης κορυθος νευοντα νοησας.   *Hom. Il.* 1.

" As he observed the plume nodding awfully from the top of his helmet."

P. 395.

Neque me Phœbi cortana fefellet.   *Virg. Æn.*

" Nor has the shrine of Phœbus deceived me."

P. 395.

Gubernaclum non vi, (sed sponter) revulsum,
Cui datus bærebat custos, cursusque regebat,
Præcipitans traxit secum.   *Virg. Æn.* 6.

" He dragged headlong into the deep with himself the rudder (not torn from him, but voluntarily abandoned) whose care was committed to him, and by which he was engaged to direct the vessel."

P. 397.

P. 397.

His armis illâ quoque tutus in aulâ.   *Juv. Sat. 4.*

" Preserved by precautions like these, even under such an administration."

P. 399.

DEUS, in spatio infinito, tanquam in *sensorio suo,* res intimè cernit.

Newton. Princip. Schol. General. sub fin.

" The Deity, in infinite space, as in his own *sensorium,* has an intimate perception of all things."

P. 399.

Deus creavit; Linnæus disposuit.

" God created the universe; Linnæus disposed it in order!"

P. 400.

Stabat anhela metu solum Natura Tonantem
Respiciens.   *Stat. Achill. l. 1. 488.*

" Nature stood in awful apprehension, looking upon *the God* who alone rules the elements!"

P. 401.

Nolumus leges naturæ mutari.

" We will not suffer the laws of nature to be changed."

P. 402.

Νοουμενα καθοραται.

" They are seen by the understanding."

P. 402.

Sunt lacrymæ rerum, et mentem mortalia tangunt.

" Tears

" Tears are a debt due to human misery, and the woes of mortality affect the mind."

P. 404.

Πολλων και συνεχων Αστερων συμφωτιζομενων αλληλοις συναυγασμον.   *Plutarch. de Placitis Philosophorum.*

" The united effulgence of numerous collected stars shining together."

P. 408.

Ταυτα μεν, ικανως εμφανισαι δυναμενα την τ8 Θε8 φυσιν τοις αγνο8σιν, ειρηκαμεν, οτι ποικιλη τ' εστι και πολυτροπος· και ταυτα καθ' ωραν απαντα τεταγμενως, α τε δει γενεσθαι προλεγει, την τε των ανθρωπων αγνοιαν και απιστιαν, υφ' ης 8δεν προιδειν εκθησαν των αποβησομενων, αφυλακτοι τε ταις συμφοραις παρεδοθησαν, ως αμηχανον αυτοις ειναι την εξ αυτων πειραν διαφυγειν.

Joseph. Antiq. Jud. l. 10. s. 3. p. 499. Ed. Hudson. Oxon.

" We have given this narration, to the intent that the nature of GOD may be made manifest to those who are ignorant of it, how various it is, and how manifold; that all events come to pass in their appointed season, and that HE declares what shall be hereafter. We have related these to shew the ignorance and unbelief of men, by which they were not suffered to foresee any part of these events, and were delivered over to the calamities, without a mode or possibility of escaping them."

P. 409.

Ανθρωπε τ8 Θε8, πιστε θεραπον και οικονομε των τ8 Θε8 μυστηριων, ανερ επιθυμιων των τ8 πνευματος, καλω Σε στυλον και εδραιωμα της Εκκλησιας, λογου ζωης επεχοντα, και πιστεως ερεισμα, και πνευματος καταγωγιον.

Gregor. Nazianz. Orat. p. 286. Ed. Prunæi Par. 1609.

" Thou

" Thou man of God, faithful minister and steward of the mysteries of God, thou man of the desires of the spirit, I call upon thee as a pillar and support of the church, holding fast the word of life, and the main stay of faith, and the resting-place of the spirit."

P. 410.

Æacidæ similes, Vulcaniaque arma capessunt.

Juv. Sat. 8.

" Like Achilles himself, they wield the divine armour."

P. 410.

Αφ' εαυτυ μεταβαινει, (a) ὡς εικων προς αρχετυπον, τελος εχων της πορειας. *Plotini. Ennead.* 6. lib. 9. c. xi.

" He passeth from himself, as the image to the archetype, being already in the possession or enjoyment of the end of his earthly pilgrimage."

P. 410.

῾Ουτω Θεων, και ανθρωπων θειων και ευδαιμονων βιος, απαλλαγη των αλλων των τηδε, βιος ανηδονος των τηδε, ΦΥΓΗ ΜΟΝΟΥ ΠΡΟΣ ΜΟΝΟΝ.

Plotini Ennead. 6. l. 9. c. xi.

" Such is the life of gods, and of godlike, happy, highly-favoured men; a deliverance and separation from the low cares of mortality. It is a life which receives not its pleasures and satisfaction from the things of this world; an ascent or flight of the soul, which is one, simple, and uncompounded, to that Being who is ONE, *and* ALONE in an eminent and incommunicable sense, GOD HIMSELF ! (b)

P. 414.

(a) Μεταβεβηκεν εκ τυ Θανατυ εις την ζωην. Evang. Johan.. "He is passed from death to life."

(b) The language of Plotinus in these passages is so sublime, and full of meaning, that without a paraphrase it is absolutely *impossible*

P. 414.

Τον των Αστρων χορον, και αυτον τον μεγαν Ηλιον, ὡκ οντα εκ πυρος.

Procli Comment. in Timæum Platonis, p. 141. *Ed. Basil.* 1534.

" The whole company of the Stars, and the great Sun himself, are not bodies of fire."

P. 414.

Πυρ τη των Αστρων προσφορον φυσει.

Plotin. Ennead. 2. lib. 1. pag. 99. *Ed. Basil. cum Comment. Facini.*

" A species of fire *accommodated* to the nature of the stars."

P. 416.

Τοιη Μυσαων ιερη δοσις.   *Hesiod. Theogon.*

" Such is the sacred offering of the Muses."

P. 417.

Musarum dona vocarem.   *Horat.*

" I would stile this work the gift of the Muses."

P. 418.

Finem dignum et optimo viro et opere sanctissimo faciant.

" May they close their labours in a manner worthy of the character of men of virtue, and suitable to their consecrated works."

P. 419.

impossible to express the ideas contained in them, particularly in these few words, " Φυγη Μονυ προς MONON." The translator feels what every Greek scholar will experience on such an attempt. It is sufficient if the sublimity of the ideas is comprehended by the reader.

P. 419.

Η μαλα λυγρης,

Πευσεαι αγγελιης, η ᴜκ ωφελλε γενεσθαι·

Κειται Πηλειδης. *Hom. Il.*

" I have a message full of sorrow to deliver to you; would it were not so!—Achilles is no more."

P. 419.

Του μεν θανοντ' Λοιδαι

Ελιπον' αλλα; οι

Παρα τε πυραν ταφοκ

Θ' Ελικωνιαι παρθενοι

Εσταν, επι θρηνον τε πολυφαμον εχευαν. Εδοξεν

Αρα γ' Αθανατοις

Εσλον γε Φωτα και φθιμενον μοιραις Θεαν διδομεν·

Pind. Isthm. Od. 8.

" But even in death he was not left unpraised or unsung: for the virgins of Helicon encircled the pile and tomb of the hero, and chaunted their memorial dirge. It seemed good to the immortals, that so great a man should not pass from the world without the hymns and harmony of the Muses."

P. 420.

Remuneratio ejus cum Altissimo!

" His reward is with THE MOST HIGH!"

P. 420.

Diis dilecte senex, te Jupiter æquus oportet

Nascentem, et miti lustrârit lumine Phœbus,

Atlantisque nepos; neque enim nisi charus ab ortu

Diis superis, poterit magno favisse poetæ.

Hinc longæva viret lento sub flore Senectus,

Nondum deciduos *servans* TIBI frontis honores,

H   *Ingeniumque*

Ingeniumque vigens, et adultum mentis acumen.

Ergo ego te Cliùs, et magni nomine Phœbi

MANSE PATER, JUBEO LONGUM SALVERE PER ÆVUM!

Milton ad Mansum.

".·Fortunate old man, favoured of heaven! Jove himself, and Apollo, and the God of eloquence must have shed their mildest influence on your birth; for no man *can* be *the* friend of a great Poet, who is not himself dear to the immortals. Favoured thus, you enjoy a green and flowering old age. The honours of your brow are preserved; your understanding is vigorous, and your mind in full possession of it's adult faculties. In the name therefore of Clio, and of the mighty Phœbus, all hail, thou *venerable* MANSUS, hail for ages yet to come!"

P. 421.

Tanto homini fidus, tantæ virtutis amator.

" A faithful friend to so great a man; and a steady admirer of such distinguished excellence."

P. 423.

Exornet ætatis nostræ gloriam!

" May he add to the glories of this our age!"

P. 427.

Natura omnium partium rudimenta simul parit et procreat."

Bacon. de Augm. Sc.

" Nature creates and produces, at one and the same time, the rudiments, and principles of the whole body, and of every component part."

P. 428.

Gnossius hæc Rhadamanthus habet, durissima regna."

Virg. Æn. 6.

" The

" The Cretan Rhadamanthus sways over these realms of unrelenting severity."

P. 428.

Abyssus abyssum invocat.

" One deep calleth upon another,"

P. 429.

Συνερχομενων νεφεων μυκητορι ρομβω
Βρονταιη, ζαφυδηπος, εζομβεεν ομβριος ηχω.

Nonni Dionys. l. 41. v. 84.

" The sound of the storm, rushing with a mighty noise from the conflicting clouds, roared with a deep intonation."

P. 429.

Vera bona, atque illis multum diversa remotâ
Erroris nebulâ. *Juv. Sat.* 10.

" The true goods of this life, and those which are found to be essentially different, when the mist of error is dispersed,"

P. 429.

Την ψυχην μη διερχεται Ρομφαια.

" A sharp-edged sword pierceth through my soul."

P. 431.

Sic furiis Caci mens effera; nec quid inausum
Aut intractatum scelerisve, dolive! *Virg. Æn.* 8.

" So ferocious and infuriate was the soul of *Cacus*. He left not a species of crime, wickedness, treachery, or fraud, unattempted or untried."

P. 432.

Ανθρωπος! ικανη προφασις. *Menander.*

It is man : the name will explain, or excuse the rest.

H 2 P. 432.

P. 432.

Ο καιρος οξυς, η πειρα σφαλερη.

" Opportunity is instant; experiment is hazardous."

P. 433.

" Licet quod videtur, publicum judicare ; quod judicaverint, vendere."   *Cicero Orat. de Lege Agrariâ.*

" Whatever they think proper, they declare to be national property ; and what they decree to be so, they expose to publick sale."

P. 433.

Perspici non potest, utrum severitas acerbior, an benignitas quæstuosior sit.   *Cic. ut sup.*

" It cannot be determined, whether their severity is more grievous, or their alliance and favour more expensive to the objects of it."

P. 433.

Επειδη ουχι των ενοχλουντων ημας, ουδε των πεπολιτευμενων και πιστευομενων παρ υμιν ων, πραγμα τηλικουτον φημι δειξειν πεπραγμενον.

Κατα Αριστοκρατυς, *Demosth. Op. Gr. Ed. Ed. Benen.* 1570.

" I am not of the number of those men who are perpetually troubling and disturbing you ; I hold not any office of trust, or of administration in the State. I therefore come forward with confidence, and denounce transactions and crimes like these."

P. 433.

Μη προτερον, ω Αθηναιοι, ψηφισεσθε, αν μη τυ ΕΛΕΟΥ τον βωμον καθελητε.

Lucian. Demonax. p. 555. Edit. *Bourdelotii.*

P. 334.

Je ne veux point admettre dans les arrêts de conseil un vrai trivial, une clarté trop familiere. Je veux un vrai de recherche

recherche, une clarté elegante, une naiveté fine, toute brillante de termes pompeux, relevés inopinément de phrases arrondies, de vocatifs intermediares & d' adverbes indefinis.

, .. *D'Alembert Lett. Hist. et Polit.* vol. 4, p. 176.

" I would not allow the admission of *a trivial truth* in the decrees of council, or a clearness which is too easy and familiar. I choose to have a subtle kind of truth, an elegant perspicuity, a natural manner but not wholly without art, set off with words of pomp, unexpectedly raised with a roundness of phraseology, with *intermediate vocatives*, and indefinite adverbs,"

P. 435.

Πεντηκοντα χρυσων δει, και λραμματων ο δει. Ει με φιλεις, δος.

Alciphron. l. 1. ep. 40. *Ed. Bergleri.* 1791. p. 61.

" I want fifty pieces of gold; I do not want letters. If you love me, give me money."

P. 435.

Περι Ζωων,

" A treatise concerning Zoology."

P. 435.

Η Πολιτικη κυριωτατη και αρχιτεκτονικη. Τινας γαρ ειναι χρεων των επιστημων εν ταις Πολεσι, και ποιας εκαστος μανθανειν, και μεχρι τινος, Αυτη διατασσει.—Ορωμεν τις εντιμοτατας των Δυναμεων υπο ταυτην ουσας.

Aristot. Ethic. Nichom. l. 4. c. 2.

" The science of Politicks is the supreme and master-founder of the rest. It is her province to declare and ordain what sciences shall be cultivated in States, which of them is proper for each person, and to what point, and how far.— We see already some of the most respectable powers bending under *her* dominion,"

" Ah,

P. 436.

Ah, si vous saviez le Grec! —Ceux qui sçavent, ou croient savoir l'Hebreu, l' Arabe, le Syriaque, le Cophte ou Copte, le Persan, ou le Chinois, pensent et parlent de meme, et par les memes raisons.

D'Alembert Melang. de Literat. et de Philos. v. 5. p. 526.

" Oh, if you did but understand Greek! — They who understand, or think they understand Hebrew, Arabick, Syriack, Coptick, Persian, or Chinese, think and speak in the same manner, and for the same reasons."

P. 437.

Το μη δυσφημα λεγειν πασι τοις Παλαιοις φροντις ην, μαλιστα δε τοις Αθηναιοις· διο και το Δεσμωτηριον, οικημα εκαλην, και τον Δημιον, Κοινον· τας δε Εριννυας, σεμνας θεας· κτλ.

Helladius Besantinous apud Photii Biblioth, sect. 279. p. 1593. *Ed.* 1653.

" All the ancients were very careful not to use words of an inauspicious sound, and in particular, the Athenians. They therefore did not call the Prison, the Executioner, or the Furies, by their direct appellations, but by softer terms*, such as a Mansion, a publick minister, the venerable Goddesses, &c. &c. &c.

P. 438.

Signa tamen, divûmque tori, et quem quisque sacrârat
Concubitu genioque, locus monstrantur.

Stat. Achill. l. 1.

" The statues, and the couches of the deities, and every spot which they had honoured with their presence and favour, are yet shewn."

P. 439.

* The synonimous words will hardly bear a translation.

P. 439.

Αντι τȣ αποδȣναι, σοφισματα ἑυρισκȣσι, και παραγραφας, κα.
προφασεις, πονηροτατοι ανθρωπων και αδικωτατοι.

.*Demosth. Orat.* Προς Λακριτȣ Παραγραφην. *Demosth.*
Ed. Benen. 1570. pag. 546.

" Instead of giving a plain, open avowal of their opinions,
they have recourse to sophisms, and glosses, and exceptions,
and *(demurring)* declarations. Such is their character;
men without virtue, principle, or justice.

P. 440.

Auream invenit, chartaceam reliquit.

" He found it of gold ; he left it of paper."

P. 441. (8th Edit.)

Cum ferro, cum metu, cum privilegio, cum præsentibus
copiis perditorum, et minis, et nefario fædere, servitute
oppressam civitatem tenerent. Libertatis signum posuerunt
magis ad ludibrium impudentiæ, quam ad simulationem
religionis.

Cicero Orat. pro Domo sua ad Pontifices. sect. 51.

" With the sword, by terror, by pretended rights and
privileges, with the collected bands of desperate and abandoned wretches, by threats, by a nefarious league
and union ;—by these, and such instruments and agents,
they would hold the country in the bonds of servitude and
oppression. They have set up the STATUE of LIBERTY, as
in mockery and derision, not with a religious reverence
and respect."

P. 442.

Non hoc ista sibi tempus spectacula possit. *Virg. Æn.* 6.

" The times demand not *exhibitions* such as these."

P. 443.

P. 443.

Non ante revellar,

Exanimem quam te complectar, ROMA, tuumque
Nomen, Libertas, et inanem prosequar umbram!

Lucan, l. 2.

" I will not be torn away from thee, *O Rome*, O my
Country, till I embrace thee in thy last agony. Thy name
also, LIBERTY, will I venerate and cherish; and will follow
after thy very shadow, when it can avail no more."

END OF THE FOURTH AND LAST DIALOGUE OF
THE PURSUITS OF LITERATURE.

~~~~

THE

SHADE

OF

ALEXANDER POPE

ON THE

BANKS of the THAMES.

A SATIRICAL POEM.

WITH NOTES.

~~~~

[Price 2s. 6d.]

THE

SHADE

OF

ALEXANDER POPE

· ON THE ·

BANKS OF THE THAMES.

~~~~~~

A SATIRICAL POEM.

WITH NOTES.

Occasioned chiefly, but not wholly, by the residence of
HENRY GRATTAN, Ex-Representative in Parliament
for the City of DUBLIN, at TWICKENHAM,
in November, 1798.

Voce fu per me udita,
Onorate l'altissimo Poeta !
L'Ombra sua torna.

Dante Inf.

BY THE

AUTHOR of THE PURSUITS of LITERATURE.

THE THIRD EDITION.

LONDON:
PRINTED FOR T. BECKET, PALL MALL.
1799.

Ἀστοις και Βασιλευ-
-οι διακρινειν ετυμον λογον ανθρωπων.

Pindar. Pyth. **1.**

PREFACE.

THIS Poem was chiefly occasioned by the

perusal of Dr. Patrick Duigenan's Answer to

the Address of Mr. Grattan to his Fellow

Citizens of Dublin (*a*). I considered the Address

and

(*a*) See " An Answer to the Address of HENRY
GRATTAN, Ex-representative of the City of Dublin in
Parliament, to his fellow Citizens of Dublin, by Patrick
Duigenan, L. L. D. a Citizen of Dublin, and one of the
Rrepresentatives of the City of Armagh." 3d. edit. with
Additions. Dublin, printed for Milliken, Grafton-street.
1798. and for J. Wright, Piccadilly, London.

B

and the Answer with that attention, earneſsness, and zeal which the importance of such a Cause, at this present hour, requires and demands. I considered it in this manner, because whatever affects Ireland, *must* affect the exiſtence and safety of Great Britain, and of all the dependencies, territories, and possessions annexed to the Crown.

I think Dr. Duigenan might have adopted the very words of Cicero againſt Antony. That Orator requeſted indulgence and attention when he spoke of himself; but as to the enemy of his country, he exclaimed with confidence; " Contra illum cum dicam, faciam ut attenté au- " diatis.(*b*)" A more maſterly, just, and irresistible

(*b*) Philipp. 2.

sistible piece of argument has seldom appeared ; and if the eloquence suffers any abatement, it is from the admission of some expressions which might, and should, have been avoided. But a mind intent on great and national matters, urgent in their nature and allowing of no delay, cannot always attend to the minuter elegances and graces of diction.

In Dr. Duigenan's Answer, there is the vigour, the manlinefs, the courage, the impetuosity, the indignation, and the thunder of an orator, feeling for the wrongs of his country, and the horrors of rebellion, againft a Man, whose political conduct and character have ranked him among the domeftick enemies of Ireland. Against a

B 2   man

man, who appears to have imposed himself upon his credulous country, under the pretence of brilliant talents and rhetorical exertions. Against a man, who boasts that in the hour of distress, *he* EXTORTED from the timid and feeble Minister of the day, and from an improvident British Parliament, such *concessions*, as have been since proved to be inconvenient, and sometimes in direct opposition to the essential welfare of Ireland. Against a man, who received the most extravagant and disproportioned rewards for very equivocal services, and who has now (*c*) fled to England from his own country, from that hue and cry of every loyal subject, which pursued him from the Castle, to the shop and to the cottage.

I have

(*c*) Nov. 1798.

I have no concern with Mr. Grattan, but in his publick capacity, as his actions, his writings, and his speeches have demonstrated and declared it to the world. He has signed with his own hand all the doctrines, which have been discussed, exposed, and confuted.

In Mr. Grattan's Address we find, as I think, false facts, even of the day, false history, false reasoning, false premises, and false conclusions. There is inanity of sound, and shallowness of argument. We observe the glosses of the sophist, and all the purple patches in the rhetorician's cloak. It is such a tissue of the most unfounded assertions, rebellious doctrines, and treasonable sentiments, as have discovered, and proved to the loyal subjects of Great Britain and Ireland, WHO AND WHAT

B 3 MR.

Mr. Grattan is. But I refer to the caustick discussions of Dr. Duigenan, whose answer, I hope, will be read in this country; for it does not concern Ireland alone.

When William Wood and his associates had been confounded by the eloquence and energy of Dean Swift, (a man to whom Mr. Grattan bears not the least resemblance in the powers of his mind,) the Copper Cáptain of that day continued his calumnies in the newspapers. I think that Mr. Grattan has been so examined, so exposed, so probed to the quick in his political capacity by Dr. Duigenan, that his letters, full of sound and fury in the Dublin and London Newspapers, and signifying little, can be considered only

as

as shrieks similar to those of William Wood, in similar agonies. Some of his doctrines, and publick conduct, are briefly exposed in this Poem ; as *such* statesmen should be held up to the publick in every point of view, that we may always know who and what they are, and judge them from their own mouth. " Licet omnibus, licet etiam mihi, " dignitatem Patriæ tueri : potestas modo " veniendi in publicum sit, dicendi periculum " non recuso*(d)*."

I have observed, that this Poem was occasioned chiefly, but *not wholly*, by the appearance and residence of Mr. Grattan in the village

B-4   of

(d) Cicero, Philipp. 1.

of Twit'nam on the banks of the Thames, the ancient and favourite abode of our great Poet. It is not unnatural to imagine his indignation at such vicinity. No man could have felt greater horror at the scenes of democratick France, the *papal fanaticks*, and rebellious disorganizers of Ireland, and the projected, but baffled, plots of the Jacobins in Great Britain, than Mr. Pope.

To suppose indeed, that the spirits of departed Poets are acquainted with the passing scenes of this lower world, is an indulgence which has always been granted. I think no apology for the supposition can be required or expected.

But

But if any person should be so very reasonable, and so very unpoetical as to demand it, I must consign him to the custody of the Governor of Tilbury Fort in the days of Queen Elizabeth, who declared, that no man can see what is not to be seen; or hear, what is not to be heard. *(e)* A sentence indeed of great truth, but which, I fear, would overthrow from their foundation, some of the best poetical fabricks in every language.

It has been declared of SATIRE, *(f)* that " She alone of all her poetical sisters is " unconquerable, never to be silenced, when truly " inspired and animated, as should seem from

above,

(e) Mr. Sheridan's Critick, Act 2. *(f)* By Warburton.

" above, for this very purpose, to oppose (the

" power and influence of) dulness, (conceit,

" democracy, and wickedness) to her very last

" breath." In these days, the various objects

which offer, or rather force themselves upon

our notice, are very numerous, and many of

them are considered in this Poem. But no

subject whatsoever is introduced, which has

not some reference to the welfare, support, and

stability of these kingdoms, and their consti-

tutional government, in this hour of danger and

experiment. There is no subject in it which

the great moral and national Poet, who is

supposed to speak, would not have thought

worthy either of his casual notice, or of mature

consideration, or of jocular allusion and easy

pleasantry,

pleasantry, or of his most severe and most powerful Satire. If I have read Mr. Pope's works aright, I think he would, at this hour, have adopted the patriotick words of him, who declared that a Poet was nearly and closely allied to an Orator: " Erigite animos ; retinete vestram dig-" nitatem. Manet illa in Republicâ bonorum " consensio ; dolor accessit bonis viris, virtus " non est. imminuta."(g)

Upon this consideration, if Satire should exalt herself, and if her language should become bold and of ancient potency, it is unjust to attribute it to ill-nature, or to malignity. It is the deliberate, keen sensation of a mind feeling for

the

(g) Fragment. Orationis in Clodium :
ap. Cicer. Epist. ad. Attic. L. 1. E. 16.

the human nature and the human character, for the ruin, the degradation, the confusion, or the disturbance of a well-ordered state, and of that morality and principle which can alone uphold it. It must then be regarded, (as a man whose thoughts were deep, and whose views were clear and comprehensive, once expressed himself,) " Not as malice, but indignation and " resentment against vice and wickedness. It " is one of the common bonds, by which Society " is held together; a fellow-feeling, which each " individual has in behalf of the whole species, " as well as of himself. And it does not appear " that this, generally speaking, is at all *too* " *high* among mankind." When the sustaining principles are in danger, we must look and act beyond ourselves. The connexion of the well-

disposed

dispofed muft be closer than ever; for safety is in coherence alone, and in the order of the ftate. It is well expressed by Plato, I think in his Timæus, when he is discoursing on the Œconomy of the Universe, the arrangement, the disposition, and the consequent stability of the whole; Διεχοσμησε, διεταξε, ΞΥΝΕΣΤΗΣΕΝ.

We should feel all selfishness of spirit subdued by the time. We should cast away the petty interests and low considerations of mere literary prudence, and the contemptible submission to half-measures. We should feel them sinking and giving way, when we acknowledge in common with every man who will reflect deeply, what a debt of gratitude we owe to our ancestors who established our Constitution;

and

and how great the duty is of each individual to lend his support to his own country, when publickly attacked, or secretly undermined. Resistance must be bold, determined, and unshrinking, or it is ineffectual; nay, it is worse than no resistance at all. With political knowledge, well or ill understood, is now involved every thing which is valuable and worth preservation. Morality, religion, the laws, literature, our domestick safety, and individual property must perish in the common shipwreck.

In whatever we are at present engaged, THE CAUSE is just and righteous. It is a war unsought and unprovoked by our aggressions; a war of self-defence, but extended beyond all powers of our original conception. I hope and trust we shall still be the instruments of a general preservation, and

of

of the deliverance of Europe from the overbearing, desolating, and unrelenting tyranny of France, by a mighty co-operation and an inflexible league. But above all, the internal peace, the quiet, the safety, the authority of the legal powers, the institutions, the manners, and the laws, within the precincts of our own Island, are the most immediate and dearest objects of all our labours, our expences, our arms, and our trophies; worthy of unremitting vigilance, and of united vigour.

Upon the general issue; upon the great united contest; upon the powers of the North, and the strength of the East; on the Isles and the Continents of Europe, and of Asia; on the shores of the Mediterranean; through the Indian

and

and Atlantick waves; on the states of America, and the invaded deserts of Africa, the Cause ONE AND THE SAME is now to be maintained, or lost for ever. There is a voice, (it was the voice of an Imperial Poet, the friend of the Minister of his day,) which may be *now* heard with effect by every Nation, but by none with more peculiar emphasis and propriety than by Great Britain and Ireland.

Credite nunc omnes, quas dira *Britannia*, Gentes,
Quas *Ister*, quas *Rhenus* alit !
   Uno tot prælia vincite Bello ;
Romanum reparate decus, molemque labantis
Imperii fulcite humeris : Hic omnia Campus
Vindicat ; HÆC MUNDO PACEM VICTORIA SANCIT !

November; 1798.

The SHADE of ALEXANDER POPE

ON THE

BANKS OF THE THAMES,

At TWIT'NAM.

A SATIRICAL POEM.

WITH NOTES.

The SHADE of ALEXANDER POPE

BANKS of the THAMES. (*a*)

═══════════

" WHAT accents, murmur'd o'er this hallow'd tomb,

Break my repose, deep-sounding through the gloom?

Would mortal strains immortal spirits reach,

Or earthly wisdom truth celeftial teach?

Ah! 'tis no holy calm that breathes around :

Some warning voice invites to yonder ground,

Where once with impulse bold, and manly fire,

I rous'd to notes of war my patriot lyre ;

While Thames with every gale, or bland or strong,

Sigh'd through my grotto, and diffus'd my song. 10

C 2   Whence

(*a*) A Satirical Poem; Occasioned chiefly, but not wholly, by the residence of HENRY GRATTAN (Ex-Representative in Parliament for the City of Dublin,) at Twit'nam; November, 1798.

Whence bursts that voice indignant on my ear?
To Britain ever faithful, ever dear,
E'en *now* my long-lov'd, grateful Country's cause,
Her fam'd pre-eminence, her state, her laws,
Can touch my temper of ethereal mould,
Free as great Dryden, and as Milton, bold.
Sadly the fcene I view, how chang'd, how loft!
The statesman's refuge once, and poet's boast;
I hear the raven's hoarse funereal cry,
Since all, whom Ireland spares, to *Twit'nam* (a) fly. 20

The polish'd Nestor of the classick shore,
Mendip, *(b)* my green domain can guard no more;
E'en Cambridge(*c*)droops, who once with tuneful tongue
The gifts of science, and her wand'rings sung;

With

(*a*) Mr. Pope generally spelt the word in this manner.

(*b*) The Right Hon. Welbore Ellis, Baron Mendip, the present possessor of Mr. Pope's villa at Twit'nam.

(*c*) Richard Owen Cambridge, Esq. a diftinguished veteran in literature and the polite arts. His poem entitled "*The Scribleriad*" is a work of great fancy, just composition, and poetical elegance; but above all, of mature judgment

With Him, whom Themis and the Muses court,

The learned Warden of the *tatter'd* Fort. *(d)*

For their best task *my* Sylphs are all unfit,

While more than Gnomes along the meadows flit:

No more my fabled phantoms haunt the plains,

Where Moloch *now*, in right of Umbriel, reigns; 30

His bands from their Hibernian Tophet pass,

And clash the cymbal's visionary brass;

Or round my groves, sublime on murky wing,

Spells of revolt and revolution fling;

And as they glide, unhallow'd vapours shed

On that false Fugitive's inglorious head.

   Whence, and what art thou, GRATTAN ? has
      the shock,

And terror low'ring o'er the sable rock,

                     Hurl'd

judgment conspicuous throughout. It should be read as well for instruction, as amusement. The preface is entitled to much attention.

(*d*) George Hardinge, Esq. a man of genius, learning, and eloquence, M. P. one of the Welsh Judges. He is the present possessor of the villa, called " *Ragman's Castle*" at Twit'nam, by the banks of the Thames.

Hurl'd thee aftounded with tumultuous fears,

From Ireland's mutter'd curse, from Ireland's tears? 40

For thee no vistos ope, no friendly glade,

No Muse invites thee to *my* sacred shade ;

No airs of peace from heav'n thy presence greet ;

Blasts from Avernus, in respondence meet,

Hoarse through the leafless branches howl around,

And birds of night return the' obscener sound.

From thee, whate'er thy fame, I spurn all praise;

My lyre ne'er answer'd to Rebellion's lays :

With other lore my purer groves resound,

With other wreaths these temples once were bound;

Nor shall my green sepulchral laurel ftand

By Gallick mercy, and a Marian hand.   52

Hence, and thy baffled Gallick jargon try

On coward flaves, in abject tyranny :

Know, thy *twice-conquer'd (d)* Britons still advance;

No chains from Pitt they fear, or humbled France;

From their beft source each mingled blessing draw,

Content with freedom, property, and law ;

                                        Secure

(d) " The English have been conquered, *firft*, by the
Minister, and *afterwards*, by the French." Henry Grattan's
Address to his Fellow-Citizens of Dublin. p. 37.

Secure they own their monarch's rightful rod,

His friend, the people; his Creator, GOD. *(e)* 60

Hear then *thy* doctrines, and *thy* patriot love:

" Kings are but satellites; *(ee)* the people, Jove;

" Priestcraft a falling cause, *(f)* from folly sprung,

" When Saturn reign'd, or when the Pope was young;

" Religion

(e) " In the people it would *only* be rebellion against *their creature*, the King; in the other (*i. e.* in the King) it would be rebellion against *his Creator*, the People." Grattan. p. 12. Such is the unblushing doctrine of a Rhetorician. Cicero says to Lucceius, *Epistola non erubescit*; and Mr. G. (if he has read Cicero) believes the doctrine.

(ee) " Kings are but fatellites; and *your freedom* is the luminary which has *called them to the fkies.*" Grattan. p. 40. It would perplex any understanding, to explain the meaning of these words; or to tell (if art could tell) *how* the *fatellites* of a metaphorical planet are *called to the fkies* by *a Luminary?* I have in charity given the Satellites a Primary, which Mr. G. forgot in the fervour of his political astronomy. But after all, I suppose, it is only a beautiful rhetorical expression alluding to the murder of Louis the Sixteenth, or the modern democratick mode of " *calling Kings to the fkies.*"

(f) " Priestcraft is a falling cause, and a fuperannuated " folly." Grattan. p. 22.—If Priest*craft* means the juggling or deceit of Priefts, I hope it is falling, and will fall for ever. But I think, no man of fober enquiry and of a cultivated understanding, who admits the truth of Christianity, can ever apply with sense, honesty, or justice, the

term

" Religion boasts no more a royal rule, *(g)*

" Or great Mathèsis an imperial school.

" Self-legislation *(gg)* to the mob restore; *(h)*

" This is Reform ; corruption is no more:

" Reaſon

term Priestcraft, to ſuch an *Eſtabliſhment* of it, as the Church of England, dependant as it is, on the general law of the land for its support, rights, and constitution. I am here ſpeaking only of the modes of religious worship as they affect civil society, between which there is an important relation, and a cloſe connection. Mr. Grattan's " popular and energetick *Romaniſts*," could tell him what *Prieſtcraft* is.

(g) " We know of no royal rule for religion or mathematicks." *Grattan.* p. 21. I only notice this, to mark the folly of the rhetorician in it's application.

(gg) One peculiar feature of Mr. Grattan's inconsistency (now a favourite term) is this: In his Address to the Citizens of Dublin, he recommends and enforces self-legislation, abſolute and unqualified, to Ireland; and in his speech on Mr. Fox's motion in the British Houſe of Commons, he asserted and maintained the propriety (and conſequently the legality) of Appeals from the Parliament of Ireland to the Britiſh Houſe of Commons.

(h) " What method (ſays Mr. Grattan,) remains to limit the monarchy of these kingdoms, Great Britain and Ireland, (it has now no limits) but by Reforming Parliament (i. e. the

Houſe

" *Reason* commands ; go, fix *her* limit strong,

" Monarchs are bound, but councils never wrong.

" What

House of Commons)? What method to *prevent* a Revolution,
but a Reformation?" (i. e. of the H. of C.) What is the Reformation of Parliament? (i. e. of the H. of C.) but *the restoration* TO THE PEOPLE of *self-legislation* ?—Without
which there is no liberty, as without Reform, no *self-legis*-
lation. *So* WE REASONED !!!" Grattan, p. 40. In a preceding part of his Address, Mr. Grattan says, " It is the
object of the Reform, that Parliament (i. e. the H. of C.)
should continue *in contact* with the people always, and with
the Minister never, except the people should be *in contact*
with him." Grattan, p. 28. The beautiful ambiguity,
equivocation, or rather the absolute nonsense, of the word
contact suits such an underſtanding as that of the Ex-Representative of the City of Dublin. " Tantamne rem tam
negligenter, tam indisertè, tam impudenter ?" Perhaps Mr.
Grattan may be of the same opinion with a seditious scrib-
bler, one M'Cormick, concerning the many headed monster, THE IRISH DRAGON, " whose teeth (as M'Cormick
" tells us) are sown, and muſt *ere long* spring up in *hosts of*
" *armed Patriots*, not with frantick rage to point their
" spears at each others breaſts, but *to fertilize the ſoil* and
" renovate the proverbial *verdure* of their Country, BY THE
" BLOOD of it's cruel oppreſſors."†—N. B. In the rural
" œconomicks of Democracy, *Blood* is always the manure.

· † See a large pamphlet in 4to. published in 1798, which
M'Cormick calls, " The Life of Burke," p. 231.

" What *Rights*, by thee proclaim'd, are equal (*i*) shewn?

" Huffey's (*k*) to freedom, BRUNSWICK's to the crown.

" Britain no commerce spreads from pole to pole,

" Oppress'd, without an empire to console; *(l)*

" For her no ports expand beneath the line,

" No friendly flags in Arctick splendours join;

" Since Ocean's self republican (*m*) is grown,

" She holds, like Delos, but a floating throne.

" No

(i) " The Catholicks have, in truth and reason, *as good*
" *a right to Liberty as* his Majesty has TO THE CROWN !"
" Grattan, p. 21. Such is the sport of a rhetorician with
" the term *Liberty*.

(k) Hussey, the Roman-Catholick, democratick, and
seditious, titular Bishop of Waterford. See his *Paftoral*
Letter, &c. &c.

> *Paftorale* canit signum! cornuque recurvo
> Tartaream intendit vocem.

(l) " The project—to put France at the head of Europe,
instead of Great Britain, while her people *crouch* under a
weight of debt and taxes, *without an Empire to confole* or
a constitution *to cover* them." Grattan. ib. 38.

(m) " We saw that these Islands, Great Britain and
Ireland, were now two kingdoms in A REPUBLICAN
OCEAN." &c. Grattan. p. 39.

" No wisdom in finance, no patriot scheme,

" No modern care in borrowing to redeem, (*n*)   80

" No Constitution *for a cover* (*o*) left,

"Of

(*n*) If Mr. Pitt's principle of *Redemption* in all loans had been originally adopted at the commencement of the Funding System, the National Debt would have been but small even at this period.

(*o*) See above ; Note (*l*).—I would here briefly consider Mr. Grattan's pretensions to credit, as a Writer and an Orator, from his own expressions. If indeed putting down sentence after sentence in succession, however unconnected, confers on a man the character of a Writer, Mr. Grattan has a claim to that honour. If a torrent of " wild and whirling words" uttered vehemently and ungracefully, and of metaphors jostling and supplanting each other, and wondering at their union in the same sentence, constitute an Orator; who shall refuse that title to the Ex-Representative of the City of Dublin? His Address is printed throughout with dashes (— — —) at the end, and frequently in the middle, of almoſt every sentence in it, for stage effect, as I ſuppose. If these dashes do not beget an awful attention, (like Mr. Sheridan's (*a*) *Morning-Gun*,) they certainly create ſurprife. But even the Shakspeare Commentators would tell him, in their little way, that such tricks are but " Laquei Ridiculosi, (*b*)

or

(*a*) Critick, Act 2.

(*b*) A Collection of (Irish) Epigrams, &c. printed in 1616.

" Of rights, of liberty, of laws bereft.

" State-
or Springs for Woodcocks," which can only take effect
in " The Isle of Gulls." (*d*)

Mr. Grattan firſt tells his Fellow Citizens, that " they
are kind and gracious *Masters* ;" such he has found them.
He also acquaints them, that " They have found in Him
an unprofitable Servant"; (*e*) and they agree to the doctrine
without demurring. I know not from what part of his
Address to begin a selection of *fine* writing ; or to produce
instances of what Thomas Aquinas and " the energetick,
" but not popular, Romaniſt" Schoolmen, term " the grace
of congruity."

  " Attend! the curtain wide the Muſe ſhall draw,
  Nor shade from light, nor cover *Him* from Law."

In the diſcuſſion of an important subject Mr. Grattan
firſt deſcribes THE STATE, as " a furious Wrestler"; then
suddenly it becomes " an angry Father," and " an old
fool"; and then, in the very same sentence, by a rapid
transition from an attempt at sense to mere sound, we
are informed, *how* Mr. G. " saw the Miniſter retreating
" from the enemy with as rapid a step as he advanced upon
" the people, going *back, and back, and back,* while the
" democratick principle was going *on, and on, and on,* like
" *a miſt* at the heels of a countryman," &c. Then follows
a beautiful deſcription of the properties of *a Miſt,* which
nobody understands better than the Ex-Representative.
He then tells his Fellow-Citizens, with the best and most
peaceable intentions, and all in the ſame sentence, that
"A *naked* man oppreſſed by the State is an *armed* Poſt ;"—
that " A ſew *decent* Biſhops ſent to the Tower againſt
" Law,

(*d*) Name of a Comedy in 1605.
(*e*) Grattan. p. ii.

" State-quacks still hold thy prophylacticks good,

To

" Law, *produced* (*g*) *the Revolution*:"—that " Mr.
" Hampden, and *four* other *innocent* perfons arraigned for
" High Treason, *produced* the Civil (*h*) War:"—that
" *Grey-coated* men, and *green* men (in certain circumftances,)
" have their political consequence." And then, in the
true style of a modern animal-magnetizing Quack, he
gravely assures them, that, " *Sensible* acts of violence
operate *by sympathy*;—that " They *possess* the air, as it
were, by certain *tender influences*, and spread the " kindred
(I wonder he did not alfo add, *the tender*) *passion*
through *the whole* of the Community." (*i*)

But if the reader wishes to observe the eye of this
Rhetorician and Sophist rolling in his fineft metaphorical
phrenzy, and with more than poetical boldness, let him hear
the following sentence, and perpend. Mr. Grattan says:
" In the American contest we saw, that REFORM, which
" had been *born* in England and *banished* to America, (*k*)
" advanced

(*g*) A *Production* of which Mr. G. seems to be particularly fond.

(*h*) Another favourite *production* of Mr. Grattan's.

(*i*) Grattan. p. 19.

(*k*) Throughout the whole of Mr. Grattan's Address, by the
word, or image, of REFORM, he always means, " A Reform in
" the House of Commons." How this Reform " was *born* in
England, and *banished* to America," remains for the Ex-
Representative to explain to Country-Gentlemen, and reconcile
it to common sense. But the transitions of meaning in a
Rhetorician's words are frequent, and always suited to the
moment. " REFORM (of the H. of C.) says Mr. G. is the
" principle of attraction, *round which* the King and People
" would *spin on* quietly and *insensibly* in *regular movements*," &c,
" &c, Grattan, p. 40.—How pretty! *Trossulus exultet*.

" To starve the spirit, (*p*) they remove the food."

Divine

" advanced *like the Shepherd Lad in Holy Writ*, and over-
" threw Goliath. *He* (that is, the *Shepherd Lad David*)
" returned *riding on the Waves of the Atlantick*, and his
" Spirit moved upon *the waters of Europe.*" Yet attend :
" The royal Ship of France went down—the Britifh man
" of war labours—Your vessel is affected—Throw your
" people overboard, say your Ministers, and *ballast* with
" your abuses.—Throw your abuses overboard, we said,
" and ballast with your People." This is certainly the
prime eloquence of the Quarter-Deck. It is however but
a specimen ; for I could proceed in this manner, from page
to page.

The more I consider Mr. G. as a writer, an orator, a
scholar, or in his *pretensions* to be a man of sense, the more
I discover in his Address talents without cultivation,
knowledge without difcernment, and history without
truth. The whole, as a Composition, with all its " mob
" of Metaphors, unlike Similes, and ill-paired Figures," is
beft described in Mr. Pope's lines.

" All these the Rhetor, like Bœotia's Queen,
Beholds through fogs that magnify the scene ;
He, tinsell'd o'er in robes of varying hues,
With self-applause his wild creation views ;
Sees momentary monsters rise and fall,
And with his own fools colours gilds them all."(*q*)

Such is the ADDRESS, parts of which would disgrace the
exercise of a school-boy, delivered and publifhed *for the
use of* A GREAT NATION, by a Rhetorician who
received FIFTY THOUSAND POUNDS, as a national
reward for his *eloquence*, abilities, and exertions,

voted

(*q*) Dunciad, B. 1.

Divine Machaon ! should thy views extend,

Baker (*q*) must bow, and learned Milman (*r*) bend,

Hence then, and trace the Rhine's polluted flood,

The ruffian plunder, and the price of blood :

Mark the mild guardians of the Gallick land !

Justice, the lion's portion in her hand ;   90

Mercy,

by a *most discerning* Parliament, in an hour of epidemick zeal, or phrenzy. The Addrefs pretends to be the produftion of an Orator, a Statesman, and a Scholar, in a day of the moft inftant peril, and of general national diftrefs, never before experienced or conceived ;—by A PATRIOT, retiring from the scene of publick affairs, to give publick counsel, and infuse wifdom, good sense, knowledge, discretion, and the motives *to action* in his Fellow-Citizens, when the fleets and armies of the Directory of France were hovering on the Coaft of Ireland, fraught with desolation, rebellion, revolution, and misery beyond all calculation. Such is the patriotifm, such is the difcernment, such is the rhetorick, of HENRY GRATTAN, Ex-representative of the City of Dublin ! ! !

(*p*) " It appeared to *us*, that the *best* way of starving that spirit, was *to remove the food*." Grattan. p. 16.

(*q*) Sir George Baker, Bart. Physician to the King, of high professional character and learned accomplifhments.

(*r*) Francis Milman, M. D. a Physician in London, of great skill and eminence, and extenfive practice; a gentleman of classical erudition, polite manners, and of a well-cultivated understanding.

Mercy, in tears o'er fallen sparrows shed,

Beneath her feet the murder'd Monarch's head;

Philanthropy, that fain would fold the globe

With arms fraternal, in a tyrant's robe !

See Directorial Chanceries elate

Stamp their diplomas for each neutral State;

Licentiate Kings in humbled order stand,

Till Rewbell nods, to sweep them from the land.

With horror *now* my purer fancy paints

Ïerne's clans, and democratick saints; (*t*)　　　100

Relicks and rags on Gallick standards fly,

And the *green* rabble of the papal sky. (*tt*)

Oh, if Helvetia yet thy soul alarms,

Who mourns her late resolve, and tardy arms;

Pause o'er the fragments of that vengeful storm,

Lo, Rocks, and Ruins, *Rhetors,* and Reform !

Then

(*t*) " The popular and energetick Romanists, the United Irishmen."　　　　Grattan.

(*tt*) See at large Dr. Duigenan's masterly and irrefragable arguments on the subject of the Roman Catholick religion and principles, in his answer to Mr. Grattan's Address. P. 41 to 45. and p. 123 to 141.

Then if one honeft pang should rend thy breast,

Look *homeward*—and let Conscience tell the rest.

Hence to the field with Treason's victims strewn;

Reap the dread harvest which *thy* hand has sown:

The robe Prætorian, (*u*) and the learned gown, 112

The' insulted Senate, and the loyal town,

(Each smuggled honour from thy temples torn,)

Brand thee alike with epidemick scorn.

Now loyal flames extend from sire to son;

CORNWALLIS (*w*) shall compleat, what CLARE
    begun;

The storm, by aweful justice taught to roll,

With Patrick's (*x*) lightning fhoot through Grattan's
    soul;   —   One

(*u*) The freedom of the City of Dublin, &c. &c. &c. has
been taken from Mr. Grattan by the vote of the Citizens,
Freemen, &c. and his picture removed from the College.

(*w*) MARQUIS CORNWALLIS, Lieutenant Governor,
&c. &c. of Ireland, 1798. I cannot better characterize
this great and good man, when the tenor of his virtuous and
honourable life, and of his publick conduct military and
civil, is impartially considered, than in the following lines.
"Non qui præcipiti traheret simul omnia casu;
Sed qui maturo vel læta, vel aspera, rerum
Consilio momenta regens, nec tristibus impar,
Nec pro successu nimius, *spatiumque morandi*,
Vincendique modum mutaris nôsset habenis."

D

One heart, one hand unite each sister realm,

Direct the force, and guide ONE COMMON HELM. 120

Hence, nor presume with hateful steps to rove

By Twitnam's shore, or Windsor's royal grove.

  Go rather, and thy wayward measures fill,

" Where *the young Wantons* sport on Anna's hill;" (z)

Blue-bells and red-caps on each bush shall blow,

While Erskine prattles, and while Seine shall flow.

See there the midnight solemn tapers shine,

(So Gilray's (a) patriot pencil rais'd the Shrine ;)

While choral Dæmons, from the gulph beneath,

                        Marseilles'

  (x) See the Answer of Dr. Patrick Duigenan to Mr. Grattan's Address.—I refer to what is said in the preface to this poem.

  (z) " Or where ye, Muses, sport on Cooper's Hill ;
      On Cooper's Hill eternal wreaths shall grow,
      While lasts the mountain, and while Thames shall flow."
                    Pope's Windsor Forest.

  N. B. St. Anne's Hill is the feat of the Hon. Charles James Fox.

  (a) James Gilray ; the political Hogarth of the present day. His pencil has been, and continues to be, of essential service in the publick cause of Great Britain and Ireland. In some of the higher efforts of his genius, such as, " The Sun of the Constitution,—The Homage of

Marseilles' dire notes in hoarser accents breathe, 130

Tartarian anthems! mix'd with sullen moans

Of bleeding martyrs, and rebellious groans.

Mark well the couch, whence Charles from slumber
    starts

At heads, which Treason join'd, and Juftice parts;

Blood-bolter'd Hamilton (*b*) for vengeance calls,

Vengeance re-echoes from the Castle walls.

Then view the scene, where Charles with senates tir'd,

Stung by contempt, with Gallick phrenzy fir'd,

Shunn'd by the Nobles, by the Commons spurn'd,

While with infuriate thought his bosom burn'd, 140

In treason-taverns bold, address'd the ring,

Bow'd to *his Sovereign*, (*c*) and forgot his King.

                                    But
Leviathan—The Shrine at St. Anne's Hill," and others
which might be named, it is justice to fay, that the design,
skill, execution, and intention deserve the highest praise.
Multæ Veneris, cum pondere et arte.

(*b*) The Rev. and unfortunate Dr. Hamilton, one of the
first victims of the Irish Rebellion.

(*c*) Le Peuple Souverain! as the French Jacobin tyrants
term it, and, " The Sovereignty of the People," as the
English Jacobins echo it. I am astonished that such
nonsensical democratick babble can be endured any longer,
even at a tavern from Mr. Barrister Erskine.

But soft; prepare unwelcome truth to hear;
That Botanist (*cc*) may whisper in your ear,
Few plants will bear the test of English ground,
It proves the *race* (*d*) corrupt, the root unsound:
And GRATTAN, mark'd for ever, shall retain
Hibernian forehead, and Hibernian brain.

Time was, when Statesmen, high in fame and place,
With proud distinction *my* retreat would grace; 150
Would court my friendship, soothe my aching head,
By study soften'd, and " with books well-bred;"
Fond to unbend, they sought familiar ease;
I never flatter'd, yet could always please.
Then oft with Ministers would GENIUS walk:
Oxford and St. John lov'd with Swift to talk;

Dorset

(*cc*) Mr. FOX, the Linnæus of St. Anne's Hill.

(*d*) i. e. The *flavour* of the foil; the word *race* is applied by W. Temple to the *natural force* of the intellect. See Temple's Essay on Gardens.

Dorset with Prior, and with Queensb'ry, Gay,
And Hallifax with Congreve charm'd the day;
The Muse her Addison to Somers join'd,
The noblest Statesman to the pureſt (e) mind.   160

But in these dark, forlorn, distracted days,
Though D'Arcy smil'd, and foster'd Mason's lays,
Few friends are found for poetry and wit,
From North well-natur'd to imperial Pitt.
Yet when his Country's deep-felt interest calls,
Himself shall plant the standard on the walls;
Duty (ee) shall urge, what talents vainly claim
By native lustre, and untitled name.

But

(e) Mr. Pope is here supposed to speak of Mr. Addison
without remembrance of their jealousies and disagreements;
and as Mr. Addiſon deserved of mankind.

" Their tears, their little triumphs o'er,
Their *human paſſions* now no more,
Save Charity, that glows beyond the tomb."
                                        Gray.

(ee) From some late attentions, which have done the
Minister honour; and even from the dedication of Mr.
Maurice's

D 3

But oh, what scenes, what varied wonders press,
What visionary forms my fancy bless !   170
Now fears deject, now blessings round me smile,
The follies, and the glories of the Isle.

Supplies are prompt for Pitt's directing hand ;
Pactolus rolls through all the wealthy land ;
But still with Tully's speech his wisdom hold,
He never said, *Œconomy is cold* ; (*f*)

No,

Maurice's Second Volume of the History of Hindostan
to Mr. Pitt, I am inclined to express the wish of the
Poet ;

> *Hinc* priscæ redeant artes ; felicibus inde
> Ingeniis pandatur iter ; despectaque Musæ
> Colla levent !

(*f*) An expression of Mr. Pitt in the H. of C. in
November, 1798, imprudent, however qualified. " Magnum
Vectigal est Parsimonia," were the words of Cicero.
The want of œconomy, (I know what I advance) is the
chief and prominent defect of Mr. Pitt's administration.
With what ease might it be remedied !

But in the great and master principles of government, by
which *alone* the constitution of these kingdoms, and of all
civilized

No, 'tis the life-blood, feeding all the state,

The source of all that's safe, and all that's great:

Hence Palaces for Bankrupt-Bankers rise, (*ff*)

And Monarchs wonder with enquiring eyes.   180

A voice exclaims, in dread financial search,

" *Commute the Tythes* :" and, lo, a falling Church !

On Sabbath's violated (*g*) eve I see

The' unhallow'd combat, by the murderer's tree :

Reflect, State-Suicides, while Empires nod,

None serve their Country, who forget their Gop.

By Scott unaw'd, behold Ambrosio (*gg*) stand ;

And Lewis braves the justice of the land :

Avonius

civilized society in Europe can be maintained, I am ready, with every loyal and reflecting subject, to declare and to style Mr. Pitt, the

EVERSO JUVENIS NATUS SUCCURRERE SÆCLO!

(*ff*) Some abuses of this kind should be looked into: what is granted liberally, should be expended wisely.

(*g*) Excidat illa dies ævo, ne postera credant Sæcula ! nos certè taceamus.——

(*gg*) Ambrosio, or The Monk, a Romance, by M. Lewis, Efq. M. P.—See the Remarks upon it in the Preface to the Fourth Dialogue of the Purfuits of Literature.

D 4

Avonius sneaks, his daily progress known,

A rustick hermit peering o'er the town ;   190

Carlisle is lost with Gillies in surprize,

As Lysias (h) charms soft Jersey's classick eyes ;

Knight (hh) half-recants ; the luscious Darwin sings ;

The Baby Rhymer flaps his flimsy wings ;

While HE, whose lightest works might soothe the land,

Like the dull ostrich, drops them in the sand.

Through air, fire, earth, how unconfin'd we range !

What veil has Nature ? and what works are strange ?

All mark each varied mode of heat and light,

From the spare Rumford to the pallid Knight ;   200

Though Watson's aid in vain his Chemia calls,

The modest * Hatchett no fatigue appalls :

The

(h) An Athenian Orator, whose works attracted Lady Jersey's attention through the medium of Dr. Gillies's translation. The Oration on Eratosthenes is rather singular.

(hh) See the Preface to the Second Volume of the Ionian Antiquities published by the Dilettanti Society.

[*] Charles Hatchett, Esq. F. R. S. a gentleman of ingenuity, and of liberal, intense application to the study of Chemistry : The R. S. presented him with their medal for his chemical researches in 1798. Much may be expected from the ability and patient labours of this gentleman.

The Elements contract; the water (*hh*) flies;

Balloons ascend; gas quickens; spirit dies.

Trace all the *rural* whims, that sprout and spread

In branches intricate through Sinclair's head,

Who ships, in ploughs; in oxen, Tritons sees;

. The waves, in furrows; and in masts, the trees. (*i*)

Behold from Brobdignag that wondrous Fleet,   209

With Stanhope's (*ii*) keels of thrice three hundred feet!

Be ships, or politicks, great Earl, thy theme,

Oh, first prepare the navigable stream.

The healing Art, to maxims seldom true,

Changes with ease old fancies for the new :

See

(*hh*) Alluding to the experiments of the learned and very ingenious Mr. Cavendish on Water, and it's constituent principles.

(*i*) In allusion to Sir John Sinclair's *novel* ideas on marine subjects, delivered in the House of Commons some time in Nov. 1798.

(*ii*) The present Earl Stanhope is one of the first experimental Naval projectors in England. He will possibly recollect the proposition he made to an eminent Ship-builder.

See Jenner (*iii*) there, the laurel (*k*) on his brow,

Leads up Sabrina's Commutation-Cow! (*l*)

Pasiphäe

(*iii*) I allude to the present important controversy in the medical world. See the Inquiries by the Doctors Jenner and Pearfon, " into the causes and effects of the Variolæ Vaccinæ, or *Cow*-Pox, principally with a view to supersede and extinguish the Small Pox." London, 1798.—The evidence appears as yet to be wholly negative; but it is not my intention to examine all the cases and writings, " *Vaccinus* quæcumque recepit *Apollo*." Dr. Pearson's Treatise is inscribed to Sir George Baker, Bart. which entitles the subject to the consideration of the Faculty. (Nov. 1798.)

(*k*) This appears from the sublime and poetical words of the ingenious Dr. Pearson; " I would not pluck a sprig of *laurel* from THE WREATH *which decorates the brow* of Dr. JENNER!" Enquiry on the Cow-Pox, p. 3. But still— Et *Vitulâ* tu dignus et Hic.

(*l*) Dr. Jenner is a Physician in *Gloucefterfhire*, and I very naturally suppose that *Sabrina*, the tutelar nymph of the Severn, pointed out to him the fair object of his discovery.

Pasiphäe (*m*) smiles at Syphilitick stains ;

But Home (*n*) sheds brazen tears, and Earle (*n*)

    complains.

                      Mark

(*m*) Hic crudelis amor Tauri, *suppoſtaque* furto
   Pasiphäe, mixtumque genus.   *Æn.* 6.

It is impossible to say, how far the *Commutation Syſtem* may be carried in this country. It first begun with a little *Tea*, which the celebrated DOCTOR WILLIAM PITT, (a Practitioner of great and extensive reputation, who settled in London about the year 1784, and still continues to give advice to the publick in Downing-Street,) recommended to his Patients, as a cheap medicine in lieu of *light*, *air*, and some other non-naturals. The physicians are now beginning to pay their addresses to the Cow ; and the Clergy are afraid that some State-Doctors may offer the same gallant attention to the calves, pigs, and lambs, merely by way of *change*. But if the medical commutation-act is to extend to *other* diseases, I fear that it will be easier for Sir George Baker, Bart. to appease the classical Manes of Fracastorius, than to console some of the medical profession on the extinction of the Nymph Syphilis. (Nov. 1798.)

(*n*) Everard Home and James Earle, Esqrs. two Surgeons of eminence in London.

Mark now, where bold, with fronts metallick shine

William and *Mary*, (*o*) on one common coin :　220

Full

(*o*) WILLIAM GODWIN and MARY WOOLSTONCRAFT GODWIN.—I refer the reader to the Notes in the third and fourth Dialogues of the Pursuits of Literature, for the exposition and exposure of Philosopher *William*. At present it is curious to compare the *living* works of Mr. Godwin, with the posthumous writings of the frail fair one; and above all with *the Philosopher's* unblushing account of his own Wife's † amours, life, and conduct. " Ego te ceventem, Sexte, verebor?" Mr. Godwin has fully explained and exemplified what he calls " the most odious of monopolies," Marriage; and has published all his philosophical transactions with *Mary*, previous to his *monopolizing* her. When Mrs. Bellamy's and Mrs. Baddeley's Memoirs were printed, we knew what we were to expect. But when a philosopher, a reformer of states, a guide in *fine* writing, belles lettres, morality, and legislation, like Mr. Godwin, publishes *such* Memoirs of *his own Wife*, what must we say ? " *Sic liceat tumulo scripsisse,* CATONIS MARCIA?"

I have

† See " Memoirs of Mary Woolstoncraft Godwin, by William Godwin.

Full freedom to the genial bed restore,

And

I have been informed, that previous to the important, or as he thinks, unimportant nuptial *contract*, Philofopher Godwin consulted a descendant of Trouillogan in Rabelais, who states in two chapters, (a) " How the Philosopher " Trouillogan *handled the difficulty of marriage*; together " with the answers of that great Ephectick and Pyrrhonian " Philosopher on that subject." A very short specimen of the doubtful doubts, as *handled* by Panurge and that great man, may not be unpleasant or inapplicable.

" Panurge.—Should I marry?

Philosopher Trouillogan.—There is some likelihood,

Panurge.—But if I do not marry?

Philosopher.—*I see in that no inconvenience.*

Panurge.—You do not?

Philosopher.—None truly; *if* my eyes deceive me not.

Panurge.—Yea; but I reckon *more than five hundred inconveniences.*

Philosophor.—Reckon them, &c. &c.

Panurge then complies with the Philofopher's demand, and enumerates fome of the *five hundred* inconveniences of not being married, with intermediate remarks and suggestions by Philosopher Trouillogan, afterwhich the Dialogue proceeds thus.

" Panurge.—Well then; *if* I marry, I shall be a Cuckold,

Philosopher.—*One would fay fo.*

Panurge.

(a) Rabelais Book 3. Ch. 35, and 36;

And prove whate'er Vanini (*p*) prov'd before.

Fierce

Panurge.—But are *you* married, Philosopher Trouillogan, or are you not ?

Philosopher.—Neither the one, nor the other ; and yet *both together.*" &c. &c. &c.

At the conclusion of this Nuptial Dialogue, in which Panurge with all the keenness of his dialecticks pushed the Philosopher home, and probed him to the quick, the great Gargantua, who had heard the whole disputation most patiently from the beginning to the end, non sine stupore, suddenly rose and exclaimed, " Praised be heaven! but above all for bringing the world to *that height of refinedness,* beyond what it was, when I was first acquainted with it; that now the most learned and prudent philosophers are *not ashamed* to be seen entering the porches of the schools of the Pyrrhonian, Aporrhetick, Sceptick, and Ephectick Sects ! It will be henceforth found an easier enterprize to take lions by the necks, oxen by the horns, or goats by the beard, than to entrap *such* philosophers in their words !" By which it appears, that the great Gargantua made no allusion, by anticipation, to Philosopher Godwin, who certainly may be *entrapped* with great ease *in his words*, at least in such as he has thought proper to print. But as Panurge said, " Parlons sans disjunctives."

It

Fierce passion's slave, she veer'd with every gust,

Love,

It is however certain, that many parts of this Dialogue must have administered great comfort to Mr. Godwin. But before I can persuade the reader to peruse the Memoirs of *Mary* by her own husband, and all Mary's own posthumous writings revised, and perhaps a little *improved*, by *Mary's* husband, on justice, marriage, rights, wrongs, and so on, to the end of the chapters by *"He and She"*, the gentleman and the lady, the *two parties* in the contract; the philosopher and philoso*phess*, the citizen and the citi*zette*, recourse must be had to abler arguments than any which I can produce. I must request him to study the chapter in which it is shewn, " *How* Pantagruel persuaded Panurge to take " counsel of a fool." Perhaps the Philosopher, may here say with Panurge, " Je mettray *mes lunettes* a " cette oreille gauche, pour vous ouir plus clair."

I still think, that these memoirs and posthumous works of Mary Woolstoncraft Godwin should be earnestly recommended to every father and mother, to every guardian and every mistress of a boarding school throughout the kingdoms of Great Britain,

as

Love, Rights, and Wrongs, Philosophy, and Lust :

But
as " A convenient Manual of fpeculative debauchery,
with the most select arguments for reducing it into
practice;" for the amusement, initiation, and instruction of young ladies from sixteen to twenty-five †
years of age, who wish to figure in life, and afterwards in Doctors Commons and the King's Bench;
or ultimately in the notorious receptacles of *patrician
prostitution*. This is the end of the new school,
certain, inevitable, irreversible.

The force of ridicule indeed on this subject can hardly
be exhausted upon *the manner* in which these
philosophers treat it seriously. The words of Shakspeare press upon the mind ;
" I have a speech of fire, that fain would blaze,
But that *their folly* drowns it."

Yet still the consequences are so fatal, and so extensive
in their iniquity, that we must also strive to repress them
by reasoning, and by every method which learning
and reflection can supply or suggest. It is one nefarious system of philosophick *foolery*, which some
persons suffer themselves to play with too long, till
by

† The Annals of Doctors Commons extend the term.

But some more wise, in metaphysick air,

Weigh

by flowery language, or rather by ridiculous terms, they are at last betrayed into a forgetfulness of original sound principles, and of sober sense. They read, till they persuade themselves, that they can see " the *tear* of " affection (like Mr. Godwin's) *chrystallized* by the " power of *genius*, and converted *into a permanent* " *literary brilliant !!!* (a)   But by this nonsense, by this *foolery*, by this substitution of words, aided by the general corruption of morals throughout Europe, the great revolutionary terrors have been brought into action.

Surely parents and guardians should, with the most affectionate earnestness, for the sake of their country, of themselves, of their dearest hopes, and of every institution divine or human, warn and caution young female readers against such writings as Mrs. Woolstoncraft Godwin's ; if they perceive an inclination in them to peruse her works.   I hate literary prohibitions , in such a case, which are generally ineffectual ; but gentle admonition will always have some force on young minds and ingenuous tempers.   It is a just and proper compliment to observe, that " if you speak to women in " a style and manner proper to approach them, they " never fail to improve by Counsel. (b)" Their instructors

E

therefore

(a) In *such* language has publick criticism been delivered to the world in one of the Reviews, on Mr. Godwin's Memoirs of his Wife.

(b) Tatler No. 139.

Weigh the man's wits (*q*) against the Lady's hair. (*qq*)

Mark

therefore should inform them, that such opinions and doctrines are founded upon the contempt and rejection of that system, which has *alone* given comfort and dignity to women in the social state, and placed them in honour, confidence, and security.

The Christian code speaks to them of no species of subjection to men, as to masters; but it teaches them to look for support, affection, and comfort from men, as fathers, brothers, and husbands. Is it any wonder, that the Creator should best understand the specifick distinctions, and relations of his creatures? Whatever is consistent with the delicacy of their frame, the care of their minds, the cultivation of their talents, and the superintendence of their family and children, is offered and enjoyed freely and fully by women in this Christian kingdom. These philosophers, of either sex, first make marriage the object of their most peculiar ridicule, and then refine it into prostitution.

What can women expect to learn from such writings? To approach them, is to tread, perhaps without design and generally with original rectitude, in the vestibule of the Corinthian temple of seduction and adultery. To no other altars can they be conducted by such a priestess as Mrs. Woolstoncraft Godwin. But they should be reminded, that in the gloomy back-ground they may plainly discern the cavern of suicide.

It

Mark next, how fable, language, fancy flies

To

It is unpleasant to criticize, even in the gentlest manner, the works of the female pen. We have ladies of ingenuity, learning, and of every varied excellence; I would name Mrs. Carter, and Mrs. Hannah More, in the most eminent sense. The genius of the authoress of the Elegy on Captain Cook, the poetry of Mrs Charlotte Smith, and the sombrous fancy and high-wrought imagery of Mrs. Radcliffe, cannot ' be mentioned without admiration. But when female writers *forget the character* and delicacy of their sex; when they take the trumpet of democracy, and let loose the spirit of gross licentiousness, moral and political, in contempt of those laws, which are their best shield, and of that religion, which has invariably befriended and protected them; the duty which is owing to the defence of our country, and of all female virtue, comfort, and happiness, calls for strong animadverfion. When their softness is laid aside, when they appear as the *Minervas* (a) of the modern illuminated syftems, and the Bellonas (b) of France; in such cases men must be excused, if they would avoid deftruction even from *their* writings.

Young female readers often find in Mrs. Godwin's treatises a lively fancy, a specious reasoning, a bold

E 2   spirit,

(a) Baruel Memoirs of Jacobinism, Vol. 3.

(b) ʿΑι τ᾽ ανδρων πολεμον κατακοιρανεʋσιν,

Ειτ᾽ αρ᾽ Αθηναιη, ειτε ΠΤΟΛΙΠΟΡΘΟΣ Ενυω.

Hom. Il. 5.

To Ghosts, and Beards, and Hoppergollop's (r) cries :

Lo,

spirit, and flights of ideas to which they have been unaccustomed. The possession and the exertion of these ideas they sometimes, in a fatal moment, conceive to be actual liberty, and effectual freedom from restraint, and the enthralment of prejudice. They drink deep, and are intoxicated with words and fancies, till. they are tempted beyond their strength, and become " *incapable of their own distress.*" Their weedy trophies of liberty, philosophy, and emancipation, fall into the stream together with themselves, their innocence, their comfort, their dignity, and their happiness, to rise no more. (Nov. 1798.)

(p) Vanini, the celebrated atheist, who wished he had not been born in wedlock. " Utinam extra legitimum " torum procreatus fuissem, &c." Such is the blasphemous, idle rant on the subject in his treatise, " De Admirandis Naturæ Secretis."

(q) I shall take my leave of Mr. Godwin (for I have no present intention to examine any more of his works specifically) with some observations on the general tendency of all such authors and their works.

In the present state of civil society, and of political order so wisely established, so vigorously maintained, and so honourably recommended in this still flourishing, opulent, and powerful kingdom ; it is difficult to restrain the emotion of the breast, and the indignation of the

under-

Lo, from the' abyss, unmeaning Spectres drawn, 229
The Gothick glass, blue flame, and flick'ring lawn !

Choak'd

understanding at such nefarious writings, and desolating principles. The arms, the instruments, and the
agents are before us, and are now understood. It was
the strong language of Cicero; " Demonstro vitia;
" tollite : denuncio vim, arma ; removete." * We
would recover the health which is gone, and the soundness
which is loft. I am of opinion, that they may both be
recovered. But we must all strive, in our several capaci-
ties, to direct the vessel of the publick mind, and of the
national understanding, in a straight and undeviating course;
or, as it is well expressed in one of the Orphick fragments
preferved by Clemens, (a) Ιθυνειν Κραδιης νοερόν κυτος.

In the sublime, but often fanciful theology, or as I would
rather term it, the *Theonomy*, exhibited in the Timæus
of Plato, and more fully in the commentary of Proclus,
we read of the Εγκοσμιοι Θεοι, or superintending
mundane deities. I would not insist upon the imaginary
visions of any man, however great ; but in the way of
adaptation, they have often a force and analogy, which
is neither unpleasing nor unfruitful. I am sure the present modern philosophical writers, such as Condorcet,
and his mongrel disciples in England, Godwin and
others, have no pretensions to the reverence of
mankind, as mundane deities. Their aim is not to
exalt

* Cic. Philipp. 1. Sect. 10.
(a) Clement. Alexandrin. L. 5. p. 443. Ed. Lugd. Bat. 1616.

E 4

Choak'd with vile weeds, our once proud Avon strays ;

                              When

exalt the soul of man, but to depress and degrade it to the beast, or in Sir Thomas More's indignant language, " ad pecuini corpusculi vilitatem." (b)

.It is remarkable that Sir Thomas More, in his Republick of Utopia, declared that a person who entertained and professed such sentiments, as the modern philosophy holds forth and inculcates, was not worthy to be numbered among rational men, much lefs to be enrolled among the Citizens. His reason was this ; that a contempt of all laws and of all institutions was a neceffary consequence of such opinions, when uncontrolled. His words are remarkable : " Illum ne hominum quidem ducunt numero, *tantum abest ut inter Cives ponant*, quorum instituta moresque, *si per metum liceat*, omnes floccifacturus sit." † Now we have lived to see, that *fear* has not restrained *such Citizens* as Mr. Godwin and others ; and they have accordingly vilified, set at nought, and held out to contempt the laws, the religion, the manners, and the institutions of their country, which defends and protects them, in conformity to the opinion of Sir Thomas More. Such Citizens maintain the doctrines of dissolution, not of compact ; the frame and body of Society drops into pieces member

                              after

(b) Mori Utopia L. 2.

† Mori Utopia, Lib. 2. p. 234. Ed. Glasg. 1750.

When Novels die, and rise again in plays :

No

after member, when the principle of continuity is withdrawn. " Nigidium vidi; Cratippum cognovi."‡

Men of the greatest minds and of the widest intellectual views, have frequently indulged themselves in forming Utopian Republicks, and have often unadvisedly dwelt too much upon the unavoidable evils of Society. Such pure spirits are naturally offended with every species of evil. But when such men, as Sir Thomas More, suffer their minds to be amused (I fear it is but an amusement at best) with speculative or imaginary political excellence, or rather perfection, how different are their *principles*, and the result of their thoughts from those of sciolists and sophists. We all regret the loss of that Republick, which the genius of Cicero had constructed. There are indeed a few noble fragments of the building, preserved by Lactantius, Macrobius, and Augustine ; though the plan of the entire edifice by the hand of that consummate practical Statesman, and experienced Philosopher, cannot be traced from the remains. I believe he would have corrected many of the errors of Plato.

But it is not without it's use to compare, (if we have leisure, and as far as we may compare them) the work of the sublimest Heathen Philosopher with that of the Christian Statesman Sir Thomas More. I speak upon the whole; for I am sensibel of their errors, particularly in

E 3   the

‡ Cicero in Timæo, Fragm. de Universitate, Sect. 1.

No Congress props our Drama's falling state,

The

the Athenian: yet when we think of Plato, we must not forget the state of the Heathen world, antecedent to Christianity. But notwithstanding, both these great men proceeded upon the true dignity of the human mind, when undebased by vice; and bottomed their opinions upon the most solid science. Their views were large, comprehensive, connected. They knew the nature and the state of man; and they saw what it would admit, and what it would not bear. When they proposed some amendment, or some institution which did not then exist, it was in the way of suggestion, and not of dogmatical imposition. They never moved through the state with the sword, and the scythe in their hands. What they saw, was with the eye of a well-instructed mind, long prepared by study and exercised in discernment.

These persons in their generations, were indeed among the superintending mundane deities of their country. Not so the modern *Directors* of human affairs; though they aspire to be thought, and to act, as the gods of this nether world. They would sit with the thunderbolt in their hands, and the storms under their feet. Yet even Mythology condemns them, and points to her Salmoneus. But we stand·not on the ground of fable: for what is the most extended and the most desolating power of tyrant and of rampant wickedness on the earth, for a few days or a few years, before HIM " who (for his own inscrutable purposes) putteth down and

" setteth

The modern ultimatum is, " Translate."

Thence

" setteth up, and ALONE RULETH in the kingdoms of
" men!"

The confideration of these modern philofophers offers
also the strongest argument for the vigorous and unremitting prosecution of *well-directed* study, in all the publick
seats of education in these kingdoms. Plato declared,
that one of the causes of atheism is, " a certain ignorance
" very grievous, which notwithstanding has the appear-
" ance of the greatest wisdom." *(d)* This apparent
wisdom must be combated, and overthrown by reason and
erudition ; the fallacy must be pointed out, and the
effect, when perfected, shewn to be DEATH moral,
mental, and political.

I am confident that the Universities of Oxford
and Cambridge will be still found to be the best
and most solid bulwarks (I trust not the only ones)
of true science, and of the legitimate cultivation of the
understanding, if they adhere to their *original* principles ;
but not otherwise. By this method of reasoning, I
should conceive, that the works of Hooker, Pearson,
Stillingfleet, and Barrow, have been lately reprinted at
the Clarendon press of the university of Oxford, with
singular judgment and true difcernment of the time.
They have been sent forth again into the world, " rejoicing

D 4   " like

(d) Αμαθια μαλα. χαλεπη δοκεσα ειναι μεγιστη Φρονησις.
Plato de Leg. L. 10.

Thence sprout the morals of the German school;

The

" like giants, to run their course." We are in general either deftroyed, or loft, or warped, or led astray, for want of the primal (dd) knowledge. I fpeak not here of the great incontrovertible abstraĉt sciences of the mathematicks, and of natural philosophy founded on a severe and sublime geometry. These cannot be disputed. But I am speaking of the *moral* cultivation of the underftanding, that the frame and good order of religion and government may be *still* supported in these realms, by a succeffion of young men well educated, and judiciously conducted in the paths of erudition. An acute and intelligent obferver of history once inscribed a most valuable work *(e)* in these emphatick words : " To the hope of England, its young gentry, is dedicated, the glory of it, its ancient statesmen ; a renowned ancestry, to an honourable posterity." I wifh to see these words continued, and embodied with strength and energy in Great Britain ; her laws will never abhor such a perpetuity.

I have

(dd) The words of Plato are worthy of observation. Προς τυτοις, όταν Πολιτειαι κακοι και λογοι κατα πολεις ιδιχ και δημοσιᾳ λεχθωσιν, ετι δε μαθηματα μηδαμη τυτων ιατικν εκ νεων μανθανται, ταυτη κακοι παντες οἱ κακοι. Ὡν αιτιατεον μεν της φυτευοντας μαλλον η φυτευομενυς, και της τρεφοντας, των τρεφομενων. Plato in Timæo. p. 87. Vol. 3. Ed. Serrani.

(e) State Worthies; from the Reformation to the Revolution, by David Lloyd; re-published by Charles Whitworth, Esq. in two volumes.

The Chriſtian sinks, the Jacobin bears rule :

No

I have often, when discoursing on education, dwelt with peculiar earnestness on the dignity and wisdom of the Greek writers in almoſt every department of science, poetry, philosophy, politicks, and morality. I think I have observed, that the modern political theoriſts, who are either not versed in them at all, or but superficially, and who therefore hold them in contempt, have generally wandered the widest and the wildest in theſe days of confuſion, diſtraction, and convulſion. Aristotle, Plato, and Thucydides, to mention no others, well knew what was the tyrannical nature of a democracy, and all its appendages. None have more strongly or more justly characterized and depicted it ; none have held it out to greater reprobation and abhorrence. They teach us alternately by reaſon, and by example.

The writings of theſe great men have a perpetual youth. Like the ſun, their light is always new, yet always the same ; the source of mental life, health, vigour, chearfulneſs, and fecundity. It guided our forefathers, and it will guide us if we attend to it. The Commentator, or rather the animated rival of Plato, has words which, on such a subject, it is neither unnatural nor improper to produce and to adapt. Οινοχοει αυτοις ἡ Ἡϐη. Τον ὁλον αισθητον Κοσμον ὁρωσιν· ατρεπτοις και ακλινεσι νοημασι χρωμενοι, πληρῶσι τα παντα της δημιυργικης αυτων προνοιας. Συνεστιν αυτοις κυριοτη θεοτη;, τη μεν νοησει το αχραντον επιλαμπυσα. (f)

I would

(f) Procli Comment. in Timæum Platonis, L. 5. p. 334. Ed. Baſil. 1534.

No virtue shines, but in the peasant's mien,

No

I would yet add a few words on thefe modern philosophers. They sometimes tell us sneering, and in scorn,
that the code of Christians is the code of *equality*. They have
attempted to shew this more than once. But surely
we may ask, what is the equality held forth in the
Christian Scriptures? Is it not the equality of the creatures
before THE CREATOR? the equality of men before
GOD, and not before each other? They every where
speak of the political distinctions and ranks in society.
They ordain tribute to be paid to whom tribute is due;
custom to whom custom, honour to whom honour; and
they defcribe all *lawful* power, as derived from God.
The great Founder of it himfelf acknowledged the
image and superscription of Cæsar. His Apostles
declare the gradations of power, delegated by authority; they inculcate submiffion to the ordinances
of man, for the Lord's sake; to *the King*, as Supreme;
to Governors and Magistrates, as unto them who are
fent by him. Is this the political equality of the boasted
deliverers or oppressors of the world? How long shall
we *suffer* the tyrant, the blasphemer, the disorga-
nizing Sophist, to triumph and to *deceive* us?

Finally; when the modern systems are delineated, and
the chart of the opinions and doctrines laid out in
departments, I would ask, What is the Picture? What
are the objects? Are the things recommended and
enforced, either true, or honest, or just, or pure, or
lovely,

No vice, but in patrician robes, is seen; *(rr)*

Through

lovely, or of good report? Is there any thing to be
found and felt, but insolent domination; sanguinary, and
unrelenting ordinances; and the tyrannical suppreſſion
and overthrow of every exiſting Institution? Throughout
the whole of their ſyſtems, Is there any virtue, or any
praise, or any motive, which the good can approve, and
the wiſe ratify?

    I would ſay, Behold ye despisers, and tremble!
I would much rather say to my countrymen; Behold
and watch, that ye enter not into the porch and
vestibule of their " Plutonian Hall," by the temptation
of such Philosophy.

Through the gate,

Wide, open, and *unguarded*, S<small>ATAN</small> pass'd,
And all about found, (or made) desolate!

(Nov. 1793.)

(*qq*) Rape of the Lock, C. 5. v. 72.

(*r*) See an admirable piece of ridicule on the
German nonsense of the day, by a man of parts and wit,
in a pamphlet entitled, " My Night-gown and Slippers;
or, Tales in Verse, written in an Elbow-chair, by
George Colman the younger."(Printed for Cadell, 1797.)
It is called, The Maid of the Moor; or, the Water-
Fiend, concerning Lord Hoppergollop's Country House.

But

Through four dull acts the Drama drags, and drawls,

The fifth is stage-trick, and the curtain falls. 240

Thence

But I would refer with still greater pleasure, and with the most decided approbation, to " The Rovers, or the Double Arrangement," a Drama in the German style, in the Anti-Jacobin, or Weekly Examiner, No. 30 and 31. A WORK which has been of signal service to the publick, by the union of wit, learning, genius, poetry, and sound politicks.

(*rr*) The modern productions of the German stage, which silly men and women are daily translating, have one general *tendency* to Jacobinism. Improbable plots, and dull scenes, bombastick and languid prose alternately, are their least defects. They are too often the licensed vehicles of immorality and licentiousness, particularly in respect to marriage; and it should be remarked in the strongest manner, that all good characters are chiefly and *studiously* drawn from the lower orders; while the vicious and profligate are seldom, if ever, represented but among the higher ranks of society, and among men of property and possessions. This is not done without design.

It is indeed time to consider a little, *to what* and *to whom* we give our applause, in an hour of such general danger as the present. The Stage surely has the most powerful effect on the publick mind. The Author of *The School for Scandal*, with the purest and most patriotick intentions, long ago endeavoured to make

dishonesty,

Thence mark, where deep within that civick wood,

(No balm the trees distill, but lustral blood,)

An altar stands : there TOOKE his emblems lays,

Shoes, (s) razors, constitutions, straps, and stays ;

M'Cormick's (ss) libel ; Wakefield's sanguine gall ;

Pitt's rise pourtray'd, (t) and the Third Charles's fall ;

Historick

dishonesty, gambling, cheating, deep drinking, debauchery,
and libertinism, *appear* amiable and attracting in his character of Charles Surface; and the German Doctors of
the sock and buskin are *now* making no indirect attacks
on the very fundamentals of society and established
government, subordination, and religious principle ; the
vaunt-couriers of French anarchy, national plunder, and
GENERAL MISERY.

(s) The *insignia* of Citizen Hardy, Citizen Kingsbury,
Citizen Thelwall, Citizen Tom Paine, &c. &c. and all
those philosophers, scribblers, and Lecturers, who serve us

" In a double
Capacity, to preach and cobble."

(ss) Life of Edmund Burke by M'Cormick.

(t) Two pair of Portraits, of two Fathers and two Sons,
by John Horne Tooke.

Historick scraps of Brunswick or Berlin,

From flimsy Tqw'rs, and Belsham's (*tt*) Magazine.

There Porson, who the tragick (*x*) light relumes,

And Bentley's heat with Bentley's port assumes; 250

Dramatick

(*tt*) Mr. Belsham and Dr. Towers, two Dissenting Compilers of some information and ingenuity, who, by a figure of speech, would be thought Historians.—" They make lame mischief, but they mean it well."

(*x*) RICHARD PORSON, M. A. The most learned and acute Greek scholar of the present age. I allude to his late accurate and most valuable editions of the Hecuba, and Orestes of Euripides, whose integral works may be expected from the Professor. He modestly says, that they are published " in usum studiosæ Juventutis, or, as I suppose, for the use of schools and Tiros. * But his notes and remarks are not adapted to school-boys, to their wants, or their comprehension. He might as well have published them for the use of the Mamalukes in Egypt, or Bonaparte's Savants. The Professor should condescend to give some more general illustrations, and a selection of the Greek Scholia, if he would confer a real favour, as it is in *his* power to do, on the Masters of Schools and the Tutors of Colleges.

I have

* Tironum uʃibus potissimum destinata.

Præfat, ad Hecubam.

Dramatick Bardolph in his nuptial noose;
And wiser Perry, (*u*) from his prison loose,

Starts

I have still a partiality for a Latin Translation, executed
with care, and placed at the bottom of the page of
every Greek Author. It may now and then promote
idlenefs in mere boys; but it is of signal fervice to men
who are studious, if a learned Editor will give the full
meaning of the words, and correct the errors of preceding Translators. I am fure, few men can read Greek
Tragedies without consulting a Lexicon; and as *utility*
should be the motive of an Editor, I think a Latin
Translation indispensable. I cannot fubmit to argue
from the abuse of any convenience.

I hope Professor Porson will proceed in this important
revision, and perhaps effect the final establishment of the
Greek text of all the Tragedians. This H E can do, or no
man. He will be entitled to the publick gratitude
of the learned world.

Such a man, so gifted, so instructed, so adorned
with various science, I could wish to number among the
defenders of the best interests of his country. But at
present most unfortunately, in many of our learned men
there is, in regard to subjects of political and sacred
importance, a something which, in the phrase of Hamlet
" Doth all the noble substance often *dout*."(*)

Why is it so? If such men would commune with
their own hearts, and in their chamber, and be still, I
think it would be otherwise.

F

* Malone's reading of the passage.

Starts at the Diligence, that tells the tale
How blithe French Printers (y) to Guiana sail :
There reeling Morris, and his bestial songs ;
Blaspheming Monks ; and Godwin's female wrongs ;
The Lawyer's strumpet, and *disputed* draft ;
And Darwin, fest'ring from the Horatian shaft ;

Blossoms

(u) Perry, the Editor of the Morning Chronicle, was imprisoned three months in Newgate, for a libel on the House of Lords.

(y) The example of the Caravan of *Deportation*, or as it is called from the place of banishment, the *Guiana Diligence* in Paris, should be a warning to the editors and printers of such papers as the Courier, Morning Chronicle, the Star, &c. &c. how they abuse the patience and forbearance of the mild and lenient Government of England.

Under the bleſſings of French freedom and emancipation, what is the liberty of thinking, speaking, and writing ? The authors, the printers, and the booksellers, are crushed at once and equally, and either chained in dungeons, or seized and swept away from their native country, without hope and without judgment, unheard, unpitied, and unknown. Pro lege Voluntas !

But WE have yet a NATION to save ; we have millions of loyal men who never bowed the knee to the Baal of Jaco-

binism

Blossoms of love descend in roseate show'rs,

And last, Democracy exhales in flow'rs. (*yy*)   260

Behold La Crusca's Paridel advance,

From Courts, or Stews, from Florence, or from

  France :

Before him Swift and Addison retire,

He brings new prose, new verse, new lyrick fire ;

Proves a designer works without design,

And fathoms Nature with a Gallick line. ·

~But hark ! at Pearson's and at Hooker's voice,

The pillars of the sacred dome rejoice ;

And hail the day, when Stillingfleet is join'd

To Barrow's vast, immeasurable mind! (*z*)   270

                                                Geddes

binism; and we have also many who have *drawn back* from
the bloody idol, and turned unto righteousness to
the preservation of their souls, their bodies, and estates,
and the general deliverance of their country.

(*yy*) See Dr. ·Darwin's Botanick Garden and Loves
of the Plants.

(*z*) Alluding to the judicious and well-timed
republications of Hooker's Works, Pearson on the Creed,
Stillingfleet's Origines Sacræ, and a selection of Barrow's

Geddès (*a*) may wave his dark Egyptian rod ;

Britain still owns th' *inspiring* breath of GOD ;

Sees Truth emerge from Oriental (*b*) dreams,

And Gospel treasures roll down Indian streams.

The Dennes, and owlish Stukeleys of the day,

Retire abash'd at Lysons' (*c*) rising ray ;

The

Sermons, at the Clarendon Prefs in the University of
Oxford, in a convenient form, and for an easy consideration.

(*d*) Dr. Geddes, the Roman Catholick Divine, the
new Translator of the Bible. See some remarks on the
Doctor's attempt, in the Preface to the fourth Dialogue
of the Pursuits of Literature.

(*b*) See the Asiatick Researches, in particular those
by Sir William Jones, and Mr. Maurice's Indian
Antiquities, and his History of Hindostan, which have
afforded the most curious and important facts, if applied
with judgment and soberly investigated.—But we may
expect a work on the Sacred Writings, of the greatest
importance, and of the deepest erudition and ingenuity,
from a Gentleman, whom I shall not name. Yet perhaps,
" Nunc intelligitur, olim nominabitur."

(*c*) I cannot but observe, that the learned world has much
to expect in the improvement, reform, and conduct of the

study

The Macedonian march, the Libyan state,

On Rennell's (d) keen decisive labours wait;

And see each grateful Muse on Vincent (e) smile,

His kindred talents, and congenial toil.   280

Pitt once again revolves the Stagirite,

And bends o'er Plato by *Serranian* light;

Philosophy

---

study of our national Antiquities, from the genius, erudition, difcernment, active age, and unceasing diligence of SAMUEL LYSONS, Esq. F. R. and A. S.

(d) I allude to the works so long and so eagerly expected by the learned, from that consummate Geographer, and most accurate investigator, Major JAMES RENNELL.

(e) The Rev. WILLIAM VINCENT, D. D. Master of Westminster School. A Gentleman whose professional merits, deep erudition, and unwearied and fuccessful application to science, in the intervals of a laborious and honourablecalling, demand the most decided teftimony of publick approbation. I believe, I fpeak the general fense of every scholar in the kingdom. Surely an honourable retreat, and some distinguished mark of publick gratitude, should be offered *in time* to such men, as Dr. Vincent, who have devoted their talents and attainments to the

publick

Philosophy uprears her ancient head,

And Grecian truth in Grecian words is read ;

Arts, Arms, and Policy maintain their course,

And Science flows from her primæval source.

·· But now·I feel the' avenging thunder roar,

In British terror on the dusky shore ;

                                                    The

publick fervice, with unremitting diligence. The Masters of our great schools should be made *independent, in every sense, of their scholars.* This would stamp a dignity and firmness on their office and on their character, and the kingdom would derive great advantage from such a regulation.

I believe it is impossible to name such a work as Dr. Vincent's Translation of the Voyage of Nearchus, with all the learned illustrations, produced under the labour and constant pressure of so important an occupation, as the conduct of a great publick school. It has been received at home and abroad with equal attention and honour.

The Bog Serbonian (*f*) yawns for Gallia's doom;

And Pompey points to Bonaparte's tomb!   290

There, as in mournful pomp o'er Egypt's woes,

Th' embodied Majesty of Nilus rose,

In sounds of awful comfort NELSON spoke,

And the Palm wav'd obeisance to the Oak;

Firm, yet serene, the Christian Victor rode,

And on his flag inscrib'd, THE WILL OF GOD! (*g*)

                                        The

(*f*) "That Serbonian Bog,
Betwixt Damiata and Mount Casius old,
Where Armies whole have sunk." P. L. b. 2.

(*g*) The Victory of Admiral Lord NELSON on the
First of August, 1798, over the French Fleet on the
shores of the Nile; that signal interposition of the Divine
Providence.

"Illi *Justitiam* confirmavere triumphi;
PRÆSENTEM DOCUERE DEUM! nunc Sæcula discant
Indomitum nihil esse pio, tutumve nocenti!"

The guilty Nation shakes; her trophies fall:

The Crescent nods; and Selim yields to Paul:

The Hellespont expands in timely pride;

Fleets not her own adown the current glide;   300

The North-Star beams on Europe's parting night,

And the dawn reddens with effectual light!

I go: my Country's fate no more I mourn;

And pleas'd revisit my august sojourn."

November: 1798.

THE END.

A

TRANSLATION

OF THE

PASSAGES

CITED IN THE

PREFACE AND NOTES

TO THIS

P O E M.

~~~~

TRANSLATION,

&c. &c.

MOTTO TO THE POEM.

Voce fu per me udita,
Onorate l' altissimo Poeta!.
L'*Ombra sua torna.*   *Dante Inf. C.* 4.

"I heard a voice saying, Pay honour to the mighty Poet. *His Shade is returning.*"

CITATIONS IN THE PREFACE.

MOTTO TO THE PREFACE

Αστοις και Βασιλευ—
σιν διακρινειν ετυμον λογον ανθρωπων.
                   Pindar Pith. 1.

" That Citizens, Subjects, and Kings may be enabled to appreciate the true value and character of men."

P. 2.

Contra Illum cum dicum, faciam ut attentè audiatis.
                   Cicero Philipp. 2.

" When I speak against the man himself, I will take care to ensure your attention."

P. 7.

Licet omnibus, licet etiam mihi, dignitatem Patriæ tueri ; potestas modo veniendi in publicum sit, dicendi periculum non recuso.
                   Cicero Philipp. 1.

" It is the right of every man, it is even mine, to endeavour to support and vindicate the honour and dignity of his country ; and while I have the power of appearing before the publick, I decline not the danger of delivering my sentiments openly and boldly."

P. 11.

Erigite animos; retinete vestram dignitatem. Manet illa in Republicâ bonorum consensio; dolor accessit bonis viris, virtus non est imminuta.

Cicero Fragment. Orationis in Clodium, ap.
Epist. ad Attic. L. 1. E. 16.

" Raise up your minds; maintain your own dignity and high estimation. There is still throughout the state an unity of sentiment among the good; well-disposed men have been deeply affected at the scenes which have passed before them, but their virtue and spirits have suffered neither abatement, nor diminution."

P. 13.

Διεκοσμησε, διεταξε, ξυνεστησεν.

Plato in Timæo.

" He disposed, he arranged all things, and then gave them consistence and stability."

P. 16.

Credite nunc omnes, quas dira *Britannia*, Gentes,
Quas *Ister*, quas *Rhenus* alit!—
    Uno tot prælia vincite bello;
Romanum reparate decus, molemque labantis
Imperii fulcite humeris; Hic omnia Campus
Vindicat; hæc pacem mundo Victoria sancit!

" Give attention and credit to my words, all ye People, whether in *Great Britain*, on the *Danube*, or on the *Rhine*.—

By one great engagement supersede the necessity of so many contests; restore the glory of *Rome*, and support the weight of the falling *Empire*. This one field avenges all your wrongs; this one victory ratifies the peace of the world!"

CITATIONS

CITATIONS

IN THE

NOTES TO THE POEM.

~~~~~~~

P. 25.

" Tantamne rem tam negligenter, tam indisertè, tam impudenter ?"

" Is it not shameful to treat so important a subject with such negligence and carelessness, with such inatten-tion to propriety of speech, and with fuch effrontery?"

P. 26.

Pastorale canit signum ! cornuque recurvo Tartaream intendit vocem.

" He sounds the *pastoral* note, the signal of onset; and sends forth a blast as from Tartarus.

P. 33.

Non qui præcipiti traheret simul omnia casu ;
Sed qui maturo vel læta, vel aspera, rerum
Consilio momenta regens, nec tristibus impar,
Nec pro successu nimius, *spatiumque morandi,*
Vincendique modum mutatis nôsset habenis.

" He was a man who would not hasten the ruin of all things by precipitate and fatal violence; but who knew well how to temper and adjust the alternate preponde-rance of good and evil, by maturity of counsel. He was not depressed by adversity, or inflated with insolence by success; but by prudent management according to circumstances, he had the skill to pause with propriety, and set bounds to the profecution of victory."

P. 34.

P. 35.

Multæ Veneris, cum pondere et arte.

Hor. A. P.

" Compositions of great beauty, with the skill of a master, and the dignity of a moralist."

P. 38.

Hinc priscæ redeant artes! felicibus inde
Ingeniis pandatur iter, despectaque Musæ
Colla levent!

" May we behold the revival of the ancient arts! may the way be opened for the promotion and encouragement of all rising ability and genius, and may the Muses once-more emerge from a state of dejection, depreſſion, and neglect!

P. 39.

Excidat illa dies ævo, ne postera credant
Sæcula! nos certé taceamus.

" May that day perish from the records of time, that Poſterity may never credit the report! We ſhall paſs it over in ſilence."

P. 42.

Vaccinus quæcunque recepit Apollo.

" All the writings of which have been received into the *Vaccine* Repoſitory."

P. 42.

Et Vitulâ tu dignus et hic.

Virg. Ecl.

" Either of you are worthy of the prize, the female calf."

P. 43.

P. 43.

Hic crudelis amor Tauri, suppostaque furto
Pasiphäe, mixtumque genus. *Æn.* 6.

" Here are recorded the cruel love of the Minotaur,
and the clandeftine *subftitution* of Pafiphäe, and tho
mingled race."

P. 44.

Sic liceat tumulo scripsisse, CATONIS
MARCIA? *Lucan. L.* 2.

" Muft we *thus* inscribe on the tomb, here refts the
Marcia of Cato ?"

P. 51.

'Αιτ' ανδρων πολεμον κατακοιρανεωσιν,
Ειτ' αρ' Αθηναιη, ειτε πτολιπορθος Ενυω.

Hom. Il. 5.

" Such *goddesses* as preside over the wars and con-
tentions of men, whether Minerva, or Bellona who lays
cities in waste and desolation."

P. 53.

Demonstro vitia; tollite: denuncio vim, arma; removete.

Cic. Philip. 1. *Sect.* 10.

" I declare and demonstrate publickly to you the specifick vices and crimes; take them away: I denounce to
you the force intended to be called into action, the arms,
and the instruments; remove them."

P. 53.

θυνειν κραδιης νοερον κυτος.

Fragm. Orph. ap. Clement. Alexandr. L. 5.

" To direct the intellectual veffel of the heart."

P. 55.

P. 54.

Ad pecuini corpusculi vilitatem.

Mori Utop. L. 2.

" To the vileness of the bestial body."

***

P. 54.

Illum ne hominum quidem ducunt numero, *tantum abest ut inter cives ponant,* quorum instituta moresque, *si per metum liceat,* omnes floccifacturus sit.

Mori. Utop. L. 2.

" They do not confider him among the number of rational men; fo far are they from enrolling him among the citizens, whofe inftitutions and manners he would ridicule and fet at nought, if not reftrained by fear."

***

P. 55.

Nigidium vidi; Cratippum cognovi.

Cicero in Timæo. Fragm. de Univerfitate.

" I have seen the philosopher Nigidius; and I was acquainted with Cratippus."

***

P. 57.

Ἀμαθια μαλα χαλεπη, δοκυσα ειναι μεγιστη φρονησις.

Plato de Leg. L. 10.

" A certain ignorance very grievous, which notwithstanding has the appearance of the greateft wisdom."

***

P. 60.

P. 60.

Προς τυτοις, όταν Πολιτειαι κακοι και λογοι κατα πολεις ιδια και δημοσια λεχθωσιν, ετι δε μαθηματα μηδαμη τυτων ιατικα εκ νεων μανθανηται, ταυτη κακοι παντες δι κακοι. Ὧν αιτιατεον μεν τυς φυτευοντας μαλλον η φυτευομενυς, και τυς τρεφοντας των τρεφομενων.

Plato in Timæo. p. 87. Vol. 3, Ed. Serrani.

" Added to this ; when bad political institutions and pernicious doctrines are the subjects of lecture and discourse from city to city, in publick and in private ; and when inſtructions and sciences, by no means calculated to remedy the evil and counteract the fatal influence, are inſtilled into the rising youth ; this is the reason why those who are of bad dispoſitions, continue to be bad. We must blame the planters, and not the things planted ; and reprobate the inſtructors rather than the inſtructed."

P. 63.

Οινοχοει αυτοις ή Ἡβη. Τον όλον αισθητον κοσμον όρωσιν· ατρεπτοις και ακλινεσι νοημασι χρωμενοι, πληρυσι τα παντα της δημιυργικης αυτων προνοιας. Συνεστιν αυτοις κυριδιη Θεοτης, τη μεν νοησει το αχραντον επιλαμπυσα.

Procli Comment. in Timæum Platonis, L. 5. p. 334. Ed. Basil. 1534.

" Hebe, the goddess of Youth, presides at their entertainments. They comprehend with the eye of the intellect the whole sensible world ; and by thought and intention of mind, which is never warped or turned aside, they fill all things by a species of creative wisdom and foreknowledge. They have always a youthful divinity ; and the power of their understanding shines forth with a brightneſs not ſubject to diminution."

G   P. 75.

P. 75.

Illi *Justitiam* confirmavere triumphi;
PRÆSENTEM DOCUERE DEUM! nunc Sæcula discant
Indomitum nihil esse pio, tutumve nocenti!

Claudian ; on the fourth Consulate of Honorius.

" These triumphs and these victories have confirmed
and ratified the cause of *Justice:* they have taught and
evinced the presence and the interference of GOD!
May hence all ages and all nations learn, and
feel, that no power can finally prevail over the
virtuous and the pious; and that there is no state of
stability or of security for the blasphemous and the
wicked!"

THE END.

THE

IMPERIAL EPISTLE

FROM

KIEN LONG,

EMPEROR OF CHINA,

TO

GEORGE THE THIRD,

KING OF GREAT BRITAIN, &c. &c. &c.

IN THE YEAR 1794

Transmitted from the Emperor, and presented to his Britannick Majesty by his Excellency the Right Honourable George Earl Macartney of the Kingdom of Ireland, K. B. Ambassador Extraordinary and Plenipotentiary to the Emperor of China in the Years 1792, 1793, and 1794.

TRANSLATED INTO ENGLISH VERSE FROM THE ORIGINAL CHINESE POETRY.

WITH

NOTES BY VARIOUS PERSONS OF EMINENCE AND DISTINCTION, AND BY THE TRANSLATOR.

IGNOTUM RUTULIS CARMEN CŒLOQUE LATINO
FINGIMUS, ET FINEM EGRESSI LEGEMQUE PRIORUM.
JUV. SAT. VI.

THE FOURTH EDITION.

LONDON:
PRINTED FOR T. BECKET, PALLMALL.

1798.

BY THE TRANSLATOR.

A PREFACE.

As no writer ever stood in greater need of an apology than myself, I hope I fhall be permitted to give a few words in explanation of my labour. I have undertaken to translate into Englifh verse the poetry of the Emperor of China, who is stiled " The torch of the East, the true descendant of " Taytsoy, and the providence of Heaven." I have studied almost every principal writer on the subjeft, but must except the general History of China, translated by Father Moyrac de Mailla in *Twelve volumes* 4*to*, which I just saw, but could not obtain ; and I regret it daily with all the fulness of that *desiderium* which so *dear a head* as Father Moyrac de Mailla's demands. I confess also that I have received assistance from the best scholars and interpreters employed in Lord Macartney's Embassy, (though I was unfortunately deprived of the aid I hoped, from the ingenious *Mr. Plumb*, stiled by way of eminence *the Interpreter*, whom I regret still more than Father Moyrac de Mailla) ; yet I am convinced that it is impossible to do full justice to the imperial Chinese phrases and expressions, which are not always intelligible to an European. I have therefore been under the necessity of supplying many passages from conjeffure, or by the analogy of meaning ; and this must be considered by any person who may have an opportunity of comparing my Englifh with the Emperor's

Chinese. Yet if the reader fhould be of opinion that I have sometimes totally misunderstood, and sometimes falsely conjectured, the meaning of the Emperor, he will be inclined to forgive me, when he considers for a moment the nature of the Chinese language.

Father Du Halde will inform him, that there was a " Dictionary composed by order of the late Emperor, " and that it did not contain all the language, since " it was found necessary to add A SUPPLEMENT IN " TWENTY-FOUR VOLUMES, though the first work con- " tained NINETY-FIVE VOLUMES, the greatest part very " thick and in a small character*." I must observe, that I was favoured only with the first *ninety-five* volumes, some of which were a little imperfect; and Sir George Staunton himself could not procure for me the *fupplemental twenty-four*, though he endeavoured to oblige me with the greatest politeness. This must be my first excuse. As to *the words* themselves Father Du Halde shall give an example or two, which will be sufficient to give an idea of the rest. He says, " The " word TCHU when *pronounced flowly*, signifies *a lord* or " *mafter*; if with an *even tone*, it signifies *a hog*; if pro- " nounced *quick*, it means *a kitchen*; if in a strong and mas- " culine tone, it signifies *a column*." Again; " The syllable " Po, according to it's various accents and modes of pronun- " ciation has ELEVEN different meanings; it signifies 1, " Glass. 2, to boil. 3, to winnow rice. 4, wise or liberal. " 5, to prepare. 6, an old woman. 7, to break or cleave. " 8, inclined. 9, a very little. 10, to water. 11, a slave " or captive*." Under circumstances like these I really think it impossible, and rather unkind, not to make some allowance for my errors, as I certainly have not the opportunity of hearing the pronunciation, and of conversing so frequently in Chinese, as I could wish; and, I think, if even

---

* Du Halde History of China, v. 2. p. 393. Eng. edit. 8vo.

* Du Halde Hift. of China, v. 2. p. 390. Eng. edit. 8vo. and Abbè Grosier's Account of China, v. 2. p. 382. Grosier's work is an agreeable compilation from various authors.

an ambassador should be found to have made a mistake or two, we may be sorry, but we cannot be much surprised.

My original is an Ode; but for various reasons I have been obliged to soften it down to the milder and more familiar form of an Epistle. Besides, a political composition requires a discussion of subjects not always lyrical in this country ; and the internal œconomy of a kingdom will not easily submit to an English stanza, however varied : but this is different in the court of Pekin.

Yet in order to give the reader some idea of the difficulty of translating poetically such sublime writings as the Emperor's, I beg leave to exhibit some part of the same imperial Author's " ODE IN PRAISE OF DRINKING TEA." But as it is impossible for an uninstructed European to conceive the form and solemnity, which accompanied the publication of that great national poem, he must for a few moments suspend his curiosity for the work itself, while I convince him of how much greater consequence the poetry of an Emperor seems to be, than his politics. I am informed by Sir William Chambers K. P. S. &c. &c. &c. in his note upon *the Difcourfe of* CHET-QUA of Quang-Chew-Fu Gentleman, annexed to his famous Dissertation on Oriental Gardening in 4to. page 118, second Edition, that "THE ODE IN PRAISE OF DRINKING " TEA was published by the imperial edict of KIEN LONG, " reigning Emperor of China, bearing date the twelfth day " of the ninth moon of the thirteenth year of his reign, in " THIRTY-TWO *different types and characters*, under the " inspection of Yun-lou and Houng-yen, Princes by the " title of Tsin-Suang ; Fou Keng, Grandee by the title of " Taypao ; Count, by the title of Valiant ; and First Presi- " dent of almost all the great tribunals of the empire ; whose " Deputies were Ak-down and Tsing-pou, Grandees by the " title of Taytzee Chaopao ; and these *were again assisted* " by Isau, Fouki, Elquinque, Tetchi, Mingtee, Tsoungming, " Tchaugyu, Tounmin, and *about a dozen* other Mandarins " of rank and reputation ; so that there is no doubt but the " work is perfectly correct."—This I believe is perfectly

new in the annàls of poetry to moſt of my readers. Now in
our Europe, we find the reverse in the present time, even in
political subjeƐts. Emperors, Kings, Vice-roys, Governors,
Dukes, Admirals and Generals publish their Manifeſtos and
Counter Manifestos with advice or without advice, just as they
please, and generally in a noble manner, without any consideration at all, like the Duke of Brunswick, Lord Hood, or Earl
Fitzwilliam. To be sure in these manifestos mere trifles are
at stake; such as the lives and properties, the happineſs or
the misery of millions. But in China (hear this, ye Right
Honourable Statesmen, William Pitt and Henry Dundas!)
when an Emperor's ODE IN PRAISE OF DRINKING TEA, is
to be published, Princes, Grandees, Counts, First Presidents
of all the great tribunals, and Mandarins of high rank and reputation, are summoned to sanction and superintend the publication of the important national work.

I shall make no excuse for these preliminary articles, but
proceed to present the reader with some sublime passages
from the Ode itself, dignified and ushered in with the solemnity which I have described, and as it stands in page 119 of
Sir William Chambers's Discourse, just mentioned. The
original commences with these words, " *Meihòa che pou yao*,
" &c." the first verse will be quite sufficient to shew the
harmonic power of the original; the translation is as follows.
" The colours of the Meihòa are never brilliant, yet is the
" flower always pleasing; in fragrance or neatness the Fo-
" cheou has no equal; the fruit of the pine is aromatic, it's
" odour is inviting. In gratifying at once the smell, the sight,
" and the taste, nothing exceeds these three things; *and if* at
" the same time *you put upon a gentle fire an old pot with*
" *three legs, grown black and battered with length of service ;*
" and if, when the fire is heated to a degree *that will boil a*
" *fiſh or redden a lobſter*, you pour directly into a cup made
" of the earth Yuë, *upon the tender leaves of superfine tea :*
" *and if* you then *gently sip this delicious beverage*, it is
" labouring effectually *to remove the five causes of discon-*
" *tent* which usually disturb our quiet."—I cannot help ob-

serving, that all other Emperors and authors would be happy to have all their causes of discontent *limited to five*, and removed effectually by a little tea. The imperial poet proceeds, and cries out in rapture, " Methinks I see *the virtuous* LIN- " FOU bending into form with his own hands the branches " of the *Meihòa-chou!* It was *thus*, say I to myself, that he " relieved his mind *after the fatigues of profound meditation* " *on the most interesting subjects.*" But the Emperor's rapture is very short indeed, and he breaks forth, or rather says, " *I skip* from Linfou to Tchao-cheou, or to Yu-chouan, and " see the first, (that is, Tchao-cheou), *in the middle of a vast* " *many tea-cups*, of which he *sometimes tastes one and some-* " *times another*, thus varying incessantly his potation ; while " the second, (that is, Yu-chouan,) *drinks with the profound-* " *est indifference the best tea**, and scarce distinguishes it *from* " *the vilest stuff.*" The Emperor then resumes his lyre, which it may be necessary to observe, he never does but at night, and generally by moon light. " Already, he cries, " *the rays of the moon* break through the windows of my tent, " and with their lustre *brighten the few moveables* with which " it is adorned." The Emperor's modesty is conspicuous at the close of this great ode, and like Pindar, he strikes us with what Lord Bacon calls a virgula divina, I mean, an useful moral sentence very unexpectedly. " I find " myself (cries the imperial bard) neither uneasy nor fa- " tigued : *my stomach is empty* (the Emperor is poetical to " the last) *and I may without* fear go to rest. It is thus *with* " *my poor abilities*, I have made THESE VERSES in the little " spring of the tenth moon in the year Ping-yu of my reign.

" KIEN LONG."

---

* The East India Directors, with that great prudence which distinguishes all their well-debated resolutions, have given positive orders to all their Supercargoes, to have no dealings with *Yu-chouan* (if alive) or any of his defcendants. What would become of the Commutation Act, (not forgetting the new Act in 1795) if this Mandarin's *profound indifference for the best tea* should gain ground in this country.

From these extracts the reader will form some conjecture concerning the nature of my labour, and of the necessity of this preface.

As my translation of the Imperial Epistle has been much handed about in manuscript, I have been favoured with a variety of notes by persons of eminence and distinction. I value too much the honour of their communications, not to gratify the public with a selection at least of their remarks on the work of an Emperor, now in his eighty-fourth year, and who is esteemed the most learned and accomplished man in his dominions. I must add, that the following Epistle is written in an happy assemblage of the *Kou-ouen*, or classical language; of the *Ouen-chang*, or that which is used when a noble or elevated style is required; and of the *Kou-enha**, or language of the court, the people in office, and the literati; which consideration will easily account for every allusion, metaphor, or style which the Emperor has thought proper to adopt.

This translation of it is now presented to the public, in the spirit of strong affection and loyalty to the person of GEORGE THE THIRD, and of reverence for the constitution and government of England. In the course of it will be found the freedom of just and liberal animadversion on public characters, and on statesmen in power and out of power, neither suggested by envy, nor dictated by flattery. The Translator of THE IMPERIAL EPISTLE is also of opinion, that the whole of it is composed with that simplicity and unity, of meaning and of intention, which only bold or bad men can misrepresent or misunderstand.

* Grosier's Account of China, v. 2. p. 387.

THE

IMPERIAL EPISTLE

FROM

K I E N   L O N G,

EMPEROR OF CHINA,

TO

GEORGE THE THIRD,

KING OF GREAT BRITAIN, &c. &c. &c.

IN 1794.

Translated into English Verse from the original Chinese Poetry.

———

FRIEND of the Muse, (*a*) by every muse rever'd,
In Europe honour'd and by India fear'd,

(*a*) The institution of the Royal Academy for painting and sculpture, the patronage of poetical and learned merit in Cowper, Beattie, the late Dr. Johnson and other writers of eminence whom it is unnecessary to mention, and the restoration of national taste for the sublime of music, by his persevering and undeviating regard for Handel, are fully sufficient to entitle his present majesty George III. "The Friend of the Muse." The Emperor notices this in a future part of his Epistle.

Note by the Translator.

Around whofe throne, in freedom's chosen land,
In stern defence a guardian people stand,
Who feel for Britain, feel their sacred cause,   5
THY juft prerogative and equal laws:
HEAR, BRUNSWICK, thy Imperial Brother's song,
Firm on the base of friendship deep and strong,
E'en in my eightieth winter fancy-free,
I build the rhyme to Royalty and THEE.   10
    Here nightly by the moon, (b) her quick'ning beams
I court reclin'd, and call Sidonian dreams,
While minstrels breathe around diviner airs,
A poet's rapture sooths a monarch's cares:
All pomp of words my sober years decline,   15
Simplicity and truth illume my line,
Soft as the tints Meihòa's (c) foliage spreads,
And fragrant as the perfume Fo-sai sheds.

(b) It is to be remembered, that the Emperor always com-
poses at night, and *generally by moon-light*; see his ode in praise
of drinking tea mentioned in the Translator's preface: this frequently gives the happy effect of the *chiar'-oscuro* to the imperial
poetry, and particularly in his *portrait-painting*, but occasions
the necessity of notes, which never should be admitted without
such a necessity. The Emperor, who is always classical in his
allusions, speaks of his *Sidonian dreams* in the next verse, and
reminds me of Milton, P. L. b. 1.
        " Nightly by the moon
    " *Sidonian* virgins paid their vows and songs.
        Note communicated by Benjamin Weſt, Esq. Presidant
            of the Royal Academy.
    (c) The *Meihòa* and the *Fo-sai* are the names of two beautiful
and aromatic plants in China.

Thanks to the Power, whose well-fraught vessels bore

Thy lov'd MACARTNEY to my friendly shore,　20

Whose various talents strength and grace impart

To blameless life and singleness of heart.

He came: but with no prodigies on high;

As once, beneath the frore Siberian sky,

When sent in Britain's happier hour to prove　25

Imperial CATHERINE's policy and love,

Cœlestial Venus mark'd th' auspicious way

In dusky passage o'er the orb of day. (*d*)

　　When such thy ministers that round me tend,

A willing ear to Albion's wish I lend.

Long has her trident aw'd the subject main,

Nor e'er unfurl'd her swelling sails in vain;

Ne'er did her voice in idle thunder speak,

But crush'd the haughty, and upheld the weak.

　(*d*) The Emperor's information is true. Lord Macartney, before he was raised to the peerage of Ireland (and no man is more deserving of that or of any other honour than himself) was appointed ambassador to the court of Russia in 1767, *at the very time* when the Empress was making great preparations to observe *the Transit of Venus over the Sun*, from the frozen regions towards the pole, and on the borders of the Caspian, within her own vast empire. (see the Ann. Reg. for 1767, p 9.) At present this imperial votary of *Mars* and *Venus* seems to be employing her political astronomy *in making transits* rather more permanent and more formidable. The Empress is supposed to have the best and strongest sighted telescope of any potentate in Europe. Her *observatory* is valuable on many accounts, but in my opinion THE BUSTS of the great orators ancient and modern are its principal ornament.

　　　　Note communicated by the Rt. Hon. C. J. Fox.

By THEE inspir'd, her fame unspotted stood,   35
No taint of avarice and no guilt of blood ;
Beneficent and mild from pole to pole
Commerce was taught through mercies tides to roll,
To pour each cultivated blessing wide,
To give new motives to a nation's pride,   40
And blend with artful, but harmonious strife,
The law of int'rest with the light of life.
Such course THOU bad'st th' immortal Sailor run,
Who made discovery where he saw no sun ;
Contending nations own'd their common trust,   45
And France, (for then her Louis liv'd) was just.
Now other climes and other groves among
While loud lament is heard, or plaintive song,
To Him let China's monarch fondly turn,
And twine the wreath round Cook's barbaric urn. 50
    While such thy views, while such thy righteous aim,
Her proud pre-eminence shall Albion claim,
And meaner jealousies and tricks of state
Yield to whate'er is good, whate'er is great.
    But oh, what phrase of love may best befit,   55
How most may China's sovereign grace thy PITT?
Arch-chemick minister ! his prime decree
Refresh'd thy land with Commutation-Tea; (e)

(e) They who are curious (as all people should be) about the
history of *Tea*, are referred to Kæmpfer's Hist. of Japan, fol.

Wholesome and pure the beverage chears the sight,

By strange filtration thro' earth, air, and light. *(f)* 60

Great Minister! whose fame may well engage

The prose of Lauderdale and all his rage ;

And yet untouch'd by Him, with Roman claim

Who left the shadow of a mighty name. *(g)*

See how *the sick'ning stars*, in Portland's train, 65

Fade one by one from Opposition's plain,

As forth his chosen charms the Enchanter flings,

Ribbands and vice-roys, earls, and garter'd strings.

Oh, that my longing eye Pitt's form might greet,

Triumphant borne through Pekin's crowed street, 70

vol. 2. append. p. 1 to p. 20.—to Osbeck's Voyage to China in
1751, vol. 1. p. 246 to 253.—Le Compte's Journey to China
in 1685, p. 227 to 230.—Du Halde Hist. vol. 4. p. 21 to 28.
ed. 8vo. Engl.—Dr. Lettsom's Hist. of Tea, 4to. in 1772.—and
Grosier's Account, vol. 1. p. 463 to 484.

> *Note communicated by Mr. Twining and a Committee of*
> Teamen, *highly* Sou-chonged.

(f) We admire the minister's system of promoting political
vegetation by natural analogy; for as no vegetation whatsoever
can be carried on without ground, air, and *the light* of heaven,
he thought with the greatest sagacity that the circulation of this
fluid tax would be best kept up by making it pass *through windows,*
which are at once the conveyance of air and light.

> *Note communicated and produced* by the joint labour
> and thought *of Sir John Sinclair, president, and*
> *of Arthur Young, Esq. secretary to the new Board*
> *of Agriculture.*

(g) Junius.—There is a person now living, emphatically
stiled on the highest authority, The Man with the Pen.

> *Note communicated by the Rt. Hon. W. G. Hamilton, M.P.*

In boots of silk *(h)* and sattin's trailing length,

C<small>HOULAH</small> supreme! *(i)* my kingdom's grace and strength.

Around his waist I'd bind to solemn view

The scarf of yellow's proud imperial hue, *(k)*

Where, broider'd bold, thy Lion's golden might　75

With China's five-claw'd Dragon *(l)* should unite ;

Rubies *(m)* should on his cap transparent glow,

And peacock's plumes adown his vesture flow :

(h) " People of condition never go abroad *but in boots,* which are generally *of sattin or other silk.*" Grosier, vol. 2. p. 296.
Note by the Marquis of Abercorn.

(i) *Choulah,* is the Chinese word for *Prime Minister.*—" The " whole number of Mandarins appointed by the Emperor, for " the administration of the affairs of all the provinces amounts " to 8,965. These are all *Great Mandarins.*" Grosier, vol. 1. 571. Mr. Pitt's ambition will never rest in the Premier's office in such a little island as Great Britain, after an offer from the Emperor of becoming, Chief of the Chief.
Note communicated by his Grace the Duke of Bedford ; (en attendant.)

(k) The imperial family alone *wear yellow,* and such mandarins to whom the Emperor grants the honour of the *yellow scarf.* See Du Halde, Grosier and Bell.
Note by the Duke of Montrose and the Lords Cardigan and Sidney.

(l) The Emperor wore a long tunic of yellow silk, interwoven " with figures of golden *dragons with five claws* ; which device no " person is allowed to bear *except the imperial family.*" Bell's Travels, 8vo. vol. 2. p. 12.—We see T<small>HE</small> E<small>MPEROR</small> considers Mr. Pitt *as one of his family.*
Note by the Rt. Hon. C. J. Fox.

(m) The distinction of mandarins of the highest order is a red transparent jewel on the top of the cap, and peacocks feathers trailing down behind it. Mr. Bell explains this : " Most of the " ministers of state (he says) were *dressed very plain,* having

Loungers with lengthen'd nails (*n*)should march before,

And to the nine add one black whisker more.　　80

Then should the bust of virtuous Lin-fou (*o*) shine,

Lin-fou, who lives in my immortal line :

Next in high portraiture, or bold relief,

Should gleam THE IMAGE of each British chief,

Of all who swell the sails, or guide the helm,　　85

Hope of thy land, or glories of thy realm ;

While trophies of the wise, the just, the brave,

In orient hues and banner'd pomp should wave.

FIRST o'er *thy* ocean with terrifick frown,

Victorious grac'd with England's rostral crown, 90

"*nothing like ornaments about them*; a few only had large rubies,
"sapphires and emeralds. These precious stones are cut into
"the shape of pears, through which a hole is drilled, to fix them
"on the top of their bonnets." Bell's Travels, vol. 2. p. 13.

Note communicated (with great feeling) *by Mrs. Hastings and Mr. Jeffreys the jeweller.*

(*n*) All the men of fashion in China wear *nine or more whiskers*, and all the gentlemen have long nails, *to shew that they are
idle.* Perhaps Lord William Gordon and other Loungers and
Rangers may introduce this fashion in London, or when they
visit Mr. Pitt at his levees.

Note communicated by the Rev. Mr. Newman, Vicar of
Bond-street, *assisted by some other learned and laborious Divines, in the diocese of John Stockdale,* political Bishop of Piccadilly.

(*o*) Lin-fou (see the Translator's Preface for the character of
that great man) is the *virtuous tea-drinker*, mentioned by the Emperor in his ode in praise of drinking tea; and is introduced
here with great propriety in Mr. PITT's TRIUMPHAL ENTRY
INTO THE COURT OF PEKIN.

Note by Sir Stephen Lushington and Mr. David Scott.

The scourge of vaunting France, unshaken Howe,
With Fabian firmness and unruffled brow.
Then be the form of great Cornwallis seen,
Sedate, experienc'd, valiant, and serene;
Depicted in the tablet stand below   95
The filial hostage and imperial foe :
Beyond Mysore he thunder'd : the dread sound
Appall'd, and circumscrib'd the tyrant's bound. *(p)*
Next, with sad registers of treasur'd lore,
Financial scrolls, and many an Indian crore,   100
Burnish'd in breathing bronze, behold HIM pass,
Fearless, who knows alone no change, Dundas.
  HE comes, the motley wonder of the time,
Moulded in nature's and in fancy's prime,
Form'd, like Lucullus, for the wordy war,   105
To shake the stage, the senate, or the bar ;
Whose wit a people's plaudits could secure
For gamesters, rakes, and brothellers impure,
Could tear from youth the dread of public shame,
Drive from their lips e'n virtue's very name,   110
And train an easy nation to allow
A public bankrupt with a graceful bow ; *(q)*

(p) Tippoo Saib.
(q) The School for Scandal is the text, and every tutor and every tradesman know where to look for the commentary.
          Note communicated by William Wilberforce, Esq. M. P.
Additional note in 1796.—MONTANUS in the time of Juvenal,

A stage-man Portland never would respect,
But with Athenian *(q)* dignity reject;
No *cabinet* for Sheridan, no truft,   115
While England in her statesmen dares be just.

a witnefs to the unbounded luxury and extravagance of Nero, is
thus described :
Noverat ille
Luxuriam imperii veterem, *noctesque Neronis*
Jam medias.
SAT. 4.

I do not remember that Tacitus or Suetonius mention the *Spe-*
culæ cubicularia et tabu.ata adapertilia in the chamber of BR I T ANNI-
cus, and indeed as I have not by me the Glossarium *mediæ et* IN FI-
M Æ *Latinitatis,* I cannot render the terms. Perhaps *some architects*
might conjecture by the help of a *marine builder's dictionary.* I may
add, that in a secret history of the imperial court it is some-
where observed, that it was customary, *about the middle of*
Autumn, for a chorus of *learned Fishermen,* while they were
spreading their nets on a greenish walk on the coast of Campania, to sing
the following words with much emphasis; " NUPT s *delicias*
" *Viduæ* aspernatur ADULTER." But I never could explain
the reason of the custom.
Note communicated by the Rt. Hon. W. G. Hamilton, M. P.

(*q*) The Athenians by an express law prohibited any member
of the great council of the Areopagus from having any concern
in a theatre, or from writing any play or comedy upon pain of
expulsion. Plutarch informs us of this in his treatise on the Glory
of the Athenians : Tην Κωμωδοποιιαν ὁυτως ασεμνον ἡγυντο και
φορτικον, 'ωστε νομος ην μηδενα ποιειν κωμωδιας Αρειοπαγιτην.
Plutarch, vol. 2. p. 348. ed. Xyland.

Note communicated by the Rev. Dr. Parr, and not without
much reluctance :   but there was no refifting the
pleasure of a little bit of Greek.
B

HE too, who kindled at a holier flame
His wit, his learning, and fuperior fame;
Onward with more than Tully's force he prest,
With more than all, but Tully's judgment, bleft:
High truth in large discourse with wisdom fraught,
Not better heard in Tusculum, he taught;
In every realm of every science found,
Plain are his steps in all—but Grecian ground.
A temple (r) last he rear'd by art divine,   125
And plac'd his Cæsar in the central shrine;
High priest himself, but not with olive crown'd,
His forehead was with martial fillets bound;
Within some feeble pillars here and there,
And idle ornaments for want of care,   130
But marble still the column and the dome,
Wrought from those quarries which he found at home;
Immortal, though unfinish'd, is the work:
Why name the architect? (s) who knows not Burke?

(r)   Templum de marmore ponam;
     In medio mihi Cæsar erit, templumque tenebit.
                              Virg. Georg, l. 3.

The Emperor considers Mr. Burke's three treatises on French
affairs, entitled, " Reflections on the Revolution in France; a
" Letter to a member of the National Assembly, and his Appeal
" from the New to the Old Whigs," under the allegory of a
Temple.
                              Note by the Translator.

(s) I feel myself obliged to the Emperor for his opinion on my
friend Mr. Burke's compositions on the French Revolution, on

Next Wyndham, fearlefs thund'ring from his car,

Pitt's new Tyrtæus, breathes the blaft of war;

With parts a fp'endid station to adorn,

He braves the taunt of democratick scorn,

With eloquence and strength, his country's friend,

To think and act, and what he thinks, defend. 140

   And veering Loughborough, whofe unquiet mind

Found late that joy ambition scarce can find;

He came, though not in Latium to repose,

But burn in conflict with a nation's foes,

which *they are now writing a dreadful commentary.* As I am on the subject I must observe, that I never remember to have seen the French Convention described in the words of Milton. He indeed knew what a Long Parliament was; but his overbearing genius seems to have pourtrayed a French Convention, when he de-scribed

            A shape,

If shape it may be call'd, that shape has none :

Or substance may be call'd that shadow seems,

For both seems either : black it stands as night,

Fierce as ten furies, terrible as hell,

And shakes a dreadful dart ; what seems it's head,

The likeness of a kingly crown has on ;

Created thing nought values it, nor shuns.

                     P. L. b 2.

   For my own part, I distrust them all : I hate alike French po-licy, French professions, French impiety, French vaunting, French versatility, French falshood, French cruelty. I am equally disposed to guard against their Republican volcano, whether belching forth the fiery lava of *Terror,* or smouldering with the more dangerous smoak of *Moderation.*

   Note communicated by the Rt. Hon. William Wyndham, M. P.

     Secretary at War, &c. &c. &c. in 1795.

Yet still, though thron'd in Thurlow's rightful place,

His words want weight which never wanted grace.

Lo, the grave Grenville, with a patriot's end

Who dar'd to sink the rival in the friend ; (*t*)

Content could leave the Commons, and the Chair,

To breathe with Lords a more convenient air. 150

There too, upon Hibernia's sainted green,

Should Buckingham, without his boots, (*v*) be seen;

(*t*) It should .be mentioned to the honour of Lord Grenville, that he accepted a peerage at the very time when he was the only man on Mr. Pitt's side of the house, who could have contested the palm öf eloquence with him, or indeed could have succeeded him as Minister, in case of any of those little *amantium iræ*, which will sometimes happen among the best regulated statesmen.

Note communicated (after profound *meditation) by George Rose, Esq. Sec. to the Treasury.*

(*v*) The prefent Marquis of Buckingham, then Lord Temple, was formerly Lord Lieutenant of Ireland. Du Halde has explained the Emperor's pleasant allusion in substance thus : If *a viceroy* in China has executed his office with equity and the love of his subjects, (the word *subjects* is too strong) many particular honours are paid him. One of the most pleasant is this: the citizens, some of whom weep or pretend to do so, meet him at a short distance from the city, and *pull off his old boots* and present him *with new ones*: those first taken off *are preserved in a cage over the gate of the City.* Du Halde Hist. ed. 8vo. v. 2. p. 17S, 179. Now though the Emperor observes that the loving citizens of Dublin met upon St. Stephen's, or in the imperial words, on *the sainted green*, and most certainly *pulled off my Lord Marquis's old boots*, it does not appear that they presented him *with a new pair.* Whether they never desired to fee him *accoutred* among them *again*, or whatever was the cause, all that the loving citizens could be prevailed.upon to say, was, " *Off with his boots*, fo much for Buckingham."

Note communicated (con amore) *by the Rt. Hon. C. J. Fox,*

Mark how the citizens suspend in state
His leathern trophies on the Castle gate.

Then He, whom e'en fraternal worth could fail,
The plume-pluckt Chatham with a raven's tail; (x)
And garter'd Richmond, whose unblason'd shield (y)
Proves honour to œconomy should yield;
And Malagrida, (z) with his wily leer,
Sense that misleads, but words that charm the ear.

Fresh from Hermippus and his doctrine brisk,
In saffron sock old Cardigan (a) should frisk,

(x) The Emperor is again local in his allusions. The Chinese mode is this: when a Mandarin *is removed from a very important station to one of less consequence in the government*, the peacock's feathers depending from his cap are taken out, and crows feathers are substituted.

> *Note communicated* (con amore *also*) *by the Rt. Hon. the Earl Spencer First Lord of the Admiralty.*

(y) It is difficult to understand the whole of the Emperor's meaning, but I think my office enables me at least to offer a conjecture. When the late repairs were made in St. George's Chapel at Windsor, with an exemplary liberality, every Knight of the Garter contributed a sum towards it, and his arms were blasoned on the window over his banner. The D. of Richmond alone thought his fame sufficient *without the honour and expence* of the sacred glass, and declined them. The glass remains unornamented to this hour.

> *Note communicated by the Rt Rev. the Dean of Windsor.*

(z) Marquis of Lansdown. See the Lettres Provinciales.

(a) Cardigan.—" No; che *mago non è questo*;
    Egli è un musico, per Bacco."

> *Quotation from a favourite opera, communicated* singing *(rather of the loudest, as usual,) by the Earl of Galloway, assisted by Mr. Francis, jun.* dall' Academia degli Arcadi e degli Buffi Caricati.

With Ailesb'ry, graceful in his walking-dress,

And Dorset, prompt the lively dame to bless:

And there, insatiate yet with folly's sport,   165

That polish'd sin-worn fragment of the court,

The shade of Queensb'ry should with Clermont meet,

Ogling and hobbling down St. James's street.

But mark the courteous philanthropick form

Of Leeds, sagacious of each brooding storm;   170

Of wit well manner'd, skill'd at once to please,

Resign with candour, and dissent with ease;

Though wary, bold and manly is his part,

And England's honour ever at his heart.

    Then should THY sacred Orators appear;   175

Horsley in front, while Watson in the rear

The chemick dews of peace around him flings,

A pluvial prelate, from his lawny wings.

And hapless HE, whose sad unworthy tale

Is heard in Winchester's opprobrious vale; *(c)* 180

(c) The translator has improperly rendered the Emperor's original Chinese word *Too-paa-josh*, a *vale*, which *my* researches in that language enable me to interpret a *sacred eminence*, or *hill* or temple. He is certainly wrong, and the Emperor was right.— My duty *in the long absence* of my bishop *on the Continent*, which the Emperor cannot mark in too strong terms *at such a time and for such a Cause*, (though the bishop is a man of private worth and amiable character) requires a few observations from me. It is notorious to this whole kingdom that the ministry, from the best motives of mercy, humanity and toleration, originally fitted up the King's House at Winchester as an ASYLUM for the Emigrant

Forc'd by a fierce, luxurious, gambling wife,
From all the hallow'd dignities of life,
His high-paid duties, and his sacred home,
Exil'd in lewd Italian climes to roam;

Priests. It is as notorious, that it is *now* something more than an asylum. It is a sacred college; it is THE HEAD-QUARTERS OF THE CATHOLICK CAUSE in this country, *a seminary* where NEAR ONE THOUSAND ROMISH PRIESTS are publickly maintained; where ordinations, conversions, instructions, and all the business of their dark divan are held, and which water all their schools old and new. I should think the following words framed for the occasion, if Milton had not written them:

" Not content
" With their audacious neighbourhood ; they build
" THEIR TEMPLE, *right against the temple of God,*
" ON THE OPPROBRIOUS HILL." P. L. b. 1.

See Milton's Account of *Moloch* at large. It is a publick cause of consideration. We know what the Emperor did with the Jesuit Missionaries in China, when they became troublesome. They should, if possible, be sent out of our country; if that cannot *yet* be, they should be *instantly dispersed.* History informs us *what Ulysses was*; it is the part of government to guard against what *he may again be*; and to see that *Troy may stand and the citadel of Priam and of Protestantism may remain.* I speak for the publick; and I speak with the expectation of being publickly heard.

Note communicated (ex officio) *by the Rev. Newton Ogle*, D.D. *Dean of Winchester in* 1795.

N. B. This note was written by the Dean of Winchester in 1795, and there are NOW stronger and more powerful reasons for attending to his publick remonstrance. It is well known that the *whole collection* of these priests *now* consists *of not above one third* (if so much) of the original emigrants ; the remainder being *now* supplied with boy-priests, (little superior to *acolythes*) who are not emigrants, pert and insolent to the members of our established

Now (*d*) while thy Sion in desponding strain   185
Invokes the Fathers from her inmost fane;
Why slumbers thy Arch-Pontiff? on that shore
Who from embodied dulness rouses Moore?
And, while the pillars of thy temples bow,
Why circles not the mitre PALEY's brow?   190
    Next see the learned Parr, in judgment weak,
Who first lampoon'd a minister in Greek;
By merit rais'd above his *buff* compeers
In shag and title, " Master of the Bears ;" (*e*)

church, without the least gratitude for the unequalled and inconsiderate protection which they receive from the state. Besides this, nunneries and monasteries are openly and avowedly rising in different parts of the kingdom, and these *Romish conies,* burrowing into the heart of it, will shortly be found to be no *feeble folk.* We discover in these members of the *Romish* church the same principles with their ancestors, the same spirit, the same dark intrigues, the same intolerance, the same immortal and unquenchable hatred of Protestant heresy, the same insinuating or domineering manner (as the occasion may require) in the priests and spiritual guides, the same love of *the sacred sulphur* at their hearts, the same assertions of their *original rights and inheritance* in this land—in short, *Viscera magnarum domuum, dominique futuri,* if Mr. Pitt and the ministry will not attend to the Dean's words, which, beyond all controversy, ARE TRUE.

Note added by the Translator in June 1796;
(*d*) In 1794.

(*e*) It was some time before *we* could decypher the latter part of this passage about Dr. Parr. The first part evidently relates to the Bellendenian Greek and Latin preface, the translation of which into Chinese cost the Duke of Portland above five hundred pounds. But *we* now find the latter part also to be truly imperial. In the Greek Anecdota of Procopius, b. 9. (*we* read it in English) or the

He marks the den, whence 'mid the bestial herds 195

THE UNFROCK'd GRAMMARIAN *(f)* hurls his red-

   wing'd words ;

And mourns, transfix'd by the prelatick spear,

Expiring Priestley on his western bier.

   Then Bedford, late by publick views inspir'd,

Cool at Newmarket, nor at hazard fir'd ;   200

Oeconomy the order of his day,

In lease, in love, in building, or in play :

Secret History of the Court of Constantinople in the reign of Justinian, *we* find that there were two factions in the state, the *Green* and the *Blue.* The *dissolute youth* of Constantinople adopted *the blue livery of disorder,* and the bonds of society were frequently relaxed and sometimes broken. At that time *wild beasts of different species were maintained by the blue* (some MSS. have it, *and buff*) *faction* IN THE CENTER OF THE METROPO-LIS, and one of the most honourable appointments was that of " *The Master of the Bears.*"—How learned is the Emperor in his allusions ! with what propriety does he conduct his applications!

    Note by the joint labour and ability of Dr. Coombe, Editor of
        a splendid, and rather silly, edition of Horace, and of
        Mr. Alderman Curtis, Brother to the Rev. Mr. Curtis:
        Arcades Ambo.

   N. B. The *Chinese Translation of Dr. Parr's Bellendenian Pre-face* had nearly produced a revolution in Pekin, which the Duke of Portland never intended; till it was *confuted in Chinese* by the Mandarin Chum-Hoar-Ti-Fu.

   (f) Horne Tooke.—In August 1771, *The Divine* wrote thus of himself; " Monument I shall have none ; but over my grave " it will be said, in Junius's own words, HORNE'S SITUATION " DID NOT CORRESPOND WITH HIS INTENTIONS." Junius's Letters. After his acquittal from the charge of high treason in 1794, Mr. Horne Tooke *felt* that he had lived to be his own Commentator,   *Note by the Translator.*

Revers'd see now the youthful statesman start,
Splendor and greatness beating at his heart,
Full to the goal he pants for dubious fame,   205
And slights the virtuous honours of his name.

   Next feeble Portland, whom Pitt call'd to share
A forc'd alliance, and distracted care :
Fitzwilliam too !—but fate conceals the page :
Hibernian policy and Romish rage,   210
Hot from the hell of Loyola, *may* rise
With discord starting to unmeasur'd size,
Struck with unhallow'd phrenzy to divide
A sister land from Britain's guardian side:
Pause, while ye may, yet friendly chiefs! the care, 215
The cause, the blood, are ONE : forbear, forbear. *(g)*

(g) The Emperor in these lines *seems* to make a delicate allusion to one of the most finished passages of consummate art in
the Æneid:

> Illæ autem, paribus quas fulgere cernis in armis
> Concordes animæ, *dum nunc et nocte premuntur* ;
> Heu quantum inter se bellum, *si lumina vitæ*
> *Attigerint,* quantas acies stragemque movebunt !
> Ne, *Pueri,* ne tanta animis assuescite bella,
> Neu patriæ validas in viscera vertite vires:
> Tuque prior, tu parce, genus qui ducis Olympo:
> Projice tela manu, sanguis meus.
>
>   Æn. 6.

The words are figurative : the *dum nunc et nocte premuntur* are
evidently expressions which denote the D. of P. and Earl Fitzwil-

In Anglo-Russick bronze should Fox come forth;
I'd spare the blushes of degraded worth : (*h*)
Oh had he ever to himself been true,
Nor chang'd the pristine patriot for the new,   220

liam, or any other Dukes or Earls, when *in opposition*, which generally has a tendency to create the *concordes animæ paribus in armis*. This is confirmed by what follows; *si lumina vitæ attigerint*, which can have no other meaning than this; *if ever they should make part of the ministry :* the lumina vitæ, the auräi simplicis ignis, the pabulum or nutriment of life can be found in no other region. *Pueri* is a term peculiarly adapted to all Ministers. The *tu prior, tu parce*, is not so clear, but I should not refer it to Earl Fitzwilliam : weapons may however be forced from hands which use them inconsiderately. The *bellum*, *acies* and *stragem* are a little prophetick of Ireland ; but I trust England will avert it, by that tender address—*Projice tela manu*, Sanguis meus !

> *Note communicated* (in 1795 *during the short and imprudent administration of Lord Fitzwilliam in Ireland*) *by Earl Mansfield* ci-devant *Lord Stormont, one of the best informed and best-read scholars in Europe in the Translator's opinion.*—This note is preserved to explain the Emperor's meaning to posterity. (1796.)

(*h*) It is impossible to ascertain the peculiar degradation of this great orator and statesman (for such he is and ever will be esteemed) to which the Emperor alludes : whether to that degradation arising from the honour which the Empress of Russia conferred on him, or from the pension which he enjoys from private benevolence, equally disgraceful to the subscribers and to himself.

> *Note communicated by George Rose, Esq. M.P. Secretary of the Treasury, from a MS. by the Rt. Hon. William Pitt, &c. &c. &c. &c.*

Discretion had repress'd Burke's headlong *(i)* ráge,
And England wanted one immortal page.
Mark disappointed Thurlow's scowling mien;
Happy(*ii*)—had Pepper Arden *(k)* never been;
Him shall the wool-sack, him the Chancery mourn,
And Thurlow, Thurlow, every bench return.
With candid Scott, *(l)* impassion'd, but serene,
Lo, where appears Macdonald's *(m)* polish'd mien;

(i) The Emperor, always just, admires Mr. B. yet can see and censure his defects. But as to his eloquence *takcn upon the whole*, to him alone of our English Orators can the following words belong. " *En* ILLE, *qui saxa devolvit et pontem indignatur, et ripas* " *sibi facit; multus et torrens judicem vel nitentem contra fert, cogit-* " *que ire qua rapit; hic iram, hic misericordiam inspirat; hic de-* " *functos excitat; apud hunc et Patria ipsa exclamat; hic deos ipsos in* " *congressum prope suum sermonemque deducit.*"

Quintil. L. 12. c. 10.

Note communicated by the Rt. Hon. William Wyndham, M.P. &c. &c.

(ii) Et Fortunatum, si nunquam &c. &c.

Virgil. Ecl. 6.

(k) The famous contest between Mr. Pitt and the ci-devant Chancellor Thurlow for Pepper Arden, always reminded me of the dispute between Agamemnon and Achilles *for the beautiful Briséis.*

Note communicated by Joseph Jekyll, Esq. M.P. and author of many other pretty little *Jokes—principally on Mr. Pitt; but* Nunquam animam talem dextra hae &c.

(l) Sir John Scott, Attorney General; from whom proceeded whatever is honourable and of good report in principle and practice, and with great ability, at the late State-trials in 1794 (particularly in Mr. Horne Tooke's) which trial, from the conduct of it, I should rather call *a legal, judicial, and criminal conversazione round the table at the Old Bailey.* When Sir John Scott made his reply to Mr. Tooke's Advocate Mr. Erskine, I could not help observing to my friend who sate next to me;

And angry Kenyon, from state-troubles turn'd, (*n*)
Just, and in all, but graceful learning, learn'd; 230
And the Bar-pleader, whom mobs call divine,
Known by the symbols of I, ME, and MINE : (*o*)

" Cum illa *dicendi vitiosa jactatio* inter plausores suos detonuit,
" resurgit VERÆ VIRTUTIS FORTIOR FAMA." Quint. l.12. c.9.'

> *Note by the Hon. Mr. Perceval, junior counsel for the prosecution.*

(*m*) Sir A. Macdonald, Chief Baron of the Exchequer, late Attorney General.

(*n*) A Lord Chief Justice of the King's Bench, who gives himself up to his legal profession and turns from politicks, must at all times be a valuable man, and particularly so at present. There are persons who entertain some doubt of the propriety of the opinion anciently delivered of the *Orator* or, as *we* construe the word, the Barrister or Pleader by profession, yet WE believe it strictly true with a few rare exceptions. " Multi erant præ-
" terea præclari in philosophia et nobiles, a quibus omnibus
" una pene *repelli* voce *Oratorem* A GUBERNACULIS CIVITATUM,
" ac tantùm in judicia et conciunculas, tanquam in aliquod
" pistrinum, detrudi et compingi videbam." De Oratore L. 1

> *Note communicated by the Rt. Hon. Edmund Burke and the*
> *Rt. Hon. C. J. Fox.—Lords Thurlow and Loughbo-*
> *rough dissent.*

(*o*) The Emperor means ME, by G— : he affects to insinuate that my eloquence is confined to the bar; and never can have the least effect in the senate. Next to myself however, I think Cicero the best Orator : *no man ever spoke so well of himself.* I admire that perpetual ornament of his unblushing phraseology, the *Ut ad me revertar :* though his *discovery of Catiline's plot* and his PLEADINGS AGAINST THAT CONSPIRACY are not much to his honour. —

> *Note communicated by the Hon. T. Erskine.*

N.B. *Qui* ACTORIS *captat elegantiam, perdit viri boni et gravis auctoritatem,*   Quintil. L. 11. c. 3.

> *Additional note communicated by the sober and steady*
> *Counsellors Mansfield and Plumer.*

With the boy-candidates for publick praise,

The Whitbreads, Cannings, Lambtons, Jenkys, Greys,

All, from the promise of whose rising ray   235

England expects a brighter, steadier day.

   But last, in regal grandeur once erect,

Now in wan splendor and with eyes deject,

HASTINGS, that *great*, *that injur'd*, dubious name,

The glory of thy India, or *the shame*;   240

Through truth, through lies, through eloquence,
        through pride,

Borne down in Burke's unnavigable tide.

How fades the laurel on that haughty brow

Jove's thunder spar'd ! who made the nations bow,

While in his grasp, by fame and honour grac'd, 245

Britain thy delegated sceptre plac'd.

State-victim now, deluded while secure,

Flesh'd for the altar, and for Pitt mature;

Though vers'd in every wile, he learn'd too late

That love in ministers is secret hate :   250

For HIM, thus humbled in Impeachment's weeds,

To tardy justice England bends and pleads. *(h)*

(h) While these lines were printing (as I should believe) the Lords publickly pronounced the ACQUITTAL OF MR. HAS-TINGS in the chamber of Parliament, after *a trial of seven years and three months*, on St. George's day, the 23d of April 1795. I shall make no remarks but in the words of Shakespeare;

        " ON THESE CHARGES

" CRY, GOD FOR (HASTINGS) ENGLAND AND ST. GEORGE !"
     Note communicated (maestoso con brio) *by Lord Thurlow.*

While thus they pass, my Mandarins should bend,

And to my throne PITT's palanquin attend;

Trumpets of Outong-chu (q) his praise unfold, 255

And steely crescents (r) gleam in semblance bold;

With repercussive notes from impulse strong

Air thunders, rolls the drum, and groans the (s) *Gong*;

Flambeaux of odorous wood, and lanterns (t) bright

In eastern prodigality of light; 260

The cluster'd radiance of the fields above,

And pictur'd planets (v) in their orders move,

(q) " Drummers and Trumpeters march before the Empe-
" ror (blowing) with their trumpets, which are three feet long,
" and made of a wood called *Outong-chu*, and ornamented with
" rings of gold." Grosier, v. 2. p. 330.

(r) " Behind these march a hundred soldiers armed with
" halberts, the points of which terminate *in a crescent*; with
" macebearers, &c." Gros. v. 2. p. 331.

(s) The Gong is an instrument of a circular form made of
brass, which the Chinese strike with a large wooden mallet covered with leather; the sound is heard to a great distance.

(t) " Four hundred large lanterns of elegant workmanship
" next make their appearance, borne by the same number of
" men; and four hundred flambeaux, made of a kind of wood
" which burns long, and diffuses a great light." Gros. as above.
—N.B. For the account of the famous *Feast of Lanterns* throughout the empire of China, see Grosier v. 2. p. 323.

(v) " After these twenty-four banners upon which are painted
" *the signs of the Zodiac*; and fifty six other banners, on which
" are represented different *clusters of stars*, according to their
" arrangement in the heavens." Gros. v. 2. p. 331.

Note by the Duke of Marlborough.

Seraphick emblems ! and in azure car

Thy Herschel pointing to his Georgian Star.

‧For Pitt the portals of the south (*x*) expand,　265

And on *my* marble (*y*) he alone should stand,

While from the mountain of the agate seal (*z*)

His titled worth my Jasper should reveal;

Then, as in natal splendor, should be brought

The chequer'd vest (*a*) by learned fingers wrought;

(*x*) " The southern gate of the palace is never opened *but* "*for the Emperor himself.*"　Du Halde Hist. v. 2. p. 24. English ed. 8vo.

Note by Lord Hawksbury.

(*y*) " There is a causeway paved *with white marble,* and none " *but the Emperor* may walk *in this path.*　Du Halde v. 2. p. 26.

(*z*) " The patents and imperial acts are all sealed with the " Emperor's own seal, which is *a fine Jasper,* near eight inches " square, and is taken from the mountain *Yn yu Chan,* that is, " *the mountain of the agate seal.*"　Du Halde v. 2. p. 19.

(*a*) " The *Literati* among the Mandarins pay a peculiar ho- " nour to a good Governor of a province.　They cause a dress " to be made for him of small pieces of sattin, red, blue, green, " yellow, &c.　*His birth day* is chosen as the proper time for " presenting him with it.　He at first refuses it; but at last " *yields to the intreaties of the literati.*　They then make him put " on *this chequered garment,* the different colours of which are " supposed to represent all the nations that wear different " dresses, and to inform the Mandarin that he is *worthy of ruling* " *them all.*"　Grosier v. 2. p. 340 —N. B.　This is a kind of imperial anticipation of that chequered Chancellor's robe with which the *Literati* of Cambridge will one day invest Mr. Pitt, if he should continue to be the Minister; if not, those *good men* will not be at a loss where to discover transcendent merit.

Note communicated (con furia) *by Lord Thurlow.*

While with slow-pacing steps in gorgeous rows
The solemn pomp my sons of science (*b*) close.
Their heads aloft my elephants should toss,
Morton cry, *Morgu*, and Sir Clement, *Boss* ; (*c*)
The full Tartarian chorus sounding far,   275
Hail, MINISTER OF PEACE—BUT NOT OF WAR!

Ah me ! too fondly does my fancy dream:
PITT hears not ; and would slight the imperial theme,
Though all my wealth Macartney's voice should speak,
Or learn'd Sir George in chinese or in greek,   280
Or CHET-QUA's self, admir'd by beau and belle,
CHET-QUA, (*d*) whom all the world knew passing well ;

(*b*) " The grand cavalcade is closed by two thousand Man-
" darins of Letters." Gros. v. 2. p. 332.

(*c*) *Morton* and *Sir Clement.*—I suppose the Emperor means
two officers of high ceremony in his palace, whom out of compliment he names after the EARL of MORTON, Chamberlain to
the Queen, and *Sir Clement Cottrell.* Master of the Ceremonies,
of whom he cannot but have heard. As to the words they are
to pronounce before Mr. Pitt, Mr. Bell informs us of their
meaning ; " The Master of the Ceremonies (he says) stood by
" and delivered his orders in the Tartar language by pronoun-
" cing the words *Morgu* and *Boss*, the first meaning *to bow*, and
" the second *to stand* ; two words which I shall not easily forget."
Bell's Travels 8vo. v. 2. p. 9.—These emphatic words *Morgu*
and *Boss* should be pronounced by the Speaker and Mr. Dundas
whenever Mr. Pitt makes his triumphal (I mean his daily) entry
into the House of Commons and at all his levees.

Note communicated by George Rose, Esq. M.P. Secretary
to the Treasury (1794.)

(*d*) *Chet-qua* was a Chinese who visited England many years
ago, and was an intimate friend of Sir William Chambers. He

C

Ne'er shall my eyes behold in Tartar gown
The chosen Minister of England's crown.

I hail thy favour'd Island, that can boast,   285
Foster'd by THEE, those arts which Athens lost :
Apelles in thy Reynolds shall revive,
And in a Bacon great Lysippus live.

Thine too the poet's care ; nor Cowper's strain, (e)
Nor Scotland's Doric Minstrel sounds in vain ; 290
But chief that care shall Johnson's virtue prove,
Led by the day-star beaming from above.

A nation's taste to rouse and to refine,
Handel by THEE was rais'd to strength divine ; (f)

afterwards returned to China. As Sir William's friend seems to
have been a pleasant fellow, and as the knight's account of him
is very pleasant too, I shall transcribe a part of it. " *All the world*
" (says Sir William) *knew* CHET-QUA ; and how he was born at
" Quang-Chew-Fu ; also how he was bred a face-maker, and
" had three wives, *two of whom he caressed very much and the third*
" *but seldom,* for she was a virago and had large feet. He dressed
" well ; *wore nine whiskers and four long nails,* with silk boots and
" callico breeches ; equalling therein the prime Macaronis and
" sçavoir-vivres not only of Quang-chew, but also of Shum-tien-
" fu. *He played divinely on the bagpipe and made excellent remarks ;*
" was fond of smoaking, and was then always *vastly pleasant and*
" *very communicative.*" See Sir William Chambers's Discourse
annexed to his Dissertation on Oriental Gardening. 2d edit.
1772, page 115.   *Note by the Rev. W. Mason.*

   (e) See the note on the first line of the Imperial Epistle.

   (f) The Emperor alludes to the grand musical performances
in Westminster Abbey in commemoration of Handel, in 1784,
&c. They are recorded very properly on a tablet on the monument of Handel.   *Note by Joah Bates, Esq.*

The monumental marble breath'd : from high   295
His wond'ring spirit stoop'd, and own'd the harmony.
Such the instruction, such the grace, secur'd
By balanc'd rights, and policy matur'd.

    While I, reclin'd on Camusathkin down,
Careless forget the labours of my crown ;   300
Or chance some playful Vice-roy's doom deplore,
Hurl'd by dread Venus *(g)* to the fated shore.
For gravest Mandarins, in hours of joy,
Here oft with tittering pleasure-misses toy,
Charter'd unquestion'd libertines of love,   305
Heirs in expectance of the myrtle grove ;
With them in lunar halls *(h)* and odorous bow'rs,
Voluptuous, shun the blaze of sultry hours,
Skill'd with light spells of wantonness to chase
The murky *Man-chew (i)* from the enchanted space.

(g) The *Syphilis* rages in China among persons of the highest distinction, as in Europe. The physician and surgeon to Lord Macartney's Embassy relieved many of the Viceroys and Mandarin's *from their embarrassments* at Pekin, Canton, and other places.
Note communicated by Sir George Baker, Bart. Physician to the King.

(h) *Myau-Ting,* the *Halls of the Moon,* or beautiful vaulted saloons, the concave of which is ornamented with stars and painted to represent a nocturnal sky, where the Chinese Princes retire with their favourite ladies in the heat of the summer days, " *as* " *often as they are disposed to see them and be particular,*" as Sir William Chambers happily expresses it. Differtat. as above p. 32.
*Note communicated (*affettuoso con brio*) by Lord William Gordon.*

(i) *Man-chew* is the name of the genius of sorrow, among the Chinese.

For them I frame, whom trifles best may please,
A smile of softness or a sonnet's ease ;
Not as for THEE, with more than Theban fire,
Sustain the weight of my imperial lyre.

THEE last I trace with reverence, and survey 315
The awful wonders of thy various day ;
Thy nation's darling still; though Scotland's star
Shed brief malignant heat, and scorch'd afar,
Till proudly rising on the vantage ground
GREAT CHATHAM stood, and shook the realms around:
Prophet of future fate ! his potent word
Thy people o'er the vast Atlantick heard ;
And as the winds his voice ill-omen'd bore,
Methought the sceptre sunk—to rise no more.

Close we that scene: for other scenes are near; 325
Darkness, and discontent, distrust, and fear,
And brooding policy in novel forms
Call o'er the deep of empire clouds and storms.
And wild those storms would rend Britannia's field,
Should patriot bands the rod of faction wield, 330
While law, religion, property they seize,
And senates tremble at their own decrees.
Sweeping with REFORMATION's iron sway,
They crush each hand that scruples to obey,
From splendor's robe each proud distinction wipe, 335
And place a barren bauble in thy gripe.

Then mitred fathers, and the ermin'd peer,

And ancestry, and all to honour dear,

The fond well-earn'd rewards of ancient worth,

All, spirits disembodied, leave the earth :   340

These are state-blots which, in their dread intent,

Will be ras'd out IN THEIR FIRST PARLIAMENT.

For each empirick, quacks of state or church,

Now hate all truth, but truths of grand research;

They round their phrase with studied nothings, call

Sophistick pomp, and meaner minds appall,

Then unawares the strong conclusion draw,

The master of the Prince is master of the Law.

  Nor THOU, in fancied strength too safely wise,

Their base-born dark original despise.   350

Whence draws the Sun dire vapour? whence conspire

The thundrous tempest, and the lightning's fire?

From lake, and lazy pool, and weeds obscene,

(The abode of putrid pestilence unclean,)

The Elemental fury from afar   355

Collects and scatters wide ethereal war,

Ranging without confine, without controll;

E'en heav'ns own firmament oft seems to roll,

And from the fated momentaneous shock

Eternal impress marks the riven rock :   360

The arch of majesty, the temple's dome,

The pillar'd hall, the peasant's low-rooft home,

Alike in undistinguish'd ruin fall,

And shapeless desolation equals all.

    Through EUROPE's bounds, 'tis her devoted age,

Fires from within and central thunders rage. (k)

On Gallia's shores I mark the unhallow'd pow'r,

Her godless regents feel the madd'ning hour,

Dread architects of ruin and of crime,

In revolution's permanence sublime,   370

And cruel nonsense ! o'er the astonish'd World

The flag of dire EQUALITY unfurl'd,

Drizzling with blood of millions streams in air,

The scroll, FRATERNAL FREEDOM, DEATH, DESPAIR.

They pass : nor Rhine nor Rubicon they know; 375

Torrents may roar, or tranquil streams may flow,

In unappall'd protrusion on they burst,

All nations cursing, by all nations curst.

Lo, Belgium yields to unresisted fate ;

Within her ministers of terror wait :   380

Nature with rod petrifick smites the land,

And binds the floods in adamantine band,

Till Gallia's Chief in right of William sways,

And Freedom, once with life-drops bought, obeys.

(k) This picture of THE STATE OF EUROPE was drawn by the Emperor *in the year* 1794, true and juft at that period, and is *now* finally consigned by His Majesty to posterity.

                      Note by the Translator in 1796,

See, where dismember'd trembling Spain resigns 385
Peruvia's radiance, and Potosi's mines.
The pillars of THE ETERNAL CITY bow,
And the tiara from the Pontiff's brow
Drops to the dust : no more in Peter's fane
The Consistorial Brotherhood shall reign.   390

Yet see ; the turban nods by factions torn ;
A length'ning, sad, and sullen sound is borne
Around Sophia's hallow'd conscious walls,
Mutt'ring the doom denounc'd : her crescent falls.
Still view, in western (*l*) climes Death's palest horse
With pestilence and slaughter marks his course,
While dusky tribes, with more than maniac rage
Rending their brazen bonds, in war engage :
For France still burns to make, with dire intent,
HELL AND THIS WORLD ONE REALM, ONE
    CONTINENT !   400

Yet once attend, great BRUNSWICK ; nor in vain
Hear thy Imperial Brother's closing strain.
THEE from thy people may no thought divide,
The statesman's rashness, or Reformer's pride;
Reason and her fond visions still distrust ;   405
What, but experience, makes a kingdom just ?
Fix'd on her ancient base let England rest ;
And publick danger arm the publick breast;

(*l*) The Weft Indies.

On British sense depend.   On foreign fame
To proud Versailles THE FATAL STRANGER (*m*) came,
New laws, new policy, new truth to tell,
And by new maxims the vast fabrick fell.

 Oh, should thy nation slight her just alarms,
Nor Gallick TRUTHS dread more than Gallick arms,
Thy diadem must fade ; the Tyrian die   415
Sink in the scarlet of democracy ;
All dignities of brighter times will fail ;
No wisdom o'er the midnight lamp grow pale,
But knowledge, fancy, genius, all retire,
And faint and death-struck learning will expire :
Look round the land, there nothing shall be found
But swords to guard, and ploughs to till the ground.

 Though *now* awhile beneath the afflictive rod
SUPERNAL POWER may bid THY Albion nod,
Humbled in due prostration may she bend,   425
And her far-fam'd beneficence extend :
Then, all her ancient energies erect,
Strength from herself and from her God expect,
And on her rocky ramparts bold, alone
Maintain HER laws, and vindicate THY throne. 430

 (m) Neckar.

FINIS.